HOW TO
PUBLISH, PROMOTE,
AND SELL
YOUR OWN BOOK

How to PUBLISH, PROMOTE, AND SELL YOUR OWN BOOK

Robert Lawrence Holt

ST. MARTIN'S PRESS   NEW YORK

HOW TO PUBLISH, PROMOTE, AND SELL YOUR
OWN BOOK. Copyright © 1985 by Robert
Lawrence Holt. All rights reserved. Printed in
the United States of America. No part of this
book may be used or reproduced in any
manner whatsoever without written permission
except in the case of brief quotations embodied
in critical articles or reviews. For information,
address St. Martin's Press, 175 Fifth Avenue,
New York, N.Y. 10010.

Design by Mina Greenstein

Library of Congress Cataloging in Publication Data

Holt, Robert Lawrence.
    How to publish, promote, and sell your own book.

    1. Self-publishing.   2. Publishers and publishing.
I. Title.
Z285.5.H63 1985   070.5   85-11748
ISBN 0-312-39618-X

How to Publish, Promote, and Sell Your Own Book
is a new version, revised by the author, of
*Publishing for Schools, Small Presses, and
Entrepreneurs,* which was first published in 1982
by California Financial Publications.

Dedicated to the book people at
<u>Library Journal, Booklist,</u> the
<u>Los Angeles Times,</u> and other
publications, who judge books on the
basis of merit rather than the size of
their publishers.

Contents

38. Attending Book Fairs   261
39. Plugging Your Book on the Radio   265
40. Appearing on Television   269
41. Marketing to Bookstores   272
42. Selling to Wholesalers   283
43. Selling to Libraries—the Cream of the
      Business   295
44. Successful Mail-Order Techniques   298
45. Fulfilling Your Orders   315

**VI. Selling Reprint Rights to a Major
Publisher   323**

46. Finding an Agent   325
47. Finding the Right Publisher   331
48. Negotiating Your Reprint Contract   335
49. Working With an Editor   346

      Glossary   350
      Index   357

Preface

This book has been prepared because I *found a need and filled it.* I hope you can do the same.

For several years I conducted classes on the subject of "How to Write, Publish, and Promote Books." This instruction normally lasted for ten weeks, one night a week for three hours. My students would frantically copy material projected onto a screen—I used 137 transparencies during the class sessions.

At the close of each three-hour session, the students would have a mass of notes, not to mention cramped legs and sore writing hands. And after devoting a full evening to such instruction, I was usually too exhausted to accomplish much the following day.

In an effort to make the learning process easier for all concerned, I taped the entire thirty-hour presentation and transcribed the material into a manuscript. The resulting self-published book is offered as an optional text at my classes, which can now be compressed into a one-day workshop.

Nine months after the book's publication, one of my three agents contacted St. Martin's Press, which agreed to reprint the book. For those who might be interested in my other credentials, they are listed below.

1978 *Hemorrhoids: A Cure and*   self-published
       Preventative

1979 *Hemorrhoids: A Cure and Preventative* (British) Commonwealth edition)	Abacus Press reprint
1980 *Hemorrhoids: A Cure and Preventative*	William Morrow reprint
1980 *Straight Teeth: Orthodontics for Everyone*	William Morrow 1st edition
1980 *Bonds: How to Double Your Money Quickly and Safely*	self-published
1981 *Bonds: How to Double Your Money Quickly and Safely*	Harcourt Brace reprint (hardbound edtion)
1981 *How Mothers and Others Stay Slim*	self-published
1982 *Hemorrhoids: A Cure and Preventative*	Editorial Limusa reprint
1982 *Publishing: A Complete Guide for Entrepreneurs*	self-published
1983 *Sweetwater: Gunslinger 201* (novel, movie rights sold)	Aero Publishers 1st edition
1985 *Bonds: How to Double Your Money Quickly and Safely*	Harper & Row reprint (softbound edition)
1985 *How to Publish, Promote, and Sell Your Own Book*	St. Martin's Press reprint

*The man who does not read good books has
no advantage over the man who can't read.*
—MARK TWAIN

━━━━━━━━━━━━━━━━━━━━━━━━━━━━━━━━━━

*The profession of book-writing makes
horse-racing seem like a solid, stable business.*
—JOHN STEINBECK

Should You Publish Your Book?

Why Publish Your Book?

1

Having your manuscript published will change your life. You may believe you're going to get rich. Become famous. Or gain immortality.

If you've chosen a good subject and follow the advice in this book, you will "get rich." However, your wealth may not be measured by the size of your bank account. Instead, you will become rich in other, more important ways. You will become an author. You may develop a new, more satisfying career. And you may become independent.

Becoming an Author

Would you like to feel the pride of seeing your book on the shelves of libraries and bookstores? Have you ever been asked for your autograph? Have strangers stared at you, as if you're somehow different from the crowd? You will be . . . if you become an author. It's a license to be different, to be yourself, whatever that may be.

What's Your Motivation?

Jack Woodford, whom the *Los Angeles Times* called one of the foremost experts on how to write, states in his book *Writer's Cramp:*

Today in a current newspaper column, I read that five million people in the United States are attempting to become writers, that 5,000 of them will get accepted, and that 50 of them make big returns at writing.

I think these figures are close to accurate. However, the non-sequitur is whopping.

These people aren't trying to become writers. They are desperately trying to keep from becoming or being something else.

Is this your real motivation? If so, good. It's genuine.

Many writers seek immortality through their writing. This is possible whether your audience is to be millions, or simply your family. If this is your motive, fine. It's certainly worth a try. A well-written book can survive its author.

Being Independent

While we're in this world, there are few of us who would not like to be successful working for ourselves. How long have you dreamed of being your own boss? Of working the hours you choose? Wherever you wish? Of once again tasting the freedom of your childhood?

This was Erle Stanley Gardner's motivation. After escaping from a successful law practice, as he revealed in *Secrets of the World's Best-Selling Writer,* by Francis Fugate:

I took up writing, not because I felt any interior urge, but because I wanted some way to make a living where I could be out-of-doors a large portion of the daytime, and be master of my own time.

This motivation worked for him. He became the world's top-selling author, with more than 300 million books sold.

So You Haven't Submitted Your Manuscript Yet?

Even with a well-written manuscript, you will probably collect rejections, as did writers like Erle Stanley Gardner. One of his came from Harry C. North, editor of *Black Mask* magazine:

> So far as *One Profitable Night* goes, I can see no hope for it. I think it is awful, a mess, not worthy of a high school kid, one of the worst—it's the kind of story I'm glad I didn't write. When I said there was no hope for it, I was a little hasty. I think there is a chance to salvage it. My suggestion would be that you nail it within arms-length of your toilet bowl. Another little tip—the next time you write a story like that, please type it on sand paper, lest I be tempted.

Act Out Your Fantasies

You may be thoroughly convinced that a New York publisher is going to offer you a six-figure advance for your manuscript, and that it will become a bestseller within the year. Then you'll buy or build that fancy house you've dreamed of ever since you started writing.

Being a romantic and dreamer myself, I'll discourage you no longer. Go directly to Part II of this book, which describes how to prepare your manuscript for publication. Chapter 11 then explains how to submit your manuscript to a major publisher. Good luck!

It's not impossible to sell your manuscript to a New York publisher. Early in my writing career, William Morrow and Company purchased my second manuscript on the subject of orthodontics. You may be fortunate, too.

A Year Later

After you've indulged your fantasies of a large advance for your "best-selling" manuscript, you may become convinced that editors in New York simply don't know a great manuscript when they see one.

You've also wasted a year (or more) of your writing career. In any case, you've paid your dues. Virtually every writer goes through a period of submitting manuscripts to major publishers.

Is Your Manuscript Worthy Of Being Published?

This is a difficult question to answer. After reviewing Part II of this book, you may be able to assess your manuscript more objectively.

Many New York publishers rejected my first manuscript on the subject of hemorrhoids. Two years later, one of those same publishers joined with two others in bidding for reprint rights to the self-published *Hemorrhoids*.

Los Angeles writer Robert Hoffman, in discussing his own rejection letters, mentioned Macmillan in the book review section of the *Los Angeles Times* on July 22, 1981:

> It's no fun being a writer. But I cling to the memory of a story a friend tells about when his father was a book editor at Macmillan in the '30s. The old man read and responded to every piece of writing sent him; by agents, writers, girlfriends of writers—anyone. That was his job, he used to say, and that was his duty. One day he received—and ultimately published, over the objections of his colleagues—a very long first novel, a love story set in the Civil War South. The author's name was Margaret Mitchell.

The "great American novel" came that close to being unpublished.

Are these exceptional cases? Probably not. Many other best-selling books were initially rejected in manuscript form by major publishers. Below is a list from *Family Weekly* of such books, with the number of times they were rejected:

Auntie Mame	17
Jonathan Livingston Seagull	18
Kon-Tiki	20
Peyton Place	24+
M*A*S*H*	21
Lust for Life	17

So you cannot always depend on editors at large publishing houses to judge the potential of your manuscript.

If it does have potential, you may be able to confirm this by publishing it yourself. The expense of publishing your book, when spread over a year, is little more than many of us spend on hobbies, vacations, or a new set of furniture. Why not "buy" a book instead? Your own. Chapter 4 quickly reveals the approximate cost of publishing your book.

You May Make More Money Publishing Your Own Book

Few references on the subject of author-publishing divulge one of the best reasons for publishing your own book. If you have an excellent manuscript on a marketable subject, you can usually make more money self-publishing it than by selling it in manuscript form.

The figures below compare the gross sales of the author's first self-published book (during its initial two years) with the royalties it would have earned had it been sold in manuscript form.

Bindings	Copies Sold	Gross Sales	Comparable Royalties
Hard	1600	$13,400	$2,072
Soft	6875	18,450	2,315
Total:		$31,850	$4,387

Publishing and marketing expenses were less than a third of the gross sales figures, leaving an overall profit that exceeded $20,000. Self-publishing yielded a return that was five times greater than it would have been if the book had sold to another publisher.

This experience was repeated with the author's second self-published book, on the subject of investment bonds.

Reprint rights to both books were later sold to major publishers. The advances received for these rights were clear profit, further compounding the return on the books.

Are Author-Published Books Non-Books?

The Library of Congress and many book review editors look down their noses at self-published books. They view them as "non-books."

It is true that many self-published books are sad cases that should never have been printed. However, the same can be said for a substantial portion of the books released by major publishers. Examples of poorly written, even harmful, books can be found on the bestseller lists.

These books depend on promotion for their success, whereas books by small presses rarely succeed unless they have merit. Few small publishers have the necessary capital to fool the reading public.

Well-Known "Non-Books"

When enterprising writers have chosen to publish their own books, the results on occasion have been extraordinary. A good book is a good book, regardless of the size of its publisher. Here is a selected list of such author-published books:

The Acorn People . . . Ron Jones
Betty Zane . . . Zane Grey
The Elements of Style . . . William Strunk

Familiar Quotations . . . John Bartlett
Feed Me! I'm Yours! . . . Vicky Lansky
Fugitive Pieces . . . Lord Byron
How to Flatten Your Stomach . . . Jim Everroad
How to Form Your Own Corporation for Under $50 . . . Ted Nicholas
How to Pick Up Girls . . . Eric Weber
How to See Europe on $5 a Day . . . Arthur Frommer
Huckleberry Finn . . . Mark Twain
The Jungle . . . Upton Sinclair
Lady Chatterly's Lover . . . D. H. Lawrence
Leaves of Grass . . . Walt Whitman
Looking Out For #1 . . . Robert Ringer
The One-Minute Manager . . . Johnson & Blanchard
Poor Richard's Almanack . . . Benjamin Franklin
Robert's Rules of Order . . . Henry M. Robert
Science and Health . . . Mary Baker Eddy
The Taming of the Candy Monster . . . Vicky Lansky
Tarzan series (1931–1948) . . . Edgar Rice Burroughs
A Week on the Concord and Merrimack Rivers . . . Henry Thoreau
Winning Through Intimidation . . . Robert Ringer
Winter of the Artifice . . . Anaïs Nin
Your Erroneous Zones . . . Wayne Dyer

If you can:

1. select an appropriate subject,
2. write on it clearly and well,
3. design your book for ease of understanding and attractiveness,
4. print it professionally, and
5. promote it with enthusiasm,

the end result should be a successful work. It may be your one chance at immortality, or your one chance to break out of the boring job you now have. It's worth *doing it right.*

What Vanity Presses
Don't Tell You

You have probably read or heard of a few horror stories about vanity presses already. These firms are also referred to as "subsidy publishers." Their advertisements abound in book review sections of newspapers and many other publications that discuss books or the craft of writing.

An ad by one of the larger vanity presses states:

HAVE YOU WRITTEN A BOOK?

A publisher's editorial representative will be interviewing local authors in a quest for finished manuscripts suitable for book publication by [name of vanity press], a well-known New York subsidy publishing firm. All subjects will be considered, including fiction and nonfiction, poetry, drama, religion, philosophy, etc.

Another vanity press frequently appeals to us with this ad:

WRITERS

Tired of form letter rejections from McGraw-Hill, Random House and other East Coast giants? [Name of vanity press] is

> now inviting authors to call to find out if their manuscript
> qualifies for national publication. Qualifying manuscripts only
> will be read by our professional editorial staff who are them-
> selves published authors, and a few selected writers will be
> invited for a personal evaluation of their work.

These advertisements sound inviting, especially to writers
who have had their manuscripts rejected for a number of
years.

What Vanity Presses Don't Tell You

What such ads fail to reveal to unsuspecting writers is that a
vanity press is not a publisher in the commonly accepted definition of the word. The dictionary defines "publish" as the act
of "issuing a printed work to the public, as for sale."

Publishing firms—and self-publishers—derive profits by
selling books to the public. Vanity presses, on the other hand,
"sell" books to their authors. They charge aspiring authors the
full expense of printing their own books, then tack on a
healthy markup—the source of the vanity press's profit. You
should be able to self-publish your book for 25 to 35 percent
less than most of the quotes you receive from vanity presses.

A Sad Experience

The *Los Angeles Times* on February 8, 1981, published an
article written by Howard Henry Most that described a disas-
trous experience with a vanity press. The vanity press obtained
his money before printing a single book. Mr. Most was told:

> . . . as soon as the first edition has sold out, he [the vanity press]
> will pay for a second edition [1,000 books] out of his own pocket.
> You are impressed. All he asks is 25% of the gross and you can
> have the other 75%. The publisher wants you to dream awhile.

It brings in money. One thing he doesn't tell you is that he never expects to sell out the first 1,000 books.

Time moves on and you still don't see any copies of your book. Lots of alibis: paper shortage, technical problems with the typesetter or printer, layout had to be done over, change of printers in midstream. You begin to panic; $8,000 invested and still no printed copies to hold and admire. Then the crushing blow. Your publisher has shut up shop. You pick up the phone, but he has vanished, left town. His office door is locked. You've been had and you feel it in your guts. It crushes your spirit.

The author has heard this story over and over again among writers.

In one recent case, a woman pleaded for advice. She had paid a subsidy publisher $6,000 to "publish" a thousand books. At the time we met, she had received only fifty books, for which she was charged 40 percent of their list price (this was in addition to the $6,000). The vanity press wouldn't (or couldn't) fill bookstore orders. It turned out that the book had been printed by a firm in Tijuana, Mexico. The owners of this firm had declared bankruptcy earlier in the United States. Her book was printed on cheap paper and had a plain cover—just a title and the author's name. It was too late to give her any advice.

An attorney seldom helps in such cases, as many vanity presses simply shut down their operation, change names, and move to a new location when the legal problems mount.

These so-called presses are often merely a small office from which the owner subcontracts all the work to other firms, with little or no concern for quality. Authors who actually receive the proper number of books for which they've contracted should consider themselves fortunate.

Co-Op Publishers

A co-op publisher is a variation of the subsidy publisher. Here the author and the "publisher" supposedly share 50/50 in the expenses and profits of the author's book. Some co-op publishers have been known to quote the author's "50% share" at a sufficiently high level to cover the entire cost of the book's printing.

If the co-op publisher is totally shameless, the author may receive only half of the contracted books—or none at all. The co-op press simply pays a small portion of the original author's deposit back, calling it the profits on the book.

What You Should Know About Publishing Before Publishing Your Own Book

3

Do you know the facts of life . . . about the publishing world? They may shock you.

Why Bookstores Carry Few Self-Published Books

Did you realize that a bookstore can return its entire inventory to publishers for a cash refund? No other retail business operates on such favorable terms with its suppliers.

With this privilege, you might suspect that most bookstores would be willing to carry your self-published book. In fact, they cannot, for several reasons.

The Number of Books Available

According to *Books in Print,* there are more than 600,000 book titles currently available that have been published in the United States.

Each year, more books are added to this list. As many as 35,000 book titles are released by commercial publishers, and an additional 10,000 are privately published. Your book competes with all of these for space on the shelves of bookstores.

Space Available in Bookstores

According to an article in *The New Yorker* in 1980, the average number of titles stocked in a B. Dalton store is 25,000. The average number of books stocked in independent bookstores located in medium-sized cities is 10,000.

This space will not even hold the number of new titles released each year, much less a significant number of the books released in previous years.

Publicity Sells Books

In order to stay in business, the managers of bookstores must allot space on their shelves to those books that are most likely to "sell through"—to be in public demand.

Few author-publishers generate sufficient publicity to warrant space for their books in bookstores. When the larger publishers promote their books in magazines and newspapers, as well as on radio and television, such publicity demands that bookstores allot space for these books. There may be little space left over for self-published efforts, which will receive virtually no publicity.

Do You Want To Sell To Bookstores Anyway?

As this book fully explains in Chapter 41, self-publishers should not plan on distributing all their books through bookstores. There are more than 9,000 bookstores in the United States, fewer than half of which are part of large chains like Waldenbooks and B. Dalton. How would you invoice that many bookstores?

Literary Market Place estimates that there are more than 10,000 publishers. How could a bookstore manager be expected to keep track of orders to that many publishers? The expense would be prohibitive.

The bookstores that do accept your book will do so only on consignment. That does not mean that they will automatically send money to you when and if your books do sell. You must go back to each store that has your books, count those sold, prepare an invoice, send it, and then wait.

And wait. As a small press publisher, you will be among the last to be paid by bookstores. Ninety days is a common waiting period if you are fortunate. Six months is not uncommon. And many bookstores will not pay at all, especially if they are out-of-state.

Regardless of the wait, you can consider yourself fortunate to sell any books at all. This is because your books will probably be displayed with only the spine, not your carefully designed jacket, showing. With your limited ability to publicize books outside your own region, how will people even know that your book is available?

When you recover unsold books, you may be disappointed to learn that they are in too poor a condition to be resold. However discouraging, these are the facts you will be confronted with when you are ready to sell books.

You can also sell your book through wholesalers, but that has problems of its own, as discussed in Chapter 42.

Eighty Percent Of The Books Released By The Major Publishers Do Not Earn Back Their Advances

The most important reason why 80 percent of the books released by the major publishers do not earn back their advances is that few publishers, big or small, do an adequate job of promoting all the books they release. Many major publishers promote only those books for which they've paid substantial advances. The rest sink or swim according to the reviews they receive.

A major newspaper such as the *Los Angeles Times* reviews

only 16 percent of the yearly output; *Library Journal* reviews
only 17 percent. The rest of the books "sink." Many authorities in the industry think too many books are released each
year. Some publishers may be listening, as the yearly output
has declined from 40,000 to the 35,000 level in recent years.
But the competition for reviews is still fierce. This is the market your book will enter.

Only Five Percent Of All Authors Make a Decent Living

In 1981, *Publishers Weekly* reported on a survey of 2,239
published book authors by a group of Columbia University
social scientists that indicated only 5 percent of them were able
to sustain themselves by writing over long periods of time.

Does that sound encouraging? These are authors of books
printed by large publishers for the most part. Their meager
returns are explained to a large degree by the difficulty that
all books have in surviving the marketplace.

The only way to ensure that your manuscript is properly
edited is to get it edited yourself. Chapters 9 and 10 explain
how to accomplish this.

Concentration Within The Publishing Industry

Although there are more than 10,000 book publishers in the
United States, the industry is highly concentrated. Not only
does this factor make it more difficult to get published, it also
makes competition keener among publishers.

The *Los Angeles Times* reported in 1982 that, according to
the Association of American Publishers, the top eleven publishers of trade hardcover books accounted for approximately
70 percent of such sales.

The mass paperback publishers were even more highly concentrated. The top thirteen mass paperback publishers accounted for almost 95 percent of total mass paperback sales.

Even more serious is the power concentrated in the three major chains: B. Dalton, Waldenbooks, and Crown Books. While they account for only 17 percent of all retail book sales (in 1981), their sales amount to over 70 percent of all chain store sales. (BP Report, June 18, 1982, *Los Angeles Times*)

Their computerized cash registers can instantly reveal the status of individual book sales. Of course, this encourages the managers of these chains to concentrate their efforts on the best-selling books. If a book does not quickly begin "performing," it may be pulled in favor of new candidates. With the promotion capital and media contacts of the largest publishers, their books tend to be favored.

Learn As Much As You Can About Publishing

To succeed against these seemingly insurmountable odds, you must be as well informed as possible. This book provides a wealth of information, but you need much more. This book suggests that any serious author-publisher read at least ten other books about the industry.

Two of these are *The Blockbuster Complex* (1981), by Thomas Whiteside, and *The Writer's Survival Manual* (1982), written by Carol Meyer. Further suggestions are listed in appropriate chapters. In addition, there are a number of weekly publications that can keep you up to date with this rapidly changing business.

Publishers Weekly

Foremost of the book trade references is *Publishers Weekly,* or *PW*. It is fascinating and informative reading for anyone in the book business. Check the front for the Contents page, as its initial pages (sometimes over a hundred) are devoted to advertising.

An author interview usually appears just after the Contents page. Industry news is then discussed. A feature-length article normally includes information that will be helpful to you. A "rights and permission" page discusses six-figure advances, which should provide motivation. Once every month, a page is devoted to publishing on the West Coast.

The last half or third of the magazine is devoted to book reviews, which are generally friendly. Scan these to check the better books being released in your fields of interest. A favorable review for another title on the same subject in *PW* discouraged this author from preparing a book on skin care.

Book Review Sections of Newspapers

The largest newspaper in your region should have a weekly book review section. This source is particularly valuable in locating regional publisher and author societies, where you can meet other author-publishers, who, in turn, can refer you to reliable typesetters, graphic designers, printers, binderies, editors, and other professionals in the book business.

Who Is Responsible For Promoting Your Book?

Few authors of books published by major publishers are satisfied with the amount of promotion their books receive. They always blame their publishers when their books are not promoted.

Perhaps they should follow the example set by Sidney Sheldon. He said in a *Los Angeles Times* interview in 1982 that when his first book was released, "I paid all promotional costs myself. I paid for the book party at the 21 Club; and I paid for the book tour." Sheldon's formula for success is, "Always do more than you're paid to do."

If you decide to publish your own book, you should realize that the responsibility for promoting it will fall entirely on you.

How Much Will
Your Book Cost?

4

Establishing Your Company
——— Post Office Box
——— Stationery and Cards
——— Bank Account
——— Fictitious Name Statement

Graphic Design Fees
——— Line Illustrations
——— Line Screens
——— Photographs (black and white)
——— Photographs (color)
——— Duotones

Typesetting Costs
——— Text
——— Headings
——— Front and Back Matter

Book Manufacturing Costs
——— Length of Book
——— Page Size
——— Type of Paper
——— Illustrations

            Binding Costs
——— Softbound Cover-Printing
——— Dust Jacket
——— Binding Softbound Books
——— Binding Hardbound Books
——— Converting

            Promotion Costs
——— Advance Reading Copies
——— Promotional Brochure
——— Mail-Order Promotions

——— Fulfillment Costs

This chapter provides a quick means of estimating the out-of-pocket expenses to publish your book. As you read the chapter, place estimates for your own book's cost on the lines preceding the expanded chapter outline. By the time you finish the chapter, you will have a good idea of the total cost of your planned book.

Establishing Your Company

The first step in producing your book is to form its publishing company. This is necessary for numerous reasons:

1. to obtain a post office box,
2. to open a company bank account,
3. to avoid sales taxes on materials purchased from suppliers,
4. to obtain credit from suppliers,
5. to obtain discounts from suppliers,
6. to obtain forms and cataloging numbers from the book industry,

7. to command more respect from all your suppliers, including printers, and
8. to convince reviewers to consider your book.

Obtaining a Post Office Box

The cost of a standard-size post office box is currently $20 a year, or $10 semi-annually. It is not necessary to rent the larger boxes, as the post office will give you a red "pick-up" slip whenever they receive an item too large for your box.

You can also obtain a "box number" from private mail-drop services; however, the cost is considerably higher than for a box at your local post office.

Printing Stationery and Business Cards

While the streamlined methods suggested in this book can save you thousands of dollars, your company stationery and cards are areas where you should not cut corners. Your stationery must appear professional in order to convince reviewers, the media, and others that you are not just another amateur self-publisher.

Plan to spend at least $100 for stationery and business cards. This will pay for a thousand letterheads and envelopes, plus five hundred business cards—printed on quality, colored paper. For this price, you will also be able to have an attractive company logo.

Opening a Bank Account

Your initial expense will be the printing of your company checks. You should order the large, business-size checks, which come in a three-ring binder. The cost should be about $30. The stubs that come with these checks provide a record of business transactions for tax purposes.

Filing a Fictitious Name Statement

If you choose to use your own name for the title of your publishing company, you can skip this step. However, by using your own name, you will be signaling to potential reviewers that your book is self-published.

Upon choosing a fictitious name for your company, you must publish a legal notice of your choice. By selecting a small daily or weekly newspaper, you should be able to limit this expense to $25 or less. The smaller the circulation of a paper, the less its advertising will cost.

Graphic Design Fees

Your book should include ample illustrations and/or photographs. They are usually relatively inexpensive, depending on the book's design and how much you can do yourself.

Black-and-White Line Illustrations

Line illustrations, which have no gray tones, can be drawn by yourself, clipped from a clip-art catalog, or prepared by a graphic designer.

Figure 4.1 was cut from a clip-art catalog that contained

Figure 4.1

hundreds of other readymade drawings. Clip-art catalogs can be obtained in stationery and art supply stores for $5 to $20 each. If you wish to use artwork for decorative purposes, this is an inexpensive way to illustrate your book.

Figure 4.2 was prepared by a professional graphic designer. Graphic designers can be hired on an hourly basis for amounts ranging from $25 to $50; graphic art students can often be hired for much less with satisfactory results. Figure 4.2 required approximately an hour to prepare.

Line Screens

If you wish to add gray tones to a black-and-white illustration, you must hire a graphic designer to create the artwork for your illustration. From this artwork, a printer will make a screen for each of the gray tones.

A light gray can be created by permitting only 10 to 20 percent of the printer's ink to "flow through" the screen. To obtain a darker tone, a screen of 70 to 90 percent would be utilized.

The printer of your book may offer to prepare your artwork, but it is suggested that you hire your own graphic designer for this purpose. By supervising your own artwork, you can be more certain the final result will be to your satisfaction.

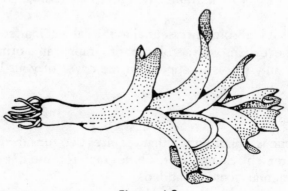

Figure 4.2

Photographs—Black-and-White

One of the least expensive methods of illustrating your book is to use black-and-white photographs. Most of the writers who attend the author's publishing workshops guess that a single black-and-white photograph costs anywhere from $50 to $300 to reproduce in a book. In fact, it should cost no more than $5 to $10 to print such a photograph in a book, regardless of the number of books printed. This is the charge for making a halftone, which is explained in Chapter 25.

If you can take your own photographs, you should consider this method of illustrating your book. As long as your photographs are not in color, you do not need a graphic designer.

Photographs—Color

The reproduction of a color photograph in a book requires four runs through most presses. A black-and-white photograph, by comparison, requires only one run. The added cost of printing a single color photograph can be as much as $250 to $350.

In addition to the increased printing cost, color separations must be prepared for each color photograph. It is wise to hire a graphic designer to assist in obtaining and judging the quality of color separations. While the color separations will cost from $75 to $150, a graphic designer may cost an additional $100.

Unless it is absolutely essential to the subject matter of your book, the expense of a color photograph can normally be justified only if it is to appear on the cover of your book.

Duotones

A duotone is a photograph that requires two runs through the press; after a black-and-white photograph is printed, a second, complementary color is added.

The effect of a duotone can be almost as attractive as a color photograph. To print a duotone should cost no more than $75 to $100 extra. There is no need to hire a graphic designer. Duotones receive further discussion in Chapter 14.

Typesetting Costs

A reasonable typesetter will charge from $4 to $8 per type page, depending on the kind of material. Straight copy—no indented material, tables, headings, or the like—is the least expensive to typeset.

Word Processors and Computers

A number of authors are using word processors or mini-computers to compose their manuscripts. When these machines are compatible with typesetting equipment at a printer, the cost of typesetting your manuscript may be considerably less than if you submitted normally typed material. However, the cost of your word processor may negate much of these savings.

If you wish to consider this alternative, the best book on the subject is *The Word Processing Book* by Peter McWilliams. The softbound edition ($8.95) is available from:

PRELUDE PRESS
Box 69773
Los Angeles, CA 90069

Another option, which many author-publishers have used, is to "typeset" the book yourself using an IBM Executive, which enables you to justify the right-hand margins and allows for proportional spacing of letters (this is fully described in Chapter 20).

Headings, or Display Type

Typesetting of chapter titles, running heads at the top of each page, and other miscellaneous material that is separate from your text will be charged to you. Typesetting for a book with 15 chapter headings, running heads for 200 pages, and the captions for 20 illustrations would cost approximately $10 to $12 a page. Most of this can be done on an IBM Executive typewriter if you do your own typesetting.

Front and Back Matter

Your book's front matter (title page, copyright page, contents page, preface, etc.) and back matter (references, glossary, index, etc.) is usually typeset after the manuscript text is set. The fee for this material may vary from $50 to $100, depending on its length.

Book Manufacturing Costs

This author suggests an initial printing of a thousand books for most author-publishers. If the purpose of your book is mail-order sales, even less than a thousand may be wise in order to test your market first.

The cost of printing a thousand books will depend on several factors, including:

1. the page length of your book,
2. the size of its pages,
3. the type of paper it's printed on,
4. the amount and kind of artwork,
5. the kind of cover and binding.

Page Length of Your Book

The table below lists the approximate figures for producing a thousand books of varying page lengths, including paper and printing. These figures are for a book with 5½" × 8¼" specifications.

Number of Pages	Cost per 1000 Books
48	$800
80	1,100
112	1,450
144	1,700
176	1,900
208	2,200

Each additional 16-page signature should cost approximately $75.

The above figures assume that you follow the advice contained later in this book, which includes:

1. pasting up your own galleys to boards,
2. pasting up the boards to signatures, and
3. proofing negatives instead of blue-lines.

You should be aware that industry prices increase every year and vary greatly nationwide.

Size of Your Book Page

If you select a standard book size, you will save money by minimizing wastage of paper. The following sizes are generally the most economical:

5½ × 8¼
6⅛ × 9¼
8½ × 11
9 × 12

The two largest page sizes may result in quotes that are 10 to 15 percent higher than the figures in the previous section.

Once you have selected a preferred size, check with your local printers to determine if it is suitable for their presses. Chapters 12, 15, and 31 provide additional details on this.

Type of Paper

Most books are printed on standard 50- to 60-pound paper. You may wish to have a thicker book. If this is the case, order a high-bulk paper, which should increase your total costs by no more than 10 percent.

If the fine reproduction of photographs is vital to your book, you may wish to order clay-coated paper. This will increase your paper (not printing) costs by 30 to 40 percent. The cost of paper usually amounts to about 40 percent of the printing costs for a book.

Printing of Illustrations

Line illustrations can be photographed, plated, and printed just like your text. If you wish varied tones in illustrations, use line screens. A printer normally will charge $5 to $10 to make a negative of a line screen.

Black-and-white photographs must be converted to halftones by the printer, for which the charge should also be $5 to $10 each.

If you insist on different colors within your book, it can easily double or triple the cost of printing. Each color requires a run through the press. See Chapters 15 and 25 for detailed information concerning the use of color.

Binding Your Book

In most instances, your initial edition should be softbound. There are two reasons for this. First, hardbinding costs five to six times more than softbinding. Second, there's no need to bind in hardcover unless a library demand develops.

The Softbound Cover

The first step in binding a softbound book is to print its cover. A cover printed in one color should cost no more than $150 to $200 for a thousand copies. Each additional color will add approximately 50 percent to these figures.

By using a line screen, you can print different tones of the same color on your cover. While such a screen reduces printing costs by requiring only one run through a press, you may incur a graphic designer fee for preparation of artwork.

Printing the Dust Jacket

The cost of printing a dust jacket is the same as for printing a softbound cover. Chapters 28 and 30 explain how your softbound cover can also serve the function of a dust jacket. Review this information before deciding to pay for a dust jacket.

Binding Softbound Books

Once you've printed your cover, it is relatively inexpensive to bind it on your book. Most softbound books are simply perfect-bound (glued together), as telephone directories are. The cost of binding a thousand standard-size books should not exceed $350.

There are several other methods of softbinding books that are more expensive than perfect binding. However, if you are printing substantially fewer than a thousand books, these methods may actually be less costly. Chapters 29, 30, and 31 discuss this subject in more detail.

Binding Hardbound Books

The cost of hardbinding 1,000 copies of a 5½" by 8¼" book ranges from $1.50 to $1.75 each. If you wish to bind fewer than 1,000 copies, the price increases rapidly. For 200 books, you might be charged $4 to $6 per copy.

Converting Softbound to Hardbound

Libraries frequently purchase the less expensive softbound edition of a book, then convert its cover to hardbound. Such conversions seldom cost more than $4.00 per book. If you are unsure of the demand for your book in hardbinding, then wait. If this demand develops, then convert as the libraries do. Chapters 28 and 30 provide additional information about converting.

Promotion Costs

A book is a product. When it is first introduced, it requires publicity just as any other new product does. Potential buyers must be made aware that it exists and where it's available.

While Part IV of this book outlines numerous free methods of promoting books, it is still necessary to budget adequate funds for this purpose. A minimum of $600 is suggested. This will cover the expense of distributing so-called advance reading copies, the printing of a promotional brochure, and the shared cost of a mailing.

Advance Reading Copies

At least a hundred advance reading copies of your book should be distributed to trade reviewers, regional media, and others who might contribute to the sale of your book. The printing of these copies (see Chapter 28), postage, and packaging will cost approximately $200.

A Promotional Brochure

Plan to spend at least $100 on a strong promotional brochure. If you are going to ask people to part with money for your book without first viewing it, your promotional brochure must be convincing and professional. Chapter 35 discusses this subject.

Mail-Order Promotions

Do not plan on placing advertisements in the media for your book in the beginning; it will be far too expensive for the returns received. You must thoroughly study recommended references in the mail-order field first, in addition to testing various messages.

If you can accurately pinpoint a target audience for your book, it is possible to sell books by direct mail. This also requires research and testing. Equally important, you must find other author-publishers to share the cost. If you plan carefully, you can send a mailing out to as many as two thousand recipients for as little as $300 (with two others sharing your total costs).

While a minimum of $600 is suggested to start promotion for your book, there is no maximum. The more you wisely spend, the more books you should sell.

Fulfillment Costs

These are the expenses incurred to fill orders for your book. The heaviest cost will be for postage, followed by packaging materials.

Book mailing rates have been increasing steadily during the last five years and can be expected to continue to do so. Currently, a book weighing less than one pound costs 69 cents to mail. Between one and two pounds, a book costs 94 cents.

A mailing package for a 5½" by 8¼" book costs anywhere from 9 to 35 cents each, depending on the protection desired. These figures assume you are ordering your mailing packages in bulk (a hundred to five hundred).

There is also the expense of printing invoices and mailing labels. Invoices should be printed on NCR paper, which does not require carbons. Two thousand invoices should cost no more than $30 (see Chapter 17). A similar number of mailing labels should cost no more than $40.

Preparing Your Manuscript for

Publication

II

Have You Chosen a Marketable Subject?

5

No, your autobiography is not a marketable subject, unless you are a movie star, politician, or other type of celebrity. A book concerning your travels abroad is not a likely candidate either.

A marketable subject is one that is of interest to the general public, or at least appeals to a sizable speciality group, and that has not been adequately covered elsewhere. Remember the six magic words: "Find a need and fill it."

What Makes Your Book Unique?

How is your book unique? What makes it stand out from the crowd? What makes your book the best choice in its field? If you do not have acceptable answers to these questions at this time, then perhaps you should consider another subject. An acquaintance decided to publish a short book explaining how to stop smoking. The competition in this field is immense— even hospitals sell programs to stop smoking. This book had almost no chance of survival. And it didn't survive.

How Marketable Is Your Novel?

You're up against considerable odds if you intend to self-publish a novel. Novels are difficult to promote, even for the big publishers. Before embarking on your publishing program, exhaust all other avenues of getting your novel published.

While significant numbers of nonfiction authors have their self-published books reprinted by major publishers, the author is aware of only two West Coast authors who have had their novels later reprinted by major publishers. One of them hawked his novels like an encyclopedia salesperson by knocking on doors and offering to autograph his book if it were purchased. This unique sales technique made the regional news, which is how he came to the attention of a publisher.

The other author had successfully published a number of nonfiction books, which helped bring attention to his novel. Both of these novels were well written, a distinction among novels published by anyone.

The limited possibilities of fiction for the first-time author even with a major publisher were discussed in the book review section of the *Los Angeles Times* on February 20, 1982:

Salesmen . . . hate fiction. They want promotable books, the ones teaching people how to pan gold or slice hips or burp babies. Television hardly ever helps a novel. Talk shows want advice or experience; hosts don't want novelists unless the authors are as large as Michener, Mailer, or Clavell . . . names who are already words of mouth. Fiction is out of favor, partly because readers are perceived to be more hungry for raw data than rich drama, more interested in life style than literary style. Those are the facts of life.

If you are still enthusiastic after reading this section, then go ahead and self-publish your novel. But first, make sure it is well written.

Self-Help Books Are Lucrative

The publishing of self-help books can be quite lucrative. This is the category of all but one of the author's books and also describes most of the other successful self-published books.

A syndicated article by Dave Goldberg of the Associated Press entitled "Self-Help Books Really Do Work—Especially for Bank Accounts of Their Authors" revealed that the publishing of self-help books was estimated to be, as of 1981,

> more than a $1 billion a year business. Two-thirds of 1980's 15 top hardcover bestsellers fell into the broad category of self-help, a ratio being maintained in 1981.
>
> Self-help authors usually help themselves first . . . then they offer what worked for them to others. Self-help books are to get healthier, wealthier, and wiser; but there isn't one self-help market. There are incredible numbers of markets.

This same article describes how Wayne Dyer self-published *Your Erroneous Zones* (4500 copies) and then traveled across the country hawking his book on TV shows. The book became a bestseller. He followed its success with several more (*Pulling Your Own Strings* and *The Sky's the Limit*), which did not require self-publishing.

Research Your Marketability

Before doing research to write your book, why not do some research concerning whether it should be written in the first place?

The largest book buyers in your city are libraries. Go to them. Ask their acquisition librarians which subject areas are most frequently requested by patrons. A children's book writer learned that more "train" books are needed for children. Another librarian said that any book on the subject of health receives heavy usage.

Go to managers of bookstores. Ask them which types of books are the most popular. If the top-selling books are arranged in order on a shelf, look them over. Ask these managers if the subject area of your book would be of interest to their customers.

Do not ask these managers if they will take your book on consignment—this is the wrong question. Most local stores will take your book on consignment, but that doesn't mean they think it'll sell.

Also discuss your book idea with all the people you know who are well read. If a number of these readers compliment your idea, your book may well have possibilities. (Be careful, however, to ask some people who won't be afraid to tell you the truth as they see it; your family and closest friends may not be impartial advisers.)

The best indication is when these readers offer to help finance or market your book. Three early readers of the author's first manuscript expressed interest in such partnerships. The eventual book went through nine printings within its first three years. Five were self-published, and four were reprint editions in the United States and Great Britain.

Checking Out The Competition

Wait a minute! Don't spend another cent on your book idea until you have checked out its competition.

Before working any further on your project, review all books currently in print on the subject. If there already is a quality book available in the field, then strongly consider writing on another subject.

If your manuscript has been completed, then consider a different slant to your subject. Libraries are not going to purchase your book in significant numbers if they already have an adequate book on the subject. Bookstore buyers won't be interested either. How many books on cat care does the public need? A new one seems to come out every few months, with good reviews.

Where Do You Go?

First, go to the nearest library and review their latest edition of *Subject Guide to Books in Print.* These are several volumes published each year by the same people who print *Publishers Weekly*—R. R. Bowker Company. Bookstores often carry either this reference or another entitled *Books in Print—Titles.*

Look up your subject and make a list of every book title that appears relevant. You may have to photocopy an entire page. Then review each book on this list that is carried by your library.

To check the most recently issued books, review back issues of *Publishers Weekly.* Both the book advertisements and reviews in this publication may alert you to books that are similar to yours.

What Do You Look For?

When you review these books, ask yourself these questions:

1. Do any of these books do a reasonable job of covering your subject?
2. Are these books directed at the same market as your book?
3. Why would book buyers prefer your book to what is already in print?

After reviewing all the books on your list that are offered by your library system, go to a large bookstore. If necessary, place orders for relevant books that you cannot locate in libraries or stores. These are good investments. If they discourage you from pursuing your current book idea, they may have saved you several thousand dollars. On the other hand, if they do not compete with your idea, they may serve as useful references during your research.

When the author decided to write a book on the subject of investment bonds, only two similar books were listed in *Subject Guide to Books in Print*. Neither book was available in local libraries or bookstores. So they were ordered through a bookstore. After reviewing them, the author decided to tackle the subject of investment bonds—his profession for fifteen years. The resulting self-published book was selected by *Library Journal* as one of the top five books published in 1980 within the field of securities. It was subsequently reprinted by Harcourt Brace and selected by the Book-of-the-Month Club. This would not have been possible if there had been a decent book on bonds in existence already.

In another case, the author strongly considered preparing a reference on the subject of humorous graffiti. Again, local libraries and bookstores had nothing. The *Subject Guide to Books in Print* listed only one book of note, Robert Reisner's *Graffiti: Two Thousand Years of Wall Writing*.

The book was ordered. Upon receiving it, I quickly decided to cancel my own idea. Reisner, an experienced author (sixteen books), had put together a delightful, easy-to-read, 204-page book with ample photographs and graffiti. The failure of local libraries and bookstores to carry the book could only be ascribed to lack of interest.

Just after gasoline prices had doubled and car manufacturers were rapidly increasing their prices, the author considered writing a book to be entitled *How to Buy a Good Used Car and Keep It Running*. After I attended several classes on the subject and gathered a five-inch-thick notebook of research, two new books on the same subject appeared in *Publishers Weekly* with good reviews. Although a publisher was interested in purchasing the manuscript (unwritten at that time), I dropped the project because of the competition.

Gathering and
Organizing Research

6

In order to write the best-selling book on your subject, you must do more thorough research than authors of other books in your field.

In the beginning, you should keep one goal in mind: to gather all available information on your subject. While you start in one direction, your search may lead you down a dozen or more paths.

Use A Three-Ring Notebook

Before beginning your research, obtain a three-ring notebook. Also purchase a few dozen manila dividers to place between the developing chapters of your book.

As you gather data, arrange it by subject matter in the notebook. When sufficient data is collected on one subject, it may justify a chapter. Place paperclips on the chapter dividers, to hold small notes and articles.

As you continue to organize your research by chapters, your book will slowly take form.

Start Writing Before Completing Your Research

Don't try to do all your research first. Start writing ideas down as they occur, and place them in the three-ring notebook too.

Until your typesetting is pasted up to boards, you can continue to add the benefits of new research to your book. Major publishers seldom include material in their books that is less than twelve months old. As an author-publisher, you can include more recent, up-to-date material in your book.

Collect Footnotes

Whenever you photocopy or remove material from a publication, make a footnote of its source. This should include:

1. title of book or article,
2. author,
3. publisher or publication, and
4. date and page number(s).

Your book must reference all important source material, either in the text, at the end of each chapter, or at the end of the book. This is a courtesy to your readers, and a must for your reviewers.

Contact Other Authors

Whenever you come upon a particularly valuable research source, contact its author. Often, an author will furnish you with additional material or be able to answer important questions raised by earlier material.

If they are distinguished, you might ask them to write a foreword to your book. If their material is a valuable supplement to your own, you may wish to add it to the end of your text, as an addendum.

Quoting Other Authors

Never quote or otherwise use another author's work without giving due credit. What constitutes "fair use" of another author's work varies in each case. You will find adequate books in your library concerning this subject. If you are in doubt, contact the author to request permission.

As a general rule, it is recommended that you not use quotes that constitute more than three-quarters of one of your own text pages.

Your Local Library First

A lengthy visit to your local library is the first step in gathering your research. Do not simply look up your subject in the card-index file for books. There are many other sources at the library worth checking out.

Periodical Guides

Books on your subject in a library may be ten to thirty years old—badly outdated. For this reason, begin your research in the magazine and journal section. This is where the most recent information will be. These articles should reveal the latest technology or thought on your subject, in addition to indicating future trends. Few books will be as up to date.

In professional journals, one good article may lead you to several others. Look for references at the end of these articles.

You may find that two or three periodicals carry most of the articles on your subject. Be sure to review the Table of Contents of their latest issues. Most periodical guides are two to three months behind current issues.

Newspapers

Of course, you're reading a major newspaper on a daily basis, aren't you? Your newspaper not only originates material, it also purchases stories off the major news services. This information is more up to date than periodicals.

A few libraries clip and file articles on certain subjects. Ask your reference librarian if material on your subject is available.

Your Reference Librarian

A reference librarian at a large library can be a rich source of information. Carefully explain what your subject area is and exhaust this source before going to specialty libraries.

The National Endowment for the Humanities has granted funds to many of the nation's library systems to gather historical data on computers. If your local library system has participated in one of these surveys, ask your reference librarian for help in checking these sources.

Specialty Libraries

There are specialty libraries in every state, usually at universities. Your reference librarian can refer you to these also.

Other Sources

There is virtually no limit to the sources of research that you can tap. This section mentions but a few.

Bookstores

Visit the largest bookstores in your vicinity frequently. The most recent books in your subject area will appear here before their availability is listed in book references.

Friends and Associates

Put the word out among your acquaintances that you're gathering material for a book. You'll be surprised how many people begin supplying information to you.

Private Corporations

Get in touch with private corporations (profit or non-profit) that provide services or products related to your subject. Use your company stationery when making such contacts. The corporations will be anxious to provide you with information, as it promotes their own products or services.

Later, you may be able to sell your book to these companies.

Government Agencies

Your reference librarian may be able to furnish the addresses of numerous government agency sources of research data. Writing to your congressman or senator is usually more effective than contacting the government agency directly.

Writing Clearly

7

At a writer's workshop in Southern California a few years ago, the moderator asked a panel of well-known authors this question: "What does it take to write a bestseller?"

After little discussion, their consensus was that a writer must be *in a fury.*

If you write with passion, your words are intensified. Your message has force. Your readers can better sense your spirit and sincerity. If you cannot write with passion, perhaps you have selected the wrong subject. Or you are not ready to write.

Writing In A Fury

The author's first book was on the subject of hemorrhoids, a matter of little concern to non-sufferers. However, it was surprising how many persons without the problem read the book. Even more unusual, they often said how much they enjoyed it.

Although this book has some humor, it's essentially a serious treatment of the subject. It was also written in a fury.

The author suffered from the affliction, and was misled by physicians for years. Various physicians had said that there was nothing to alleviate the condition or keep it from worsening, all the while encouraging the author to submit to the dreaded surgical solution. When research for the book began, the truth was learned that not only was this drastic solution unnecessary, due to a painless therapy that had been available for years, but diet and exercise could also directly affect the condition. The author was incensed. The book reflects this intensity. While much of the fury required toning down, it was carried throughout the book.

Can Orthodontics Be Written About Enthusiastically?

In the case of the author's second book, on orthodontics, poor advice from several dentists and questionable procedure by an oral surgeon caused one of my daughter's front teeth to emerge twisted. Upon investigation of the subject in a dental library, it was discovered that half of all tooth disharmonies in children can be prevented. If this information had been available earlier, it would have saved me thousands of dollars and permitted my daughter to avoid several discomforting years of braces. My eagerness to tell other parents how to avoid these and other orthodontic problems is apparent throughout the book.

Avoiding Speculations

A third book, on the subject of investment bonds, was also written in a fury. Almost every month during my fifteen-year career as a stockbroker, a retired person who had been "taken to the cleaners" by another brokerage would walk into my office. How to avoid unscrupulous brokerages, plus alerting investors to the dangers of speculating in unproven areas, was to be a constant theme of the book. *Library Journal*'s review in July 1980 noted:

> Holt combines a healthy skepticism about security industry representatives with an exceptionally helpful primer lucidly explaining the bond market.

By writing with fury, enthusiasm, intensity, vigor, passion (whatever you wish to call it), your text becomes more readable. Especially to reviewers, who may or may not be interested in the book to which they have been assigned.

Don't Pull Your Punches

Don't pull any punches when writing your first draft. Be direct. Let the chips fall where they may. Say it exactly the way you'd say it to family or friends in your living room. Don't worry about offending anyone.

Also be firm in your convictions. Recently, the book review editor of the *Los Angeles Times* noted with some aggravation how many authors overuse the words *may, could, possibly, maybe,* and so on. His point was that these authors did not appear to have the courage of their convictions. Don't make the same mistake yourself.

Write With Humor, Too

In addition to writing your book with enthusiasm, humor should be injected when appropriate.

Examples of how to entertain your reader can take many forms. Jerry Steiner closes the introduction to *Home For Sale By Owner* with the following:

I hope you find this book informative, interesting, and enjoyable. This could have been a dry subject except that I watered it down. But if perchance you fall asleep before the end of this book, I won't take offense. I'll just assume you finished reading before I was able to finish writing.

Gregory Hill, author of *How to Sell Your Car for More Than It's Worth,* included this experience:

I once had a prospective buyer who would smell the transmission dipstick of every car that I showed him. When he finally decided on a particular car, he asked me to take a look at his trade-in. He watched me as I opened the hood on his car, so I thought I'd humor him by smelling his car's transmission dipstick. His eyes were studying my moves so intently that I thought I'd go another step further and taste the fluid. I then nodded my head and shut the hood. A few minutes later, the young man and I were in my office discussing monthly payments. "Do you want to buy the car?" I asked.

"Let me look at it one more time," he replied.

My office overlooked the lot, and I remained seated as I watched my prospect begin to re-examine the car he was considering purchasing. He didn't realize that I could see him frantically removing the car's transmission dipstick and tasting its fluid. I don't know how many swipes he made at the dipstick with his tongue, but the edges of his mouth and the spaces between his teeth were bright red with fluid when he returned to the office. "By the way," I said to him as he seated himself, "I tasted the fluid in that car myself when it came in a few days ago, and it's fine."

"Yeah," he replied, "I just now double-checked it and it seems O.K. to me, too."

Popular speakers use humor effectively in their deliveries. Do the same with your delivery.

How To Turn Your Readers Off

If you commit several of the following blunders in your book, you are well advised to not risk your money publishing it. Carelessness with language makes your readers suspect that you are also careless with thoughts and facts.

Do Not:

1. Preach *religion* in a non-religious book, or *politics* in a non-political book.
2. Overuse the pronoun *I* in a nonfiction book.
3. Use the words *very* or *hopefully.* A novelist wrote Dear Abby the following note:

Dear Abby:

I agree, the word "hopefully" is woefully over-used—and incorrectly at that. It would be much simpler if "I hope" were used instead because that is what is meant. Another word that is over-used is "very." I once knew an editor who told his reporters that he would fire any reporter who used the word "very"—they should substitute the word "damned" instead! But since it was a family newspaper, he blue-penciled all the "damneds" before the stories went to the composing room.

Novelist

 4. Use "weak" words, such as *really, thing, glad, happy,* and so on.
 5. Use "The" to begin most of your sentences.
 6. Overuse *adjectives* and *adverbs.* If you're selecting strong nouns and verbs, there's little need for adjectives or adverbs.
 7. Mix *singular* nouns with *plural* verbs, or vice versa.
 8. Mix your *metaphors,* as in: "The smell of war returns to Washington, and this time I am listening carefully."
 9. Use *non sequiturs,* such as: "Born in Argentina, he was an ardent golfer."
10. Use *jargon,* such as: *verbalized, ongoing, energy-wise, bottom-line, finalize, hereinafter, institutionalize.*
11. Use *vogue* words, such as: *parameter, apropos, viable, interface, dialogue* (as a verb), *thrust* (as a noun).
12. Be redundant, as in: *careful caution, planning ahead, final outcome, important essentials, future plans, end results, serious crisis.*
13. Use *sexist* pronouns, such as *his* or *man* when referring to both sexes. Instead, change the subject of your sentence to the plural form and use *their* or *persons.*

Rewriting—And Humility

It is disheartening to read careless writing submitted by a verbally articulate person. Many of them believe they can skip the second step in the writing process—the rewriting of the first draft.

The novelist Laura Kalpakian expressed the importance of this requirement in the *Los Angeles Times* on April 19, 1981:

> Novelists must teach themselves their craft any way they can, whether in creative writing programs or after a long day at the doughnut shop. They need only be equipped with enormous egotism and a useful dollop of humility. Egotism is necessary if the writer is to confront a naked page, convinced someone will read the words applied there—more, that someone will pay to read the words applied. Humility allows—requires—the writer to tear that same page apart, alter, restructure, trash, snip, paste, graft, knead, and pummel all that deathless prose until each sentence performs dual duty. Each sentence must convey intent and pull story—and reader—forward.

Thanking Your Critics

After your text is completed, ask a few friends or family members to review the work. Tell them to note with a pencil the following items:

1. areas they cannot understand,
2. where they disagree with the text,
3. where they're bored, and
4. all grammatical errors.

Actually, it is best to give your editor-friends a copy of the above list. The more specific you are, the more specific their comments will be.

When friends or family return their comments to you, your first and only reaction is to thank them for their criticism. Do not argue with them. Resist the temptation to justify your text. Simply receive their suggestions, and be thankful.

You're going to need these people later. They will be your copy editors and editors. You cannot afford to offend them.

If they cannot understand or agree with what you've written, it's your problem, not theirs. When more than one person says that a portion of your manuscript is in need of more attention, without a doubt it must be rewritten.

If you've bored them, add or substitute examples, anecdotes, quotations, humor, or illustrations to enliven your text.

Make a note of those persons who offer the most constructive criticism. A good speller is invaluable in cleaning up your manuscript. Individuals who are both well read and well educated may become your editors.

Chapters 9 and 10 describe in detail how to have your manuscript copyedited and edited.

Design As You Write

A successful teacher instructs in three steps: explaining what will be taught; teaching the subject; and then reviewing what has been taught.

Design your text the same way. Use outlines at the beginning of chapters, section headings, and sub-section headings to tell your readers precisely where they're going.

Whether your book is a "teaching tool" or strictly for entertainment, maintain your reader's alertness by breaking up straight text wherever possible. As you write, insert examples, illustrations, lists, and other artwork. This artwork should be incorporated into your text at the time it is written, not as an afterthought.

Chapter Title Pages

There are several ways to decorate chapter title pages. Illustrations suggesting the theme of a chapter can be used. Some authors use quotes by well-known persons, or epigraphs, like the ones by Mark Twain and John Steinbeck at the opening of this book.

It's common to set the chapter number of a chapter title page in italics, then the title of the chapter is set in a bolder typeface. Solid bars to set off the chapter headings can be purchased in roll form at most stationery stores.

Make your chapter titles easy to read. Occasionally, a book designer with a major publisher will select a typeface that is virtually illegible. Don't make this mistake yourself.

Section Headings

A section heading, or subhead, is the short phrase that introduces this section. It is also a valuable aid in providing transition to your text.

Several reviews of the author's book on orthodontics specifically praised the use of section and sub-section headings:

> The text shows the result of assiduous research, but the format—short paragraphs, subheadings—makes the material easily accessible to the lay reader. (*Publisher's Weekly,* April 25, 1980)

> Information in abundance on dentistry-and-orthodontics—simple and clear, section-by-section. . . . (*Kirkus Reviews,* May 1, 1980)

Section headings should be placed so they do not interfere with sub-section headings or running heads (both discussed in following sections). To distinguish section headings from other text and headings, either capitalize them or set them in bolder type. Italics are not suggested, as these are usually reserved for running heads.

An asterisk or other decorative device should be placed at the end of sections. They serve three purposes:

1. to serve clear notice that sections have ended, particularly when a new section begins at the top of the next page;

2. to distinguish new section headings from titles of diagrams or charts that immediately precede a section heading;
3. to provide space for later adjustments in the cast-off, or estimated page count, of a book. Space before and after an asterisk can be used to tighten or expand a chapter.

Sub-Section Headings

School textbooks often use section and sub-section headings to improve reader comprehension—a goal of any book designer. Not only do these headings make your book more readable, they also add emphasis. On a 200-page manuscript, the cost of typesetting these headings would amount to approximately $50 extra—a small price to pay for better reviews.

Sub-section headings can be typeset with a symbol preceding them, to key the reader visually. Again, italics are not suggested. Not only may they conflict with running heads, they can also conflict with italics appearing within the beginning of a sentence.

Using Italics Within Text

Use italics to emphasize important points within your text. They also help relieve the monotony of straight text. Italics are useful in breaking down information within a sub-section, when a list is not appropriate. When preparing your manuscript for the typesetter, underline words that should be italicized.

Front and Back Matter

Front Matter

The front matter of a book consists of all or part of the following:

1. inside front cover, or flyleaf,
2. half-title page,
3. verso (or back) of half-title page, or ad card,
4. title page,
5. copyright page,
6. dedication,
7. foreword,
8. preface,
9. acknowledgments,
10. table of contents,
11. list of illustrations,
12. introduction (optional).

How this front matter is arranged can have a significant effect on reviews and sales of your book.

Inside Front Cover, or Flyleaf

In hardbound books the first inside sheet is called a flyleaf, or end paper, and its left-hand side forms the backing to the front cover. This space often displays such illustrations as maps or family trees. When your book is to be hardbound, the bindery will ask if you wish to print on this area.

Half-Title Page

The first page of most trade paperbacks displays only a title. Publishers of mass paperbacks, on the other hand, use this page for promotional material. You should too, regardless of your book's size. Provoke your reader's interest with these pages.

Verso of Half-Title Page or Ad Card

A traditional use of this page is as an ad card listing an author's previous books. Also state where ordering information is located in your book. With remaining space, give credit to the designers of your book.

Title Page

In addition to the title and author, this page can include the book publisher, editor, year of publication, name of the foreword's author, and a company logo. Review the title pages of other books for ideas that can improve your own.

Copyright Page

This is normally the reverse side of the title page. It should include:

1. Library of Congress Cataloging in Publication (CIP) data.
2. An International Standard Book Number (ISBN).
3. A Library of Congress Catalog Card number.
4. A note describing where ordering information is located in the book.

5. The publisher's name and address.
6. The edition or printing of the book.

The CIP data gives libraries the numbers under which a book should be indexed (catalogued) or ordered. This data is provided free by the Library of Congress and R. R. Bowker and Company.

In addition, the CIP entry describes the different categories of information furnished by the book—which helps libraries to index your book properly—and gives the Library of Congress index number, the year of the book's first publication, the Dewey Decimal index number, the Library of Congress Catalog Card number, and the International Standard Book Number (ISBN).

It is important to include the above data on a copyright page. Otherwise, your book will obviously appear to be hastily self-published and will be much more difficult for libraries to order and shelve. How to obtain this data is explained in Chapter 18.

Ordering Information

Even though you may have listed ordering information on the back of the half-title page, list it again on the copyright page. This is where most people will look for it. Only a few people will know to look at your last page.

If your book receives favorable reviews in trade journals such as *Library Journal, Booklist, Kirkus Reviews,* and *Publishers Weekly,* libraries will purchase thousands of copies. Library patrons often like to purchase personal copies. Make it easy for them to do so.

Copyright

The Library of Congress suggests that the copyright format should include three elements:

1. The letter *c* fully encircled, the word *Copyright,* or the abbreviated *Copyr.*
2. The year of first publication of the book.
3. The name of the copyright owner (you).

See the front matter of this book for its copyright form. How to obtain copyright protection is also explained in Chapter 18.

In listing your publishing company's name and address, always include a post office box number below any street address used. If you don't include a post office box, then you will not receive book orders sent to the street address one year after your next move. The post office forwards mail only a year after an address changes.

At the bottom of the copyright page, state that your book is a "First Edition" and list the numbers 1 through 10. When you order a second printing, instruct the printer to remove the 1 from this line. With each succeeding printing, eliminate the appropriate number.

Dedication

When you dedicate a book to a person (or persons), try to instill some reader interest. Don't simply say: "To my father."

An example of a well-written family dedication is Jerry Steiner's in *Home For Sale By Owner:*

> This book is dedicated to my father, William A. Steiner. He was always disturbed when he saw the little guy being walked on and taken advantage of. I feel he would have been proud of me for having written this book.

If you place a dedication on a single page, make good use of this dramatic effect. The author's *Hemorrhoid* book was dedicated:

> To the silent sufferers.

Several reviewers used this phrase to introduce the book in their reviews. Make your dedication memorable, too.

The Foreword

A common error in forewords is that the word is misspelled. Your typesetter may misspell it even if you don't.

If you are not a specialist in the field of your book, find someone who is to write its foreword. Having a foreword by a professional can make your book more marketable, both to book buyers and to major publishers interested in reprint rights.

There should be no fee offered for such a foreword. On the other hand, if a professional in the field agrees to review your entire book for accuracy, then remuneration is appropriate, whether cash, books, or a percentage of profits.

Preface and Acknowledgments

A foreword is written by someone other than the author; a preface gives the author his first opportunity to address the reader directly. Many reviewers turn immediately to the preface of a book, before reading the contents. They want to know the author's motivation for writing the book, how it was written, and any other material that will make their review more interesting.

A preface is an excellent opportunity to impress reviewers with your credentials, or to list the authorities from whom research was gathered.

When writing your preface, remember that book buyers quite often purchase books because they like an author. Establish intimacy between yourself and the reader of your book at this point. Let some of your personality come forth.

Table of Contents

This is the most important page of your front matter. Potential buyers review a Table of Contents to see more precisely what they're getting for their money. The chapter titles for your book should be imaginative, descriptive, and stimulating. And short. Get your message across in three to seven words.

List of Illustrations

Readers expect to find a list of any illustrations in your book on the back of the Table of Contents page. The format for this list can vary. In selecting your own, review a few different lists at a library.

Introduction

If your book has a foreword, preface, and acknowledgments, it may become front-heavy with the addition of an introduction. An introduction should be short. Don't keep your readers waiting too long before getting into the book. Introductory material can often be better placed in earlier portions of a book—the foreword or preface.

Back Matter

The arrangement of back matter can also be an important factor in reviews. Back matter may include:

1. an appendix,
2. a bibliography, or references,
3. a glossary,
4. an index, and
5. ordering information.

The last three listed items are absolute necessities to almost all nonfiction books. Reviewers will often note when they are not included in a book, and libraries may be deterred from ordering. Not only do such omissions short-change readers, they also indicate to reviewers that their authors may have finished their manuscripts with undue haste and carelessness. How to prepare an index and glossary quickly at the same time is explained in Chapter 21.

An Appendix

When you have supplementary material that does not fit properly within the chapters of your book, make it an appendix. For example, you might want to reprint an article that supports your thesis, or a list of organizations that would be helpful to the reader.

Before reproducing a previously published article as an appendix, obtain permission from the author. After receiving this in writing, send a copy to the editor of the publication in which the article appeared requesting permission to reproduce it. If you do not hear from this editor within thirty days, call him (or her) on the telephone to spur action. It helps to enclose a stamped, self-addressed envelope with your initial request. Use your company stationery.

Many books place material in an appendix that should have appeared with relevant text. This is a common failing of art books. Fascinating material concerning paintings is often listed in an appendix, when it should have accompanied the paintings themselves.

A Bibliography or References

A bibliography is a list of sources for material contained in a book, or a list of books available in a certain category.

When footnoted references are listed in a book, there are three schools of thought concerning where the references should be located. References are easier to use when listed at the bottom of the page or at the end of each chapter; however, most major publishers list references at the end of books, which makes the typesetting and layout easier.

If you choose to combine references at the end of your book, do not prepare these references until your final draft has been given to the typesetter. If you prepare this list too early, revisions of the text may require additional revisions of the references.

When preparing a reference list, do not use "ibid" or "op. cit." when repeating a reference. Most of your readers will not recall the meaning of these abbreviations. If a reference is repeated, simply use the following form: "See Ref. 3, p. 41."

A Glossary

There are few nonfiction books that do not benefit by a glossary. Even though you adequately define a word the first time it appears in your text, it should be defined again in a glossary. A reader will not recall the page on which your initial definition appeared when a technical word is repeated in the text.

If two words that have essentially the same meaning appear in a glossary, define only the most frequently used word. When the other term appears, refer your reader to the definition of the more common word.

An Index

An index is more vital to a nonfiction book than a glossary; it ensures that readers can readily find information when they need it. Preparation requires no more than a few hours. See the format used in this book in designing your own index. How to prepare an index and glossary is fully discussed in Chapter 21.

Ordering Page

With an ordering page at the end of your book, you will have a source of continuing income. Be sure to quote an adequate figure for mailing and packaging costs. A book under one pound now costs 69 cents, plus another 10 to 15 cents for its mailing package.

Don't forget to use a post office box on your ordering address. A street address can be listed also, as long as it's above the line for the post office box number.

Note: If you're reading this page after the publication of your own book, it's not too late to place ordering information in your book. Order labels for your copyright page that state: "Please turn to last page for ordering information." Then order another set of labels that tell your reader how to purchase additional copies of your book. These labels can be ordered for less than $5 from:

WALTER DRAKE & SONS
80 Drake Building
Colorado Springs, CO 80940

Editing—
The Polishing of
Your Manuscript

9

How well does your manuscript convey its message? Are you concise? Is what you've written relevant? Have you eliminated sections that ramble? Is your transition good—everywhere? Have intelligent people given you positive answers to the above questions? If they haven't, your manuscript is not ready to be typeset.

Why Your Manuscript Needs Editing

It's difficult to judge your own work. As Shakespeare said, "The eye seeth not itself." You are too close to the book. You already know what you're trying to say, and you have a natural bias toward your writing ability.

Virtually all professional authors require editing. In 1981, James Clavell's *Noble House* went to the top of the fiction best-selling list within the first week of its release. Clavell admitted in a UPI interview on May 24, 1981:

When I started writing *Taipan,* the first four days of the novel took 500 pages of story time, and I had 128 more years of Hong Kong history to go. There was plenty of material left over from *Taipan* for *Nobel House.* I didn't know much about editing myself and I am still learning to write. The manuscript of *Noble House* ran 2,125 pages and was edited down to 1,206.

How Many Editors Do You Need?

Have three persons edit your manuscript with a fine-toothed comb. These persons must be well read and well educated. If possible, they should also be good writers in their own stead. Such editors will have a reservoir of words and phrases that are entirely different from yours and will quickly be able to suggest a satisfactory rephrasing of a passage that has given you hours (or days) of misery.

These persons need not be experts in the subject area of your book. As a matter of fact, it's best if they're not. They should become experts—after reading your manuscript. Choose people from different backgrounds, sexes, and ages. You need a variety of viewpoints.

Instructions For Your Editors

There are three questions that should be given to your editors, in writing:

1. If you could eliminate whatever you wished, what would you eliminate?
2. How would you rearrange the chapters of the book?
3. Do you generally agree with the conclusions of the book and the methods by which they are reached?

There is much more that can be asked, but these are the three basic questions your editors must answer.

By this time, earlier editing should have trained you to handle criticism. Have you learned to react in a positive manner, even when criticism is ill-conceived? If so, then you have a chance to become a polished writer, with a little help from your friends.

Remember to give all suggestions a week to sink in. Think on it. In a week's time, you'll be far more objective.

Don't expect your editors (or copy editors) to stroke your ego by telling you how great your manuscript is. If you ask for criticism, hope that you receive it. The more the better. It will improve your book's chances in the hands of reviewers.

How Do You Know When Your Manuscript Is Finished?

Your manuscript is ready for self-publication or submission to a major publisher when your most critical editors no longer suggest changes.

If you have followed the advice provided in this chapter and the previous four chapters, then you should be encouraged to publish. Your book should be better prepared than most published by major publishing houses. To survive, it has to be.

Most novice writers will be surprised to learn how many times Sidney Sheldon rewrites before submitting his manuscripts to an editor. He told a reporter for the *Los Angeles Times* on October 3, 1982:

> I trim and trim and trim. The twelfth rewrite is the final one. Well, almost the final one. Traditionally, a publisher allows an author to make cuts on only ten percent of the final galley proofs. I cut exactly ten percent from this final version, so it will read even faster. I have this goal. It's for a reader to not be able to go asleep at night. I want him to keep reading another four pages, then one more page. The following morning or night, he's anxious to get back to the book.

The result: Sidney Sheldon's books have hit No. 1 on the bestseller list in five out of his first six tries. Do you rewrite twelve times?

Copyediting, or Cleaning Up Your Manuscript

10

By the time you've written your entire manuscript twice, you may feel that no one could improve on your work. Many new writers suffer from this delusion.

Copyediting involves the correction of your spelling, word usage, punctuation, and other grammatical errors. It includes checking to see that your text is consistent in style and flows smoothly. When a book contains numerous spelling and grammatical errors, reviewers and readers may question your accuracy in other areas, even if some of the errors are actually due to your typesetter.

How Well Do You Spell?

If you can spell each of the seven commonly used words in the following test, you may be one of those rare writers who requires little copyediting.

Fill in the blanks, then check the answers at the end of the chapter.

1. "something that is unusually good of its
   kind"   exc——l——t
2. "to cooperate with"   accom——date
3. "anything that happens or takes place"   oc——r——e

4. "an introductory remark at the beginning
   of a book"   for——d
5. "that which cannot be resisted"   ir——st——ble
6. "a close bond or connection"   li——son
7. "standing firm in the face of opposition" persist——e

How did you do? In the author's workshops, only one in fifteen aspiring authors spell these words correctly. Many misspell three or four of them.

If your text contains an array of misspellings, it probably has numerous other grammatical errors, too. When they are sufficiently distracting, they can discourage reviews. Why gamble with your time? Have these errors corrected. Your book must appear as carefully copyedited as any book coming out of the major publishers.

Where Do You Find Copy Editors?

A copy editor must be both well read and well educated. Ask other writers for recommendations.

Consider the well-educated among your friends and relatives also. Finding those among this group who are interested in your planned book may require some patience. Even more patience will be required when they start giving you the criticism your manuscript needs.

Your local high school or library may have employees interested in helping you. It may be necessary to pay for such assistance; however, it should be less than what you would pay for professional copyediting.

Professional copy editors are also listed in writing magazines, telephone books, and directories such as *Literary Market Place.*

Instructions For Copy Editors

When you've rewritten your manuscript to the point that you're satisfied, give each of your potential copy editors one of the chapters of your manuscript. Never give an entire manuscript to an untried person. It may not be returned.

When you find a person who does a good job of copyediting a chapter, give them the balance of the manuscript. Try to find at least three people to copyedit your entire manuscript. This number will settle any disputes.

Don't Hand Out Super-Clean Manuscripts

A sure way to discourage friends and others from copyediting your manuscript is to hand them super-clean pages. They will hesitate to mark them up.

To encourage their assistance, make a few marks of your own on its early pages. Use a pencil to make these changes highly visible.

Don't Say It's Your Final Draft

Another way to discourage a copy editor is to make the mistake of saying the manuscript is your final draft as you hand it over. If it's "final," why would you be seeking copyediting? If you make this error, you can expect to receive back an unmarked manuscript.

Give Specific Instructions

On the first page of your manuscript, write out (in pencil) the following instructions:

PLEASE:

1. underline grammatical errors,
2. circle unclear passages,

3. place arrows where transition is rough, and
4. write on the manuscript any suggestions you can offer,
5. make a "style sheet," an alphabetical list of words that may have different spellings to ensure consistency.

When your manuscript contains deliberate deviations from normal grammar, ask if they are overly distracting. Get more than one opinion.

As you hand your manuscript over, say, "I don't want to publish this until it's as good as it can possibly be."

How Should You React When Your Manuscript Is Returned?

There is only one acceptable reaction to give persons who have copyedited or otherwise reviewed your manuscript. That is to say, "Thank you."

That's all. Even if you've paid for copyediting.

When a copy editor wishes to discuss the manuscript with you at this time, be quiet and humble. Do not argue. Do not criticize the criticism. Listen to the suggestions offered, make notes if appropriate, and do not respond except in a positive vein.

Consider All Suggestions for At Least One Week

Consider all suggestions—copyediting, editing, and other criticism—at least a full week before rejecting them.

When you first receive criticism from a copy editor, you may see little merit in many of the suggestions. If you initially agree with 10 percent of them, that is normal. That's your ego.

After a few days, you may see value in 20 percent of the criticism. And after a week, you may accept as much as 50 percent of the suggestions, many of which you totally rejected at your first reading.

Be patient with your ego. Let it come around. In the meantime, don't tell your copy editors that you haven't utilized all of their suggestions. They have egos, too.

Note: When I began instructing college classes on the preparation of manuscripts, handling students' egos was a problem. One student even composed a typed, two-page, single-spaced response to the comments I'd written on her manuscript. Her response was well written, as she was in a fury. It was better written than the manuscript. It took a few weeks for her to cool down.

I quickly learned to tell students to consider suggestions for a week before deciding to use or reject them. This woman later incorporated virtually all the suggestions, but I was fortunate that she even returned to the class. The nature of her reaction was due to my error, not hers. She had not been properly cautioned (instructed) how to take criticism.

Consider yourself cautioned. Appreciate your copy editors —and show it.

A Professional Author's Help

Most of us will agree that James Michener is one of the finest storytellers of our time. Does he do his magic by himself? In an interview published in *Family Weekly* on October 10, 1982, he said: "I invite four outside experts—a subject-matter scholar, editor, style arbiter on words, and a final checker— to tear it apart, and to them I am deeply indebted."

Your book should also reflect the input of experts. If it doesn't, it may not be ready for publication yet.

Spelling Answers:

1. excellent
2. accommodate
3. occurrence

4. foreword
5. irresistible
6. liaison
7. persistence.

Submitting Your Manuscript to a Major Publisher

11

Nothing said in this book will discourage most aspiring authors from first submitting their manuscripts to major publishers. Every writer wants the prestige and recognition gained by obtaining a national publisher. If you want to try this route first, at least be efficient. It is all too often a waste of time—valuable time.

What Happens To Unsolicited Manuscripts?

Many unsolicited manuscripts are returned unread—providing return postage is enclosed. When they are read, it is normally by an overworked or inexperienced editorial assistant. Stacks of unsolicited manuscripts are stored somewhere out of the way and receive attention when time allows. They are called the "slush pile."

How do you prevent your manuscript from ending up on the bottom of a slush pile? It's simple. Don't send it out on an unsolicited basis. Start out with a query letter, addressed to an editor by name.

Preparing An Effective Query Letter

Editors are busy people, so make your letter easy to read. Use simple words in short sentences. It should be one page, single-spaced if necessary. Generally, do not write paragraphs in excess of six to seven lines.

Your query letter should be rewritten at least ten times, over a period of no less than one month. It is the first indication to a publisher of your writing abilities.

Every word chosen in composing a query letter must sell; they must stimulate the editor's interest in your subject. The proposed title for your book is of particular importance. Review Chapter 15 in choosing a title and subtitle.

The First Paragraph

Editors at most large publishers must "sell" their marketing departments on the merits of your book idea before they can make an offer for it. You must help editors sell your book by providing sound reasons why it will be successful.

A first paragraph should describe your book in basic terms —enthusiastically. It must list promotional factors that will cause the book to sell to large numbers of people. It should be factual. Do not use the phrase: "I believe . . ." or superlatives. They will not impress an editor, or a marketing department.

What Are Your Credentials?

Briefly detail anything of importance that you've written in the past. If you have no credits, then describe the source of your expertise. What qualifies you to write on your subject?

Do You Have a Prominent Person to Write a Foreword?

If you've written no previous books and have few qualifications to write on your subject, then it's important that a prominent person be available to write a foreword to your text.

This person should be an expert in the field. Such an endorsement encourages a publisher to accept the reliability of your text. If there are additional persons available to endorse your book, list them also, with phone numbers.

Describe the Competition

Before making an offer for your manuscript, you can be sure that an editor will check its competition. List competitive books in your query letter and briefly describe them. Be honest. Describe them fairly but reveal why your book is better. If you cannot convincingly state why it is better, you may have written on the wrong subject.

Where Do You Send Query Letters?

Most publishers prefer to receive manuscripts by new writers through agents. An agent is expected to screen manuscripts and submit only those that are "worthy" of an editor's attention. However, most agents hesitate to handle a new writer's work. They want established authors, for obvious financial reasons. It can be a vicious circle. How to find and work with an agent is explained in Chapter 46.

Referrals

Writers and other people in the book business will suggest agents and editors (maybe their own) if they like your work.

Writer's Market

The annual *Writer's Market* reveals how publishers like to receive manuscripts and queries. Personal names of editors are furnished for each publisher, along with the type of books printed by each publisher. This reference book can be found in any library.

Literary Market Place (LMP)

This is a thick annual that lists all major publishers, book associations, book trade events, reviewers, wholesalers, and related businesses. Publishers are listed four times, by:

1. field of activity (book type),
2. subject matter printed,
3. geographical location, and
4. alphabetically.

LMP also lists personal names of editors and other officers for each publisher.

Submitting The Manuscript

If the response you receive to your letters is positive, make sure the manuscript you send is as good as possible. If you send a sloppy, ill-prepared manuscript to an editor, not only will it be rejected but you will not be able to resubmit it later. A sloppy manuscript will have established the level of your writing ability. Don't waste an opportunity to sell your manuscript by submitting it too soon.

It is customary to let an editor know if you are submitting the manuscript to other houses at the same time.

Enclose Photo and Sample Illustrations

Enclose a professionally taken photograph of yourself with your manuscript. If you appear promotable, the chances of your manuscript being accepted will increase.

Send sample copies of your illustrations to dress up your manuscript. If they are well done, they should help make a sale.

A word of caution: *Never* send off your only copy of the manuscript.

Be Patient

Send off your manuscript—and be patient. The 1982 Nobel Prize for Literature was given to Gabriel Garcia Marquez, whose *One Hundred Years of Solitude* has sold more than ten million copies in thirty-two languages. He searched for seven years before finding a publisher for his first book, *Leaf Storm.*

The sample query letter on the following page resulted in the sale of the author's manuscript on orthodontics to William Morrow and Company.

Julie Weiner
Asst to the Editor-in-Chief
William Morrow & Company
New York, NY 10016

Proposed Book: <u>STRAIGHT TEETH:</u>
Orthodontics for
Everyone

347 Mermaid   Box 963   Laguna Beach, CA 92652
(714) 498-0642

Ms. Weiner:

The enclosed material includes: Title Page
Preface
Table of Contents
First Chapter
First Pages Other Chapters
Last Page

The complete manuscript is approximately 305 pages, including illustrations, references, glossary, index, and addendum.

Dr. David W. Liddle, internationally recognized orthodontist, has agreed to permit his article, "Second Molar Extraction in Orthodontic Treatment," <u>American Journal of Orthodontics,</u> December 1977, to appear as the Addendum to the book. This article is considered by many to be the most important published in recent years. His proven technique eliminates the need for formal orthodontic appliances in most cases of overcrowded mouths. I expect Dr. Liddle to write the Foreword also.

The book will be unique in that it is the first complete reference on the subject for the layperson. Most of its information has been gleaned from the leading journals of the dental and orthodontic professions. It will emphasize the<u> prevention and early treatment</u> of orthodontic problems in order to avoid the need for lengthy and expensive formal orthodontic care. The manuscript devotes 195 pages of its 305 pages to this subject.

There have been two other books for the layperson in this area:

<u>Embraceable You,</u> by Jay Weiss, DMD (New York: Health Sciences, 1975). 162 pages, 6 pages of illustrations in center of book. Un-edited, un-organized, un-referenced, and un-informative. Wishy-washy. Much history.

<u>So You're Getting Braces,</u> by Alvin and Virginia Silverstein (Philadelphia: Lippincott, 1975). Shorter than other book, more illustrations, but written <u>for adolescents only.</u>

Neither of these books devotes time to prevention or early treatment of orthodontic problems. Information concerning prevention and early treatment is the most important benefit that a self-help book on this subject can offer. The enclosed Preface discusses this in more detail. This book will be "library" quality.

Thank you for your consideration.

Best regards,

R. L. Holt

Enclosures
RLH:lc

Design

Interior Design— Keeping Your Text Alive

12

Open many books to any page and there is nothing but text. There are no illustrations or photographs, no diagrams or graphs, no section headings, no sub-section headings, no lists, no chapter outlines, no indented quotations, nor any other attempt to break up the monotonous routine of straight text.

A book by a major publisher has built-in credibility and therefore does not need an elaborate design. A small press book must try harder in order to get attention. When you publish your book, dress it up. Remember, it must compete with 35,000 other books the year it's released. It must be distinctive. It must catch and please the eye of reviewers, and ultimately readers.

How Large Should Your Book Be?

Book buyers are generally willing to pay more for a larger book than they will pay for a smaller one—even when each book contains the same amount of information. Make your book as big as is practical.

By doubling the dimensions of your book, you can substantially increase its price. However, your cost to produce the book does not double. The only significant increased cost is for paper, which should increase your overall costs by no more than 20 to 30 percent.

In maximizing your book size, don't overdo it. The shelves of most bookstores have a standard height of 12 inches. Therefore, the maximum height of your book should be 11½ inches. You can also bulk out the text by using a heavier paper.

The standard page sizes, or "trim sizes," meaning the size of the trimmed sheets of paper, that are the most economical to print are:

5½"	× 8¼"	6⅛"	× 9¼"
8½"	× 11"	9"	× 12"

Design Your Book To Its Subject

A writer recently asked the author for advice concerning a proposed book on how to play better tennis. She was planning to print on pages with a width of 6 inches and a height of 9 inches. Half her book was to be illustrations. It was suggested that she reverse her dimensions (using a height of 6 inches and a width of 9 inches). This would permit relevant text to be placed beside each illustration, instead of above or below it. An extra-wide book also stands out better on a bookstore shelf. Its spine sticks out, exhibiting part of the cover to the passing browser.

Your Choice of Paper

Most books are printed on 50- to 60-pound paper. Fifty-pound paper is paper in which 500 standard-size sheets (a ream) weigh 50 pounds. The standard sheet sizes for book text papers, which will later be cut down to your book page size, are: 23 × 35 inches or 25 × 38 inches.

The lighter the paper, the more the text from the other side of the page will show through.

If you wish to make your book thicker without increasing its weight, order a high-bulk paper into which air has been whipped during manufacture. While line illustrations are not affected by the use of high-bulk paper, a slight degree of clarity is lost in photographs.

The following chart lists the thickness and weight of a 208-page softbound book when printed on varying weights of paper:

Paper Weight	Thickness	Book Weight
50 lb	12 mm.	8½ oz
55 lb high bulk	15	9
60 lb	14	10

The same book in hardbound weighs 13 ounces when printed on 50-pound paper, and 14½ ounces on 60-pound paper.

Design Your Book to Weigh Less Than a Pound

You will save 25 cents (at current postal rates) per book if your book weighs less than 1 pound. Mailing less than 1 pound now costs 69 cents, while between 1 and 2 pounds costs 94 cents. This savings can amount to $250 for a thousand books, which is approximately 10 percent of the cost of printing the signatures for that many books.

In designing your book's weight, make adequate allowance for the weight of its mailing package (at least an ounce), label, invoice, and any promotional material you wish to enclose when filling orders.

Choosing A Typeface

There are hundreds of styles for the typeface of your text; however, there are few that can be comfortably read at length. For the sake of your readers, choose an easy-to-read face. A few of these are:

1. Century Expanded,
2. Times Roman, or English Times,

3. Baskerville, and
4. IBM Executive Modern.

If your typesetter suggests another style, ask for an example (at least a page worth). Examine it for a few days. If it is too unusual, it may irritate reviewers and other readers.

Sample Typefaces

Century Expanded	This is a patient-oriented book. It should provide the reader a clear and complete understanding of the nature, causes, symptoms, and proper treatment of hemorrhoids. Confusion and misconceptions concerning this subject exist not only among the public, but also within the medical profession.
Times Roman	A recurring theme of this book has been the necessity for thoroughly investigating all investment options prior to committing one's capital. Information provided in this book should enable investors to make intelligent choices of these options. Hopefully, readers will also be able to distinguish between the many reasonable and unreasonable bond investment ideas which will surely be introduced in the future.
Baskerville	He told us at the beginning of the class, "You're either going to pay me now or pay me later. You either get into shape now, or you get into shape later." But the biggest impression he made on me was that he stressed the fact that *you can only be what you are.* You can improve on yourself, but you've got to take what you have and do the best you can with it. If you're 5'3" (like me), you're not going to look like a 5'9" model.

IBM Executive
Modern

If you decide to do your own typesetting, purchase a special clay-coated paper on which to type your final draft. The clay-coat on one side of the paper gives your typesetting the necessary hairline definition.

Typefaces to Avoid

Do not use a typeface that has no serifs. Serifs are the curls or lips at the ends of letters. The l, t, r, and s in the word "letters" have serifs. Our eyes have become accustomed to reading words that have serifs—in newspapers, magazines, and other books.

The Helios typeface (without serifs) below is contrasted with Century Expanded with serifs. While this short passage without serifs may not prove aggravating to read, your eyes would tire of reading this style in a magazine-length article or in a book:

EACH BOOK IS AN INDIVIDUAL PROBLEM, AS YOU well know. Therefore, our estimate for your book will be based on several things—including the number of pages, type of text (prose, tables, poetry), the condition of the original manuscript, etc. Your inquiry for an estimate will be cheerfully and immediately answered . . . and your book will be promptly and proudly set.

EACH BOOK IS AN INDIVIDUAL PROBLEM, AS YOU well know. Therefore, our estimate for your book will be based on several things—including the number of pages, type of text (prose, tables, poetry), the condition of the original manuscript, etc. Your inquiry for an estimate will be cheerfully and immediately answered . . . and your book will be promptly and proudly set.

Also avoid typefaces that display certain letters in awkward positions. Examples of these are:

Benguiat Book
notice the e and g

Clearface Regular
notice the a and e

Italia Book
notice the t and i

The selection of a typeface that is comfortable to read is one of the few areas of book design where you should be conservative.

Size of Type

Eleven-point type is usually the minimum size selected for nonfiction books. Smaller sizes may cause eye strain, especially under artificial light. If you're designing a book for children or the elderly, use a 12-point type size. Examples of various type sizes are shown below:

8 pt.—The purpose of good typography is to present the message clearly
9 pt.—The purpose of good typography is to present the message
10 pt.—The purpose of good typography is to present the
11 pt.—The purpose of good typography is to present
12 pt.—The purpose of good typography is to pre
14 pt.—The purpose of good typography
18 pt. — The purpose of good typo
24 pt. — The purpose of g

30 pt.—The purpose
36 pt.—The purp

Leading

The distance between lines of text is called leading. If there is not enough leading on a wide text page, the eye may have difficulty finding the next line of type. When interviewing a typesetter, take an example of the style, size, and leading that you prefer for your book text.

Letter-Spacing (or Pitch)

The typesetter will normally set the degree of spacing between letters at an appropriate distance. When this spacing is too tight, some letters may "connect" with each other. This is rarely a problem, but when it is, know that you can instruct the typesetter to correct it.

Running Heads

Chapter titles that are repeated at the top of right-hand pages are called running heads. They aid readers in locating particular chapters. Most major publishers also place a running head on the upper-left-hand pages to repeat the title of their books.

When a chapter has a lengthy title, reduce it to three or four words as a running head.

Page Numbers

Page numbers should be placed at the outside corners of either the top or bottom of pages. When you have section headings, sub-section headings, and running heads at the top of your pages, you might want to place page numbers at the bottom.

You may want to use Arabic numbers instead of Roman numerals for your front matter. If you use Roman numerals, then you must use a double-numbering system during the paste-up of your book, which will be inconvenient and may cause errors.

Begin your Arabic numbers with the first page of your book —the half-title page. By the time you reach your preface or foreword, you should be at page 5 or 6.

Reviewers often state how many pages are in a book. Using Arabic numbers from the first page of your book, you will receive full credit for the entire book. When prices are comparable, book buyers will usually purchase the longer book. Don't short-change your page count.

Illustrations and Photographs

When pasting up artwork, do not commit the common sin of many publishers: placing illustrations or photographs on pages of text to which they do not relate. Take the time to plan the placement of your artwork, so it is next to the relevant text. How to do this is explained in Chapter 23.

When your book contains numerous illustrations and/or photographs, label them in proper order by chapter. If your third chapter has four illustrations, for example, label them as Figures 3.1, 3.2, 3.3, and 3.4. The next two chapters discuss illustrations and photographs in detail.

Illustrations—
Reinforcing Your Text

13

A joint research project by the University of Minnesota and Sperry Systems determined that when people simply listen to a presentation, their learning efficiency is 25 percent. When this listening is supplemented by visual aids, an additional 35 percent is absorbed and information may be retained 55 percent longer. A similar study by Mobil Oil found that people remember 20 percent of what's heard, but 50 percent of what's both heard and seen.

This data suggests that an author can almost double a reader's comprehension by using illustrations.

Keeping Your Text Alive

In addition to indented quotes and examples, section and sub-section headings, lists and chapter outlines, imaginative artwork can maintain your reader's alertness.

As you write your manuscript, make a sketch wherever an illustration or diagram would improve the reader's understanding. It's not necessary that you be an accomplished artist to make a sketch. Just draw an outline to the best of your ability. As you rewrite your text, you will also refine your sketches further.

Illustrations to Clarify Text

Some ideas can be best conveyed through illustrations. For example, during the preparation of the author's manuscript on the subject of orthodontics, it was important to illustrate the proper method of holding dental floss in order to not damage the gums. Only illustrations could do this clearly.

Illustrations for Dramatic Effect

In the same book on orthodontics, it was also important to show how tartar causes gums to recede from tooth surfaces, resulting in tooth loss. This was illustrated to demonstrate the seriousness of the condition.

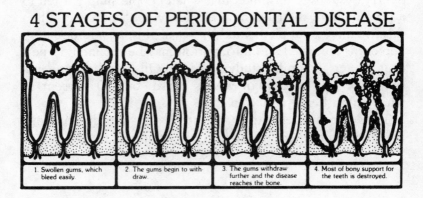

4 STAGES OF PERIODONTAL DISEASE

1. Swollen gums, which bleed easily.
2. The gums begin to withdraw.
3. The gums withdraw further and the disease reaches the bone.
4. Most of bony support for the teeth is destroyed.

Illustrations That Are Decorative

An illustration is justified, too, if it renders your book more attractive. Make such illustrations as functional as possible. The example below was included in the author's first book in a chapter stressing the value of exercise. It eventually became the logo for the company that published this book.

How Do You Make An Illustration?

If you want high-quality illustrations and are not an artist, find a graphic designer. If you cannot afford a professional graphic designer, seek the services of a student graphic designer at your local community college. If an artist-friend offers help, make sure this person knows the requirements for camera-ready artwork.

Provide Good Examples of What You Require

After selecting a graphic designer (see Chapter 15), submit the sketches you've prepared during the writing of your manuscript. These should be as precise as you can make them. Cut out examples from magazines or make photocopies of book illustrations to show your graphic designer exactly what you're striving for. The more details provided the graphic designer, the less time the designer will require to complete your artwork—and the less expense you will incur.

Black-and-White Line Drawings

The least expensive illustrations to print in a book are those that can be pasted up and photographed with your text. These are called line drawings, or line art. They have no tones of gray. The preceding illustrations in this chapter are line drawings.

Halftones

If you require varying tones of gray in your illustration, then the artwork must be photographed through a crossline or contact screen, which converts the image into dots of various sizes. All photographs require halftones.

The quality of a halftone varies according to how many dots are obtained per linear inch. Newspapers customarily screen their photographs at 85 dots per linear inch, while book reproductions are generally screened at 120 to 133 dots per inch. An artbook may use 150 dots. You can see these dots with a magnifying glass if you hold the halftone negative up to the light.

What Size Should Artwork Be Prepared?

Many reference works—and graphic designers—believe that illustrations should be prepared larger than they will eventually be printed. Their reasoning is that when the illustrations are reduced, they will become sharper. This is not always good advice.

When a black-and-white illustration is reduced by the printer, it does become darker—possibly darker than you prefer. Another problem may arise when your illustrations have patterns of closely arranged lines or dots. These patterns may become solid black upon reduction, particularly when reduction exceeds 50 percent.

A further good reason for not making your artwork larger than it will be printed is that it's easier to plan required space for illustrations in your book when they are drawn to scale. Text can be accurately arranged around illustrations early during the paste-up, when you know exactly what size your illustrations will be.

If illustrations are prepared smaller than the desired book size, enlarging them has the opposite effect—they lighten. When it is not possible to avoid enlarging artwork, a general rule is not to enlarge more than 100 percent if quality reproduction is desired.

Printing in Color

If you plan to use color within your book, read the pertinent pages concerning color work in Chapter 25. Color printing is expensive and in many cases prohibitive for the self-publisher. Chapter 25 provides several tips that can minimize the expense of color work.

Can You Use Clip-Art?

If your artwork is primarily for decorative purposes, check readymade artwork in clip-art catalogs. Folders or magazines of clip-art can often be obtained in stationery or art supply stores.

Artwork in most government publications can be reproduced freely, as it is not copyrighted; but you should always check with the agency responsible for the publication to be sure that you are allowed to copy their artwork. You can also borrow freely from any book or magazine printed more than fifty-six years ago, as the copyright has expired on these publications.

You can borrow from publications printed prior to 1950 also, as long as their publishers did not renew their copyrights. However, it can be almost impossible to determine if such copyrights have been renewed once these publications have gone out of print.

On the next page are some examples of clip-art that are available in catalogs. Check this source of artwork before hiring an artist or graphic designer.

Photographs—
How to Enhance
Your Book

14

If you print one thousand copies of your book, the addition of ten black-and-white photographs will add approximately $50 to $100 to the total cost of printing. That's a small price to pay in order to dress up your work.

Color photographs are more expensive, as they require four runs through the press. This explains why color reproductions are often found in the middle of a book, clustered in one signature.

Taking Good Photographs

There are no books in the author's experience that explain to the novice photographer how to take adequate photographs for reproduction in a book. Available titles either are too technical or fail to provide specific information according to one's individual interests and camera capabilities.

Read what's available in local bookstores and libraries, then experiment until your photographs are adequate. The following guidelines may assist you.

Save Sample Photos from Magazines

Photos in magazines are usually done by professionals, who take hundreds in order to arrive at the "perfect picture." Cut out and save magazine photos that are good examples of what you wish to appear in your own book. (Do not reproduce these photographs without permission, however.)

By studying magazine photos, you will notice the arrangement of backgrounds, clothing, facial expressions, body angles, and other details that may be worth duplicating. Place these photos in a three-ring binder and take them with you during photo sessions.

Take Instant Photos First

Take test shots of your subject with an instant-photo camera. This permits you to test accurately lighting, background, angle, and so on at the site of the photo session until the right effect is obtained. Otherwise, a second photo session will be necessary when none of your prints proves adequate.

Since you will probably reproduce black-and-white photographs in your book, you will need a Polaroid camera that takes black-and-white photographs. Polaroid no longer markets inexpensive cameras that use black-and-white film, so it may be necessary to pick up a used model at a swap meet, secondhand store, or pawn shop.

When you're satisfied with the lighting and pose of your subject, switch to a quality camera for fine photos. If you can find a camera that provides a larger negative than 35 millimeters, use it. Unless you're a camera buff, it may be difficult to take 35mm shots from which clear 8-by-10-inch blowups can be made.

Use a Tripod

Using a tripod or other form of stationary support for your camera will give the photos you take a new clarity they haven't had before. This is especially important if your camera is a 35 mm.

Find Solid Backgrounds

By choosing a solid background, you can highlight your subject. Generally, select darker backgrounds, as light backgrounds tend to darken a subject excessively. This is why white shirts are not suggested when making a TV appearance.

Backgrounds are crucial to a good photograph. Review the best photographs in magazines for their manipulation of backgrounds.

What Time of Day Is Best for Outdoor Photos?

The most attractive shading normally occurs during the early morning hours or in the late afternoon. At the middle of the day, shadows are harsh and the brighter sun makes it more difficult to shoot acceptable photos.

During the spring and fall, the best hours are 8:00 A.M. to 9:30 A.M. and 3:30 P.M. to 6:00 P.M. Optimum summer hours would be slightly earlier in the morning and later in the afternoon. Winter hours would be later in the morning and earlier in the afternoon.

Photographing People

When your subject is a person, plan in advance for a good photograph. Have the person bring several outfits, both light and dark. If possible, take Polaroid shots of these outfits before they leave home to ensure that proper clothing is taken to the photo site. You should also plan to spend at least two hours at the photo session. It takes this long to determine proper background, body angle, facial expression, props, and lighting for the subject.

Body Angles

Generally, take photos of people at 45-degree angles, as frontal shots are seldom attractive. You will also find that many people have vastly different profiles and that one side is often far superior to the other.

For a full-length photo, ask the subject to stand with one leg slightly behind the other in order to create a tapering effect. This tends to slim a person.

Shadow Half the Face

Basic photography demands that a photo be balanced. The most flattering photos of faces are those in which half the face is within a subtle shadow. As you can imagine, it takes time to position the body at an attractive angle that still permits the face to be properly shadowed.

Make People Smile

Individuals always look better in photos when they're smiling. You don't want a glum face staring at your readers.

Quite often, you'll find people who prefer not to smile for photographs. Don't give up on these people. Keep changing profiles and facial expressions until everyone is happy.

Props

Don't take a photo of someone standing there looking back at you. Find a prop for them to hold. Give them something to do. Use trees to lean on, hang from, or even sit in—they're great props. The prop or pose should relate to their appearance in the book, of course.

Closeness Distorts

When you're closer than ten feet to your subject, the closeness may result in distortion of the portion of the subject's body nearest the camera. Experiment when it is necessary to take close-up shots. If your photo is sharp, it can always be blown up to the desired proportion.

Working With A Photo Lab

If you live in a state that collects a sales tax, have you obtained a "resale" number yet? Present this number to the photo lab and other suppliers to avoid paying unnecessary sales taxes.

A photo lab may even give you a healthy discount (as much as 25 percent) when you present your business card and plan to do a considerable amount of business. Ask if they offer a discount to companies.

When your film is developed and printed in an automated shop (most are nowadays), a number of prints may be delivered too dark or light. Don't hesitate to ask for additional prints in such cases. There should be no charge. If you've taken your film to the photo counter of a chain store, however, such personal service will normally not be available.

Order prints the same approximate sizes that they will be reproduced in your book. Not only will this tell you exactly how the photos will appear, it may also save you some expense at the printer. Remember, reducing darkens and enlarging lightens. Chapter 25 describes how to prepare both color and black-and-white photos for your printer.

Exterior Design, or Designing Strong Covers

15

A book cover is a marketing tool. If you intend to sell your book through retail outlets, you must design its covers, both front and back, for maximum sales potential.

Front Covers That Sell

Before designing your book covers, visit a few libraries and bookstores. Study successful covers. Don't look at the latest bestsellers. Concentrate your attention on those books that are still selling years after they were first published. Among others, check the following titles:

*Cellulite: Those Lumps, Bumps, and Bulges You
    Couldn't Lose Before*
Sugar Blues
Our Bodies, Ourselves
Fit or Fat
The Complete Book of Running

The rich pink background for the attractive figure on the *Cellulite* cover makes it stand out in any group. *Sugar Blues* is enticing because the title is set in the same style as that found on traditional Coca-Cola bottles. *Our Bodies, Ourselves* not only has a catchy title; the cover photo of a group of marching women draws the eye. *Fit or Fat* is a lesson in simplicity, both in title choice and design.

The *Running* book by James Fixx has a classic cover. The original design called for a full-length photo of a runner in green and yellow colors—an uncomely combination. Fortunately, a high-level executive at the publishers noticed this potential disaster at the last minute and sent it back to the design department. It was decided to feature James Fixx's legs, using a dark red background. The result was magnificent, and the book quickly became a bestseller.

Does Your Title Sell?

James Fixx planned to give his book a long-winded title:

> *The Lazy Athlete's Look Younger, Be Thinner, Feel Better,*
> *and Live Longer Running Book.*

This was fourteen words in length, almost exceeding the recommended average word count for nonfiction sentences. Fixx's initial choice may have been influenced by his twenty-year stint as a magazine editor. What makes a good title for a magazine article doesn't always make a good book title. Reason prevailed, of course, before *The Complete Book of Running* was published.

The best-selling diet book of 1981 was almost entitled *The Pineapple Diet Book*. Again, a promotion-minded editor changed this to *The Beverly Hills Diet Book*. It was a clever change because many people picture California women as healthy, robust, and sleek.

Other excellent titles are:

Looking Out for Number #1
How to Avoid Probate
The Save Your Life Diet Book

If your title doesn't have a nice ring to it, go back to the drawing board and use your imagination. The title must grab the attention of the bookstore browser.

Should You Use a Subtitle?

Unless you have selected a strong title such as *Sugar Blues,* you should definitely use a subtitle. Not only can you better catch the reviewer's eye; you can also describe the contents of your book in greater detail.

It's not necessary to list a lengthy subtitle as part of the official title of your book. It can be paraphrased inside the book and on order forms.

Ask friends to suggest titles and subtitles. Gather as many as you can. When you've narrowed your choices to a few, ask bookstore managers which they prefer. In the end, you must make the final decision, but consider all alternatives first.

Titling a Reference Book

If yours is a basic reference book, it's a good idea to begin your title with the one word that best describes its subject. This word can then be followed by a descriptive subtitle. Why should you do this? So book buyers can find your book in book indexes.

For example: a bookstore customer wants to purchase a book on the subject of investment bonds. Finding no book on this subject on the bookstore's shelves, a clerk, after looking in *Subject Guide to Books in Print* may check *Books in Print—Titles,* a thick reference listing all the books that are currently in print. Upon looking up the word "Bonds," the only book listed that has a title beginning with this word is *Bonds: How to Double Your Money Quickly and Safely* (by the author).

In fact, there are more than ten other books available on this subject, but they are hidden in a maze of other titles within the above reference. Their titles contain the word "Bonds," but not at the beginning.

Is Your Title Legible at Ten Feet?

People strolling down a bookstore aisle should be able to read your book's title at a glance—whether the book is face out or spine out.

If you want to check how your book will stack up against the competition, place your planned cover on a table with several other books, then step back and see how it looks compared to other titles. Does your title stand out? Is it easily read at ten feet?

Do not capitalize all the letters of your title unless it is a short one-word title, or you are sure your design will stand out. There are three different cases:

1. upper case . . . all capitals;
2. lower case . . . all uncapitalized letters;
3. upper and lower case . . . only the first letter of each word capitalized.

The best case for most titles is upper and lower case, which is the most readable and familiar. If you are unsure which case to use, make samples of each and place them ten feet away.

The lettering for your title should also be in a bold typeface. Use the thickest lettering that space and legibility permit.

How Prominent Should Your Name Be?

If you were as well known as James Michener, your name could dominate your book covers. Until you are well known, however, give your title prominence.

This is not to say that your name should not be easily recognized on the book cover. Your name should be somewhat less bold than the title. By sheer exposure and repetition, your name can help sell books, too.

Should You Change Your Name?

Which sounds better? Robert Stevenson or Robert Louis Stevenson? Edgar Poe or Edgar Allan Poe? Ruth Hill or Ruth Beebe Hill? James Cooper or James Fenimore Cooper? If your name also benefits by the insertion of a middle name, then by all means use it in your pen-name. It will distinguish you from others with similar first and last names, in addition to improving the rhythm of your name.

A number of writers simply change their names. Pearl Grey became Zane Grey. Samuel Langhorne Clemens chose Mark Twain. If you do not like your name, or feel another would be of more benefit to your writing career, then change it. In most cases, however, your choice of subject matter will be much more important to your book's success than your choice of pen-name.

Placing Name of Foreword's Author on Cover

If you are fortunate enough to have an authority in your field as the author of your foreword, certainly state this fact on the cover of your book. It will enhance the book's credibility as well as its sale potential.

Placing Your Publishing Company's Name on the Cover

If you've selected a strong name for your publishing company, place it on your cover, too. For the author's first self-published book in the field of health, "California Health Publications" was selected. The word "California" is a selling point in itself. This choice resulted in frequent requests for the publisher's catalog. The author's second self-published book was about investment bonds, for which "California Financial Publications" was selected. Both of these names were placed on the front covers of the books. How to select a publishing company name is discussed further in Chapter 17.

Promotional Copy on Your Cover

If your nonfiction book is the "best reference" in its field, state this on your cover. Or state that it is "A Complete Reference." When space is available, list a few major benefits to the book buyer on your cover. It is common to place excerpts from reviews on a book cover. With only a softbound edition, you must await a second printing. If you have a hardbound edition, you can simply print up more dust jackets with your reviews.

Should Your Book's Price Be Printed on the Cover?

The price of your book can be placed on its front cover, spine, back cover, or on an inside flap of the book. However, it's suggested that you not place a price anywhere on the outside of the book with its first printing.

Quite often, you'll either underprice your book, thereby limiting its profit potential, or overprice it and inhibit sales.

When the author's first book was printed, its softbound price was initially fixed at $7.95. Upon release, Nutri-Books, the largest book wholesaler to health food stores, felt that $7.95 was too high and wouldn't order the book. A month later, the softbound price was lowered to $5.95 to encourage bookstore sales. At the new price, Nutri-Books began ordering and selling the book in volume.

If the $7.95 price had been printed on the outside of the book, it would not have been possible to adjust the price. So, until you've tested the market, be flexible about pricing.

Color On Your Cover

Placing color on your cover may involve an extra few hundred dollars. It's worth it if your book becomes more noticeable on bookstore shelves, or on the desks of reviewers. This section will discuss how you can add color to the cover inexpensively.

What Is the Best Color?

Red and its variations are the best eye-catchers for a book cover. This is evident on the covers of the *Cellulite* and *Running* books. If you cannot use a red tone in the background, then incorporate this color in your title.

White is also helpful in creating strong contrasts. If you use a white background, lettering will stand out better. Or on a dark background, use white lettering. It works both ways.

A Two-Colored Cover . . . Or a Duotone

By running your cover through the press a second time, you can add a different color. This will increase the cost of your cover by 50 percent. If you select the two colors carefully, they can be blended during the printing of the cover to create a third color.

Another technique of printing two colors to create the effect of additional color is the use of duotones. A duotone requires two runs through the press. The first run applies the darker shade (often black ink), and the second run applies the lighter shading.

A Three-Color Cover . . . Or a Line Screen

A three-color cover will cost almost double what a single-color cover will cost, as it requires three separate runs through the press. Chapter 25 discusses the procedure for printing in multiple colors.

If you wish to vary the colors on your cover, consider using a line screen. A line screen can be used to print two or more shades of the same color. These are inexpensive to print, as they require only a single run through the press.

While the printing costs for a line screen are more economical than printing three separate colors, this may require the assistance of a graphic designer. A black-and-white line drawing must be made for the 100 percent line screen, plus ruby-liths (or overlays) for the remaining line screens.

A Four-Color Cover

A four-color cover is the equivalent of a color photograph or full-color drawing. If you intend to place four separate colors on your cover, consider using a photograph instead of a drawing.

It is seldom necessary to print four colors on a book cover. The expense of such a cover can approach $1,000. This includes:

1. the creation of the artwork, or taking of the photograph;
2. the making of color separations for photographs; and
3. the printing of the cover.

See Chapters 13, 14, and 25 if you intend to print in four colors.

Advance Reading Copies For Reviewers

In designing your cover, be sure to allow space for the addition of "advance review copy" data. Advance review copies are referred to as ARCs in the balance of the book. Data for ARC covers include:

1. the phrase "Advance Reading Copy—Not for Sale";
2. a publication date; and
3. suggested retail prices for the editions of your book.

When your book arrives at review sources, it must not look as if it's self-published. It must appear as professional as any advance review copy released by a major publisher. If it doesn't, you greatly lessen its chance for review. It was a *Library Journal* review of the author's first book that motivated a major publisher to purchase the reprint rights. This review also resulted in library sales of seven thousand copies.

ARC data can be printed on the first fifty to two hundred covers of your book; then the press can be stopped to scrape this wording off the printing plate. It takes only a minute to stop the press and remove the wording. Your printer may not even charge for this service. The maximum charge for printing ARC data on two hundred covers should not exceed $50.

Setting a Publication Date

Your publication date must be at least four full months after you have printed and bound books in hand. This is necessary so you can mail ARCs to reviewers for trade magazines. This much lead-time is required for these publications to receive your ARC, forward it to their reviewer, have the reviewer read and write a review, and then have the review printed.

Actually, most major publishers release their books well ahead of stated publication dates. *Publishers Weekly* covered this subject on September 25, 1981, in an article entitled "Do Pub Dates Mean Anything Anymore?" They answered their own question with the article's subtitle:

> Under the onslaught of publicity, author tours, book club choices, and reviewers and booksellers who jump the gun—probably not.

Designing Your Book's Spine

If you think your book's spine is unimportant, stop to consider how most books are displayed in bookstores—spine out. That is all most bookstore patrons are going to see of your book.

The title of your book must be clearly legible. It must stand out among other spines. A long title presents a problem, as the lettering will have to be smaller. This is another reason why your main title should be one word, when possible. Any subtitle can be omitted from the spine or printed in small enough type so that the main title can be easily read at a distance of ten to fifteen feet.

Place your last name on the spine also. Most bookstores arrange book sections alphabetically by the author's last name. If you omit your last name from the spine, a bookstore clerk may be unable to locate your book.

Review other spines in bookstores before designing your own. Your spine doesn't have to be beautiful, just easily identified.

Selling Your Book With Its Back Cover

Back covers usually contain reviews and endorsements. Getting these preliminary comments is the first promotion you will do for your book. Contact librarians, professors, other professionals, and authorities in the book's field for these comments. How to do this is explained in Chapter 34.

When formal reviews from the media are forthcoming, you can substitute these for earlier endorsements, or add to them.

An Author Photo

It is often a good idea to include a photo of yourself. With your photo, provide some background material about yourself, especially information that lends authority to your qualifications to write on your subject.

Repeat the Table of Contents

The most relevant information you can place on the back cover is your book's Table of Contents. If book buyers turn your book over, they want to know more about it. What better source than the Table of Contents?

Selecting And Working With A Graphic Designer

While spending thousands of dollars to print a book's interior, many author-publishers hesitate to spend a few hundred dollars to enhance the exterior of their book. This is foolish, as it is the exterior design that must draw the initial interest of a reader. The book's interior may receive no attention at all if the cover is nondescript.

Finding A Graphic Designer

Writers often ask artist-friends to help design their books. This may work out, but more often it does not. To produce camera-ready artwork for a book requires a certain amount of technical knowledge. A graphic designer will know exactly what quality is required.

When color work is involved, whether for illustrations or photographs, the aid of a graphic designer is essential. The graphic designer will know:

1. how to make duotones,
2. how to make line screens,
3. where to obtain color separations,
4. how to inspect color keys or a cromalin,
5. how to check rubyliths, and
6. how to prepare needed artwork.

During the preparation of a full-color cover for the author's *Slim* book, a graphic designer saved several hundred dollars on the book's cost. A reliable but reasonable firm was recommended in the making of color separations. Inspection of the color transparency, color separations, proofs, and rubyliths by a professional revealed many potential problems that would have resulted in a poor-quality cover had they not been spotted.

Sharing Royalties

For the author's first two books, the out-of-pocket expenses of the graphic designer were paid in advance while a 5 percent share of future profits (or royalties) was promised for the labor involved. This worked out quite well for both the author and the graphic designer.

Such an approach may not work with a graphic designer chosen from the Yellow Pages of a telephone directory. The graphic designer of the author's first two books was a previous acquaintance.

Referrals

If you've joined professional groups, the other authors you meet can often recommend graphic designers with whom they've had a favorable experience. Authors of self-published books may even be willing to share their knowledge with you about the preparation of artwork. In return, you can offer editing services or share in the expense of mail-order promotions with these authors.

Graphic Design Students

Instructors of college-level graphic design classes may be willing to recommend talented students. Some instructors seek this work for their students. In such instances, the supervision of the instructor is free, and the fee of the student will be far less than that of a professional graphic designer.

If you have the time, enroll in a graphic design class. Check the catalogs of local community colleges and universities.

Working With A Graphic Designer

Be open concerning how much you can afford when discussing the cost of artwork with a graphic designer—*do this before* any work is done. Graphic designers generally charge by the hour, at rates that may range as high as $40 to $50 per hour.

Pick up a copy of *The Graphics Artists' Guild Handbook*, which is available at any art supply store. This lists standard graphic design fees. Be aware, however, that it is usually possible to find someone who will work for less.

It is difficult for a graphic designer to quote a total fee until all your artwork requirements have been reviewed. It may be necessary to have the graphic designer show you a sample of at least one of the illustrations for your book, so both of you can agree on the desired quality and cost of artwork needed.

Provide Detailed Examples

Do not force your graphic designer to guess what you need. Provide good examples of what you wish, either hand-drawn or cut out from magazines and other sources.

If you ask a graphic designer to provide several variations of an illustration for your consideration, be ready to pay for the time required to design these alternatives.

Learn From Your Graphic Designer

While you should submit precise examples of what you wish, also be receptive to suggestions from your graphic designer as to how to give your artwork greater impact.

As previously mentioned, a graphic designer can also suggest ideas to reduce your artwork costs. Do not forget that black-and-white photographs will be far cheaper than hand-drawn artwork, unless you can obtain such artwork free. Photographs will have a better appearance in your book than most hand-drawn artwork as well.

With experience, you may be able to prepare much of your own artwork. Use a graphic designer for technical areas where you do not yet feel competent.

Working with a graphic designer is discussed further in the chapters concerning illustrations and photographs.

Producing Your Book

IV

Planning Your
Printing and
Promotion

16

As a publisher, you must engage in many different activities simultaneously. By the time printed and bound books arrive, your preparations for their promotion and sale must have been completed. Otherwise, you'll have the books but nothing to do with them.

Therefore, you must plan a work schedule for your book. Without such a plan, many of your efforts will be inefficient and disorganized. You will waste valuable time and resources.

Remember, you must plan for success. It will not happen accidentally.

How To Use This Chapter

The *Book Plan* on the following page is a general guide. Each of the first four groups of tasks should require approximately one month to accomplish.

As you complete each activity, note the date of completion. If you write in this book, use a pencil. Few authors stop at one book.

The numbers following each task indicate which chapters are relevant to that activity. Of course, the index in the back of the book provides more detailed references.

YOUR BOOK PLAN

———— Establish Your Company (4, 17)
———— Select Graphic Designer (15)
———— Order Forms:
    ———— Lib. of Congress Cat. Card (18)
    ———— Cataloging in Pub. Data　 "
    ———— ISBN Log and Manual　 "
    ———— Advance Book Info.　 "
    ———— Copyright Forms　 "
———— Select Typesetter (21)
———— Prepare Manuscript (19)
———— Design Softbound Cover (28, 29, 30)

- -

———— Request LCCC#, CIP, ISBN, ABI (18)

———— Make First Cast-Off (20)

———— Give Typesetter Manuscript

———— Begin Proofreading Galleys (22)

———— Select Printer (26)

———— Prepare Rubyliths (25)

———— Complete Proofreading (22)

———— Make Final Cast-Off (20)

———— Send for Mailing Lists (43, 44)

———— Design Promotional Material (34, 35)

———— Make Mailing List for Advance Reading Copies (ARCs) (33)

———— Prepare ARC Cover Letter (33)

- -

———— Paste up Galleys to Boards (23)

———— Paste up Boards to Signatures (24)

———— Print Invoices and Labels (17)

———— Order Mailing Packages (17)

——— Set Price (27)

——— Give Printer Signatures (26)

——— Inspect Printer's Negatives (26)

——— Inspect Printer's Plates (26)

——— Select Bindery (30, 31)

——— Inspect Printed Signatures (26)

——— Obtain Conversion Quotes (28, 29, 30)

——— Print Promotional Material (35)

——— Schedule Personal Appearances (36, 39, 40)

- -

——— Fix Publication Date (26, 28, 33)

——— Print Softbound Cover (28)

——— Bind Books (29, 30, 31)

——— Print Dust Jacket—optional (32)

- -

——— Mail Advance Review Copies (33)

——— Send Copyright Books (18)

——— Deliver Local ARCs (33)

——— Order Second Printing (26,47)

——— Print Reviews on New Cover (28, 32)

——— Offer Book to Major Publishers (46–49)

——— Gather Local Reviews (34, 36, 39, 40)

——— Print Mail-order Material (39, 43, 44)

——— Print More Promotional Material (35, 39–44)

——— Test Mail-Order Ads (44)

——— Run Mail-Order Ads (44)

——— Send Library Mailing (43)

Establishing
Your Publishing
Company

17

Establishing your publishing company should be one of the
first steps in publishing your book. It will save you money in
several areas. You can:

1. receive discounts as a business buyer,
2. purchase on credit,
3. avoid paying sales taxes on resalable supplies,
4. impress suppliers, thereby obtaining lower quotes plus
   higher quality work,
5. establish a bank account to "loan" money to your company, and
6. save 15 percent on advertising costs.

Naming Your Company

Select an impressive name for your publishing company. Relate it to your book's general subject area. By choosing a name
that sounds professional, you minimize the number of reviewers who automatically reject books that are obviously self-
published.

A benefit of selecting a general publishing name is that you
will receive frequent requests for a "catalog" from people

who have read your first book. This gives you the opportunity to market additional books you write subsequently.

Upon choosing a name, go to your library to make sure that it is not being used already. Check the publisher indexes in:

1. *Subject Guide to Books in Print,*
2. *Literary Market Place,*
3. small press directories,
4. corporate name directories, and
5. other references suggested by your reference librarian.

You can also write to the commissioner of corporations in your state and ask if the name has been registered by another party (you need not incorporate to do this).

Filing a "Fictitious Name" Statement

When you decide to operate a business in a name other than your own, it's necessary to file a "fictitious business name" statement with your county clerk. This statement is also called a DBA (doing business as) notice.

Before filing this notice with a county clerk, you are required to have it published in a local newspaper. Locate the least expensive newspaper for this purpose—the smaller the circulation, the less expensive the ad will be. Weekly newspapers are usually the least expensive. Check your local paper for a sample listing.

The newspaper will normally publish a notice of your business name three times, then send a proof of this publication to the county clerk. The county clerk will then send you a validated "fictitious business name" statement. The total cost of this notice runs from $15 to $30, depending on the size of your newspaper.

Obtaining A Resale Number

If the state in which you live has a sales tax, you should obtain a "resale number." This number permits you to avoid a sales tax when purchasing goods and supplies that will be "resold" to your customers in the process of selling books. It is also used to turn over to the state the sales tax you collect when selling books to residents of your state.

If you must obtain this number, look up the nearest business tax office for your state in the telephone book. In California, the office is called the Board of Equalization. It's not necessary to have a validated fictitious name statement before applying for a resale number.

Dress casually and downplay your anticipated success when applying for a resale number. Otherwise, you may be asked to make a substantial advance deposit on expected sales taxes from the sales of your book. Simply tell them that you intend to publish a book and have no idea whether it will be successful. Don't discuss dreams of getting rich.

Obtaining A Federal Employer Number

You should also visit an IRS office to apply for a federal employer identification number.

This number is needed when filing a federal income tax return at the end of your financial year. Occasionally, libraries ask for the number when ordering books.

Be Your Own Bookkeeper

When visiting the IRS, ask for free brochures oriented to the small-business person: There are several IRS publications that relate to sole proprietors and partnerships.

Learning how to set up your accounting books is not difficult. Attend a local community college class on bookkeeping if you have no prior education in this area. An excellent reference book, which should be in your local library system, is John Dessauer's *Book Publishing: What It Is, What It Does*.

The Small Business Administration also has a toll-free number that you can call to get publications on how to start a new business: 1-800-368-5855.

Obtaining A Post Office Box

While you may wish to use your home address for much of your correspondence, you should also open a post office box. A post office box not only provides safety for mail while you're on vacations; it also guarantees that you will receive book orders long after you move from your current residence. The average American moves every six years (many of us more often). If you move, the post office will forward mail from a residence for only one year; after that, orders for your books will be returned to sender.

On the other hand, with a post office box you can arrange for mail to be delivered to you periodically regardless of where you've moved. The post office will not forward this mail, but a friend can be hired for this task. Mailing services are also useful for this purpose; however, they are much more expensive, and you cannot guarantee that they will stay in business indefinitely. A post office box currently costs $20 a year.

To assure that mail is delivered to your post office box, simply list the box number below the street address (if you bother including a street in your address). If you list both a street and post office box in an address, the post office will deliver your mail to whichever appears directly above the city and state line. So arrange your address on stationery as follows:

JOHN SMITH
107 Harbor Drive
P.O. Box 222
Ocean Beach, CA 92345

It can be important to include a street in your address if you plan to market your book by mail order. A street address will increase your returns, as buyers usually have more confidence in a street address than a box number.

Before walking into your local post office to apply for a box, call first to see if one is available. If not, check other nearby post offices. It may be necessary to place a reservation for a box. While the post office is supposed to notify you when a box becomes available, it pays to check every few weeks with a clerk to see how long the waiting list is.

Establishing A Bank Account

As soon as you decide to publish a book, all of its expenses should be paid through a bank account in the name of your publishing company. Most of these expenses will be deductible.

With your fictitious name statement in hand, simply open a company account in the same manner in which you would open a personal account. Order a rubber stamp with your company name and account number for endorsing checks for deposit. Select checks that come in a three-ring binder, as they will have stubs on which you can keep a running record of company expenditures. Also order deposit slips capable of listing twenty-five to thirty checks.

Placing Funds into a Bank Account

There are several methods of accounting for funds that are placed in this bank account. These funds can be considered "capital" that is being invested in your company, in which case personal withdrawals may be considered income to you.

Another method is simply to advance (or loan) funds to your company. As sales mount and cash income permits, your company can then repay this loan to you. This return of money to you is not considered income, as it is repayment of a loan. In addition, you can charge your company interest during the term of the loan.

Delay making a decision as to how to treat the money placed in your company account until the end of your first taxable year. At that time, decide which method is best for your individual circumstances after discussing the possible results with a competent accountant.

Handling Business Phone Calls

Avoid installing a business phone number as long as possible. It is normally far more expensive to install a business phone than a personal phone. If you list a business phone at your residence, you also may be required to pay for a local business permit and other taxes. This can pose a problem if your residence is not zoned for commercial purposes.

Should you receive a telephone call from someone who wishes to drop by your home to purchase a book, always invite such persons to order their book through your post office address.

If you do not wish to answer the telephone with a "hello" at your residence during business hours, simply recite the last four digits of your telephone number when answering.

Forming An Advertising Agency

Advertising agencies are entitled to a 15 percent discount from rates quoted by magazines, newspapers, and other media members. By forming your own agency, you thereby save 15 percent of your advertising costs.

Choose an agency name that suits you, place it on a letterhead of an insertion or advertising order, and you're an advertising agency. It is not necessary to have new stationery or insertion order forms printed. Photocopy the insertion order form included in Chapter 44. Use rub-on lettering to make your letterhead.

Be sure to use an address for your ad agency that is different from the address of your publishing company. The phone number given on the insertion order must be your normal daytime number, as there is often a need to receive telephone calls from magazines and other media where ads are placed.

Opening a Bank Account for Your Ad Agency

It isn't necessary to obtain a fictitious name statement for your ad agency. Simply open a bank account in your personal name and direct the bank to place the name of the ad agency below your name. Then request the bank to print checks showing just the ad agency name.

If your bank questions this procedure, explain that the ad agency is a "subsidiary" of your company. It is being formed only to channel your own advertising, not to do business with anyone. Order checks in the personal size.

Printing Your Stationery

Printing stationery is a minor expense, so don't hesitate to go first class. It will help to make a good first impression on your suppliers, reviewers, and other industry contacts.

You will need the following:

1. letterheads,
2. envelopes (#10 size),

3. business cards,
4. invoices to fill purchase orders, and
5. mailing labels for book packages.

If you watch local newspapers for their ads, printers often advertise specials for a package of five hundred letterheads, envelopes, and business cards.

Letterhead

Sit down with the printer you've selected and design a letterhead. There's no need to hire a graphic designer at this point unless you want a custom-designed logo.

If your book is illustrated, one of your illustrations may be suitable for a logo.

Envelopes

Use colored paper for envelopes, even when your letterheads are on white paper. Colored envelopes will usually cost $10 extra and will make your correspondence distinctive. Printing a logo on your envelope will not cost extra if it's the same color.

For routine mail, you may wish to use plain envelopes. A box of five hundred #10 envelopes will cost approximately $5 through a wholesale outlet. Return address labels can be purchased from one of the inexpensive mail-order houses that advertise in newspaper supplements.

Business Cards

Do you remember the names of everyone you meet at social and business gatherings? Few people do. Your card serves as a reminder for important people you meet, in addition to furnishing your address and telephone number. Include a logo if you have one.

A good-looking card also encourages suppliers to give you credit, instead of asking for down payments or payment on delivery.

Invoices

With only one book, you won't need a large invoice. The example shown should be adequate. If printed 8½" × 3½", three invoices will fit on a normal sheet of paper.

The following page demonstrates how this invoice size can be efficiently arranged on a standard-size sheet of paper in order to minimize printing costs.

When ordering invoices, ask how much five hundred 8½" × 11" invoices will cost. When a figure is quoted, then tell the printer to fit three invoices on the 8½" × 11" sheet. You'll receive fifteen hundred invoices for the same price, although there may be a small cutting charge.

On the example, space is provided for both a billing address and a shipping address. Quite often on library orders, the book must be mailed to the library and its bill goes to city hall. Your invoice number should be placed in the upper right-hand corner, for ease of locating specific invoices when problems arise.

Do not place a phone number on your invoice. It's best to avoid telephone orders as there is no proof in writing of the order authorization. It also avoids telephone calls from unpleasant wholesalers who desire better terms.

Invoices should be printed on chemically treated (NCR) paper that does not require carbons for typing duplicates. Do not order invoices in tablet form. When they are loose, it is much easier to pick up the desired number of invoices.

Your printer may suggest that you print invoices in sets of different colored paper. This is not a good idea, as the number of invoices required for orders will vary among book customers. Some want bills in triplicate, while others will request quadruplicate billing.

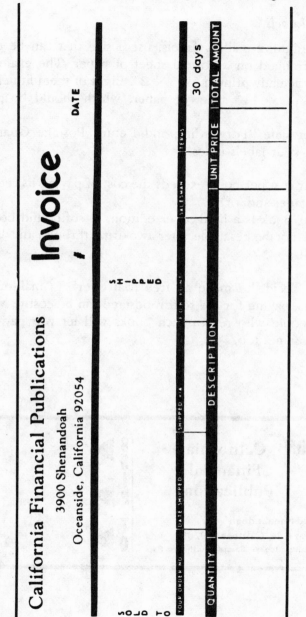

Mailing Labels

When designing mailing labels, use a size that can be efficiently arranged on a normal sheet of paper. The example label was actually printed 5½" × 2". Eight of them fit neatly on an 8½" × 11" sheet of paper, which should be pre-gummed.

Do not state "Forwarding and Return Postage Guaranteed" on your labels unless:

1. your cost per book exceeds the cost of paying its return postage; and/or
2. your book is a hard-cover edition, as softbound books will not be resalable after two trips through the U.S. mails.

If you decide to make a "free trial offer" to mail-order customers, paying for the return postage can be costly. Most of the people who return such books will let you pay the return postage, too.

Be Sure to Proofread Artwork

Whenever you order anything printed, proofread or inspect the finished artwork before the printing begins. This will reduce the likelihood of a misprinting.

For example, the author once asked a print shop to shorten the width of a mailing label, from 6½ to 5 inches. Instead of compressing the return address side of the label, the designer removed 1½ inches from the address side of the label. The result was a label with not enough room to type most addresses. Consequently, the printer had to run the job again. While the author was not charged, the delay was an inconvenience.

The Copyright Page

18

Library Of Congress Catalog Card Number

When you reach the point where your manuscript is within thirty days of being typeset, it's time to start collecting the data that will appear on your copyright page. This includes:

1. a Library of Congress Catalog Card number (LCCC#),
2. Library of Congress Cataloging in Publication (CIP) data,
3. an International Standard Book Number (ISBN), and
4. copyright registration forms.

Upon request, at no charge, the Library of Congress will issue your book a Catalog Card number. Many libraries use this number to identify books they order.

Using your company stationery, write the following letter to:

THE REGISTRAR, CIP DIVISION
Library of Congress
Washington, DC 20540

Dear Registrar:

This is to request a Library of Congress Catalog Card number for the book described below. A complimentary copy will be forwarded to you as soon as possible.

Author's name . . . .(your pen-name)
Title of Book . . . .(full title of book)
Edition . . . .(hardbound or softbound)
Place of Publication . . . . . .(city and state)
Publisher . . . .(your company's name)
Proposed Date of Publication . . . . . .(date)
Number of Pages . . . . . .(pages)

This book will be copyrighted.

Please send the preassigned card
number to: (company name and address)

Thank you.
                    Sincerely yours,

                    (name)
                    President

Within a few weeks, you will receive a card from the Library of Congress with your number.

Library of Congress Cataloging in Publication (CIP) Data

This refers to the information that appears at the top of your copyright page. It enables libraries to classify your book either according to the Dewey Decimal system or by a Library of Congress (CIP) number. These numbers appear on the spine of books in libraries.

Since the Library of Congress has a policy of not assigning CIP data to books that are self-published, it's vital that your application be forwarded to them in as professional a manner as possible.

Obtaining Necessary Forms

There are two steps to this procedure. The first is to send a request to:

CIP DIVISION
Library of Congress
Washington, DC 20540

for the pamphlet *Cataloging in Publication—Information for Participating Publishers.* Also request a few "Publisher's Response" forms.

Fill in the "Publisher's Response" form according to instructions and return it to the CIP Division. You will then receive Library of Congress Catalog Data forms. Upon receiving and filling in these forms, submit them with a copy of your manuscript, including front matter.

Also submit copies of descriptive material, such as dust jacket copy, Advance Book Information forms, and an author biographical page.

Be sure to include the Library of Congress Catalog Card number (which was previously assigned) when submitting the above data. Even if you've altered your title or publication date, still use the original number.

What you receive back from the CIP Division should resemble the following:

Library of Congress Cataloging in Publication Data

1. Holt, Robert Lawrence.
2. How mothers and others stay slim.

3.   1. Reducing diets—Case studies. 2. Women—
Interviews. 3. Mothers—Interviews. I. Title.
4. RM222.2.H578 613.2'5'0926 81-65299
5. ISBN 0-930926-04-8
    ISBN 0-930926-05-6 (pbk.)

Explanation:

1. author's name
2. book title (exclude subtitle)
3. subject headings for libraries
4. 1st no.—Lib. of Congress CIP #
   2nd no.—Dewey Decimal #
   3rd no.—Lib. of Congress Catalog Card #
5. International Standard Book Numbers, second number
   for softbound edition

International Standard Book Numbers

ISBN numbers are another classification system for books.
Bookstores and wholesalers often use these numbers for ordering purposes, as do many libraries.

What Do They Mean?

Every ISBN assigned to small publishers has at least ten digits,
divided into four parts of varying length. The four parts include:

1. Group identifier . . . usually the nation of the publisher.
2. Publisher prefix . . . the publisher.
3. Edition number . . . book's number.
4. Checking digit . . . computer checking number.

The ISBN numbers for the *Slim* book described in the
previous section were:

ISBN 0-930926-04-8
ISBN 0-930926-05-6 pbk

The first number is for the hardbound version of this book, the second for the softbound version. The *first* digit (0) indicates the book was published in the U.S.A. The *second* part (930926) identifies the book's publisher: California Health Publications. The *third* part of the upper number indicates that this is the fourth book published by California Health Publications. The last digit is a checking digit.

A separate ISBN is assigned to each edition of a book, but not to an unchanged reprint of the same book by the same publisher. Price changes do not require new ISBNs either.

Where ISBNs Should Be Placed

Your ISBNs should be printed on:

1. the copyright page,
2. the base of the book's spine,
3. the back cover in the lower corner,
4. the back of the dust jacket in the lower corner.

Obtaining ISBN Numbers

Request the pamphlet *The ISBN System User's Manual* and an *ISBN Log Book* by writing to:

ISBN AGENCY
R. R. Bowker & Co.
205 E. 42nd St.
New York, NY 10017

The manual provides more detailed information, and the "Log Book" consists of a series of ninety-nine numbers. The first number is double zeroes (00) and is assigned to the first book you publish.

Copyrighting Your Book

Your book is copyrighted by printing a copyright notice on one of its first pages, customarily the back of the title page. (See the example in this book.) Most publishers use both the encircled *c* and the word *Copyright* when printing a notice of copyright.

Why Register Your Copyright?

Page 7 of *Copyright Basics—Circular R1,* a publication of the Copyright Office of the Library of Congress, says:

> In general, copyright registration is a legal formality intended to make a public record of the basic facts of a particular copyright. However, except in one specific situation (under sections 405 and 406 of the Copyright Act, copyright registration may be required to preserve a copyright that would otherwise be invalidated because of omission of the copyright notice from the published copies or phonorecords, or omission of the name or date, or a certain error in the year date), registration is *not a condition* of copyright protection. Even though registration is not generally a requirement for protection, the copyright law provides several inducements or advantages to encourage copyright owners to make registration. Among these advantages are the following:
>
> - Registration establishes a public record of the copyright claim;
> - Registration is ordinarily necessary before any infringement suits may be filed in court;
> - If made before or within 5 years of publication, registration will establish prima facie evidence in court of the validity of the copyright and of the facts stated in the certificate; and
> - If registration is made within 3 months after publication of the work or prior to an infringement of the work, statutory damages and attorney's fees will be available to the copyright owner in court actions. Otherwise, only an award of actual damages and profits is available to the copyright owner.

Registration may be made at any time within the life of the copyright. Unlike the law before 1978, when a work has been registered in unpublished form, it is not necessary to make another registration when the work is published (although the registered owner may register the published edition, if desired).

To obtain copyright registration forms and the publication *Copyright Basics,* write to:

REGISTER OF COPYRIGHTS
Copyrights Office
Library of Congress
Washington, DC 20599

How Long Does Copyright Protection Last?

Your book is protected under the new copyright law for a period extending during your lifetime, plus fifty years. If a book has two authors, the term lasts for fifty years after the last surviving author's death.

How Do You Register a Copyright?

Normally, the following should be sent to the copyright office in order to copyright your book:

1. a completed application form,
2. a fee of $10 per book, and
3. two complete copies of the best edition (hardbound when both hard and softbound editions are released at the same time).

Advance Book Information Forms

These are standard forms within the book industry for listing data concerning a new book. An ABI form includes data such as the title, author's name, a brief description of your book, author biographical data, editions available, prices, and other information.

Being an author-publisher, you should use these forms when corresponding with various book agencies, both private and governmental. It's a sign to these agencies that you are a knowledgeable and professional publisher.

An ABI form should be sent with all advance review copies of your book. It provides potential reviewers with a standard way to quickly review your book and how it was published.

If you send an ABI form to R. R. Bowker and Company, your book will automatically be listed in *Books in Print, Subject Guide to Books in Print,* and as many as eleven other references published by Bowker.

ABI forms should be ordered when you begin typesetting. To obtain the forms, send your request to:

ABI DEPARTMENT
R. R. Bowker & Co.
205 E. 42nd Street
New York, NY 10017

Make photocopies of these forms when sending out advance review copies of your books.

Casting-Off—
Determining How
Long Your Book
Will Be

19

There are several reasons why it's important to determine the length of a book at an early stage:

1. to furnish approximate page counts to printers when requesting quotes for the printing of your book;
2. to design desired artwork around your text; and
3. to scale the length of your book to your available funds.

The First Cast-Off

Do your first cast-off when your manuscript is complete. In counting the total number of pages, don't forget to include space for:

1. chapter title headings,
2. front and back matter,
3. artwork, and
4. those pages that are to remain blank in your book.

Make mock-ups for each illustration that will appear in your book, so that you will know how much space to allow for your artwork.

Your book pages will be printed on large sheets of paper called signatures. In designing your book, try to work out a total page count that results in an even number of signatures. Most book signatures contain either 8 or 16 book pages. An 8-page signature has 4 pages on each side (called "4-up"). Of course, a 16-page signature has 8 pages on each side.

Let us assume that your manuscript is 244 pages long, and you've selected a text page size and typeface that prints approximately one and a quarter manuscript pages (determined by a comparison of your first typeset galleys to your manuscript). By dividing 244 by 1.25, you determine that your book will have approximately 195 pages.

Assuming your printer has the capability of printing 16-page signatures, divide 195 by 16 to determine how many signatures your book will require. In this example, the result is 12.1875 signatures. The remainder (.1875) equals 3 book pages (16 multiplied by .1875).

You must decide what to do with the fractional 3 pages. They could be eliminated, thus making an even 12 signatures, by shortening your manuscript or increasing the amount of text on each book page.

On the other hand, if you have enough relevant material, you could add 13 pages to your book, making an even 13 signatures. Whatever you do, don't leave 13 blank pages at the end of your book; it's a waste of money and looks unprofessional.

It is possible simply to cut the extra 13 pages off the last signature, but you must pay an unnecessary trimming expense, in addition to being charged for the unused paper.

Sound Intelligent When Talking to Printers

When you obtain quotes from printers, they will ask the length of your book, among other questions. In the above example, you could answer, "195 pages," leaving the printer to calculate how many signatures that would require. Of course, 195 pages works out to a fraction over 12 signatures. It is better to tell the printer that your book requires 12 signatures, providing the printer can print 16-page signatures.

If you require the printer to explain all this to you, he may also think you're uninformed enough to accept an overpriced quote.

Instead of appearing ignorant, do your homework. After doing a preliminary cast-off, decide whether to cut or add material to make an even signature, before calling printers for quotes. Find out whether each printer has the capability to print 8- or 16-page signatures, and tell them the length of your book in terms of the number of signatures.

The Second Cast-Off

When you're one-third of the way through the typesetting of your book, you will need to do another cast-off. To cast-off this time, make a clear piece of acetate the dimensions of your book's text page. A "text page" is the space that words occupy on a book page.

In measuring galleys—which you receive from the typesetter in long sheets that you will later trim down to your exact page size—with the piece of acetate, make light marks on the edge of the text with a blue pencil. Don't make heavy marks, as you will probably be adjusting these marks frequently. Write the page numbers required for each chapter on a separate sheet of paper. As suggested in Chapter 12, begin your book page count with the half-title page.

After a second cast-off, you can make a fair estimate of the eventual length of your book. Begin making design changes to ensure that illustrations are properly positioned and your book will have an even number of signatures.

The Third Cast-Off

After receiving all your corrected galleys from the typesetter, begin a third cast-off. First, tape the galley sheets for each chapter into a single roll, in order to eliminate the possibility of misplacing a galley page.

During this cast-off, the following visual problems should be corrected:

1. tag ends;
2. headings at page bottoms;
3. artwork that doesn't fit properly.

Tag Ends, Also Called Widows

These are single lines (either the first or last lines of a paragraph) that stand alone at the top or bottom of pages. They appear awkward and should be pasted up with the balance of their paragraphs, even if it means adding or subtracting a line from a text page.

Headings at Page Bottoms

Section or sub-section headings should not stand alone at the bottom of a page. Arrange to place them either at the top of the next column or on the next page. If that is not feasible, bring the first line or two of the section or sub-section over from the next page to paste up under the heading.

Artwork That Doesn't Fit

Your book will be both more readable and more professional-looking if you make sure that artwork always appears as close as possible to the relevant text.

When artwork does not fit naturally with related text, then adjust previous pages to make it fit.

Another solution is to change the size of the artwork. Simply ask your printer to reduce or enlarge the artwork. A third solution is to add more text.

Solve all your placement problems first. If you start cutting up your galleys too soon, you may have to repeat the process if you have erred in your planning. Then, you will have twice as many pieces of galley to paste up.

Doing Your Own Typesetting

20

There are two ways of having your manuscript typeset. You can hire a typesetter or choose to do it yourself.

Doing Your Own Typesetting

If you decide to do your own typesetting, it should be justified (even) on both the left and right margins, in addition to being proportionally spaced. An ordinary typewriter, which assigns equal space to each letter on its keyboard, will not do.

If you already own a word processor *and* a letter-quality printer with proportional spacing, it may be possible to use this equipment to typeset your book. Since the quality of typesetting from letter-quality printers varies widely, it is suggested that you compare the result from your equipment with the typesetting you see in this book. If it's of equal quality, you are fortunate. If it is not, you will gamble by using your word processor as a source of typesetting.

If the words printed in your book appear sloppily typeset, reviewers may hesitate to review it and potential buyers may recognize your effort as an amateurish, self-published work.

This author does not recommend that readers purchase a word processor and printer in order to typeset a book, because the cost of acquiring sufficiently high-quality equipment is normally far in excess of the cost of hiring a typesetter.

Author-publishers who are expert typists may find it more economical to purchase a used IBM Executive typewriter (Model C). If your manuscript exceeds one hundred pages, it will be less expensive to purchase an IBM Executive and do your own typesetting.

IBM Executive typewriters offer two unique features to author-publishers. First, they provide proportional spacing of letters. (An ordinary typewriter assigns equal space to each letter, regardless of its length.) The IBM Executive also permits you to justify the right-hand margin, which gives your typesetting a professional appearance. By typing your next-to-last draft on an IBM Executive, it's a simple matter to type the final draft of the manuscript with justified margins. Your final draft can then be pasted up to boards as camera-ready copy.

How to Buy an IBM Executive Typewriter

While IBM Executives can be leased, it may be cheaper to purchase one outright. In the used market, they are available at prices ranging from $250 to $400. Before making a purchase, you should rent the typewriter you have chosen and test it for at least a week. Also purchase an operating manual for the model you select.

The author does not recommend the Model D, as it is not as sturdy as the earlier Model C. It is also easier to justify lines visually with the Model C. The earlier model also offers the symbol ☐, which is useful in designating sub-section headings.

Purchase neither of these models unless you receive a written guarantee of at least three months; ask for six months. Replacing a key for such typewriters can cost $12 to $18, and these are used typewriters.

In selecting a Model C, test all the keys for similar tone. If one key is too light, this can often be adjusted in a minute. If only a portion of a key is light, this often indicates that the head of the key is getting ready to fall off.

Ask for a new platen, or roller, when purchasing your typewriter. The store will often replace the platen at cost, or less. A new platen will keep your paper from slipping.

Proofing and Typesetting Paper

If you decide to do your own typesetting, purchase a special clay-coated paper on which to type your final draft. The clay coat on one side of the paper gives your typesetting the necessary hairline definition.

The best place to purchase this paper is at your local printing shop. Ask for typesetting paper, reproduction paper, or repro paper. This paper comes in large sheets, so ask that they cut the paper into widths that are 2½ inches wider than your typeset line. These sheets should be as long as possible, so do not have them cut length-wise.

Choosing and Working With a Typesetter

21

Preparing A Manuscript For The Typesetter

While a manuscript submitted to a professional publishing editor should be super-clean, a manuscript given to a typesetter need only be reasonably neat. Double-space, leaving one-inch margins on both sides of the page and at the top and bottom. Most typesetters quote fees on a "per manuscript page" basis, so fill your page up to these margins. Otherwise, you'll be paying for empty space.

Do not hyphenate single words at the end of manuscript lines. Type out the entire word. Otherwise, typesetters may place hyphens incorrectly in the middle of these single words when they appear within a book text line. For example, if the word *thoroughfare* appears at the end of a line in your manuscript, do not split it in order to have a relatively even margin on your manuscript page. If you type this word at the end of the line as *thorough-fare,* then the typesetter may typeset the word as *thorough-fare* in the middle of a line on the galleys. If you cannot avoid such hyphenation, mark it as follows to indicate that the typesetter is to delete the hyphen: *thorough⁄fare.*

Numbering Illustrations

Number illustrations according to the chapters in which they appear. Place the number of the chapter first, then consecutively number each illustration as it appears in the chapter. For example, if you have four illustrations in Chapter 2, number them 2.1, 2.2, 2.3, and 2.4. Number photographs the same as other illustrations.

Page Numbers

Always number manuscript pages in the upper right-hand corner with a pencil. Use a pencil to number your Table of Contents also.

After selecting a typeface and size for page numbers, have them typeset on a single sheet of paper. The back of this sheet should be waxed by the typesetter, at no extra charge. If you forget to have your page numbers waxed, you'll have to place a small dab of glue on the back of each number during paste-up.

Contact Several Typesetters

When hiring a typesetter, printer, or bindery, the best way to minimize your costs is to gather a large number of bids.

There are many typesetting firms that customarily charge as much as $12 per manuscript page, excluding the cost for typesetting indexes, captions, chapter headings, and running heads, which can come to much more. If you contact only a few firms to obtain typesetting quotes, you may pay far more than necessary for your typesetting. All of the author's books have been typeset for less than $3.50 per manuscript page, which would probably be no more than $4 to $8 at current prices.

The best way to find low bids is to contact at least ten typesetters for quotes. It is also a good idea to contact other author-publishers in your area to see whom they have used.

Collecting Quotes

When contacting typesetters, prepare carefully in order to save both time and money.

Obtain Quotes for Straight Copy

As you gather your initial quotes, ask typesetters to furnish quotes on the basis of "straight copy." This is text consisting of plain sentences and paragraphs, without indented material of any kind such as charts, lists, quotes, and so on. The reason for obtaining initial quotes for straight copy is that it provides comparable quotes from each typesetter.

Know Whether You Type Pica or Elite

In preparing your manuscript, you have used either a pica or elite type size. The pica size is the larger, having ten characters per inch; elite type has twelve characters per inch. Measure an inch of your typing before calling typesetters, as you will probably be asked.

Which Typesetters to Call

Obtain quotes from firms that do not occupy high-rent locations. Avoid firms that do printing as well, since they tend to charge more.

Your lowest quotes will probably come from "mom-and-pop" typesetting firms. The smaller the operation, the lower the overhead, and the lower the quotes should be.

Choosing a Typesetter

After obtaining your initial quotes, make appointments with the two or three lowest bidders. Take your manuscript with you.

If you've designed your book for maximum readability, these typesetters will raise their initial quotes. Your book, of course, should have a liberal amount of indented material.

The most reasonable quotes you find will probably be in the $6 to $8 range per manuscript page. This means that a 200-page manuscript should cost in the area of $1,200 to $1,600 to typeset. However, a book such as this one, with running heads, captions for illustrations, chapter headings, and sub-headings, could cost as high as $10 to $12 a page. This is a small price to pay for a good-looking result.

At this point it's also a good idea to find out if the typesetter will charge to make changes on the galleys—both the correction of printer's errors, or PEs, and author's alterations, or AAs. You should *never* have to pay to have PEs corrected. AAs are often charged at a very high rate, so be sure that your manuscript is exactly as you want it to appear in its final form when you submit it to the typesetter.

Never let yourself be "low-balled" by a typesetter. A firm may attempt to increase its quoted price after your job is begun. The best way to control this is to get your final bid *in writing*.

Working With The Typesetter

Once you have selected a typesetter, you must decide precisely how your book is to be typeset. Use the following checklist to discuss instructions for the typesetter:

Checklist for Typesetter
——— 1. Typeface
——— 2. Type size
——— 3. Leading
——— 4. Chapter title style and size
——— 5. Running head style and size
——— 6. Section heading style and size
——— 7. Sub-section heading style and size

——— 8. Footnote size and placement
——— 9. Front matter:
——— a. half-title page
——— b. title page
——— c. copyright page
——— d. foreword
——— e. preface and acknowledgments
——— f. dedication
——— g. table of contents
——— h. list of illustrations
——— 10. Back matter:
——— a. appendix
——— b. bibliography
——— c. glossary
——— d. index
——— e. ordering page
——— 11. Page numbers (folios)

Bring examples to show your typesetter exactly how you wish your book to appear.

Obtain Sample of Typesetting Style

When you give your manuscript to the typesetter, ask that three or four pages be typeset first to check the style, letter size, and leading that you've selected. Spend a few days reviewing the sample, especially if you've selected a style other than those recommended by this book in Chapter 12.

Most typesetters have modern equipment that permits them to furnish samples of other styles without the need to retypeset your manuscript.

Request Galleys as They Are Typeset

The first thing you will receive from the typesetter will be galleys, which are proofs of text copy before it is made up into the actual pages. Galleys, which often come in long sheets that you will later trim down to your page size, offer you the opportunity to proofread your book before it is in its final form.

Rather than receive all your galleys at one time, ask that your typesetter furnish you whatever has been typeset on a weekly basis. This permits you to proofread the galleys more efficiently.

Some typesetters prefer to make their corrections after the entire manuscript has been typeset. When you have a choice, have your corrections made every week rather than at the conclusion of the job. This will better allow you to plan the layout of your book. Without corrections, it can be difficult to make an accurate cast-off (see Chapter 19).

Preparing Your Glossary And Index

Once you've turned your manuscript over to a typesetter, you may feel a great sense of relief. You haven't given birth yet! This is the best time to compile your glossary and index. While it is possible to wait until you have pasted-up boards to make your glossary and index, as author-publisher you will have time on your hands while the manuscript is being typeset.

Making a Glossary

The same list of words gathered for your glossary can be used to compile an index. Follow these steps in making a glossary:

1. underline in *red* all words belonging in either your glossary or index;
2. at the same time, transfer these words to legal-size sheets of paper, in general alphabetical order;
3. when transferring words in #2 above, be sure to include the *page numbers* where the words were found;
4. also transfer all other page numbers where the words are mentioned as you read the balance of the manuscript;

5. write numbers out in their entirety, using hyphens between numbers for consecutive pages.

By listing page numbers with the words, you'll be able to refer quickly to the original definitions of these words. These numbers will also be used when composing your index.

Making Your Index

When galleys have been pasted up to boards and page numbers have been assigned to each board, you can then number your index.

You already have a list of manuscript page numbers for the index. Why not convert these numbers to book (board) page numbers? To do this, simply transfer the page numbers on your boards to your manuscript pages with a red pencil:

1. Using the red pencil, draw horizontal lines across the manuscript pages where one board page ends and another begins.
2. Write in board page numbers above and below these horizontal lines.

Using the list of words gathered to make your glossary, simply convert the numbers on this list into board page numbers.

Proofreading
Your Galleys

22

As mentioned earlier, don't wait for your entire manuscript to be typeset before beginning the proofreading of galleys. If you receive galleys from your typesetter once a week, they'll be in short segments, which can be efficiently proofread.

Do not cut or trim galleys with a scissors at this time. Each galley from a typesetting firm has a code that reveals where the original typesetting is stored in a retrieval system. Do not remove these storage codes from the galleys. However long a galley is (some may be five to six feet), leave it that length until you're ready to paste up to boards.

Errors To Watch For

Professional typesetters commonly type at speeds exceeding 100 words per minute. Typing that fast, they're not looking for your spelling or grammatical errors; in fact, they are supposed to reproduce the text exactly as you have submitted it. If you've misspelled a word, they're likely to misspell it in the same way. It's like the blind following the blind.

If you want a typesetter to find and correct your errors, you will have to pay extra for this additional service.

Moreover, typesetters almost always make inadvertent new errors of their own.

During proofreading, you may notice:

1. misspellings,
2. other grammatical errors,
3. omissions of phrases, sentences, and entire paragraphs,
4. changes in typeface and leading (space between the lines), and
5. varied pitch (distance between letters of words), among other problems.

It is your responsibility to find all errors, regardless of their origin.

To boot, you may be charged for the correction of your errors. You won't receive credit for finding the errors by the typesetter.

When a segment of galleys contains excessive errors, regardless of their origin, ask for a new galley sheet when turning in corrections. Otherwise, you'll have to spend unnecessary time pasting up single-line corrections to such galleys.

How to Proofread

If you proofread by yourself, catching spelling and other grammatical errors may be no problem—if you are an excellent speller and know your grammar. However, you still may not notice omissions. This is why you need another person to proofread your galley sheets properly.

This other person must read the original manuscript to you, while you check the galley sheets. No one is going to proof the galley sheets as closely as you can. Only you, the author, know what your galleys are supposed to say. As you proofread, use a sheet of paper to cover all the lines below the line you're reading. This aids your concentration.

Pace Yourself

Just as you need a clear mind to write, you need a clear mind to proofread. Eat, exercise, and rest to stay alert. If you're tired, many errors may be overlooked. Usually, a half-hour is the longest you can efficiently concentrate. Also, proofread when and where you will not be disturbed.

Proofread a Second Time

Proofread the galleys again by reading them yourself—slowly. This time, you'll normally find at least a third more errors.

Proofread a Third Time

Ask your best copy editor to proofread the galleys also. A third reading by another person will usually turn up 10 percent more errors.

Making Corrections

It is not necessary to employ proofreading symbols used by professionals, unless you are already familiar with them. The system recommended in this book is more than adequate.

Use a Light Blue Pencil

Light blue pencil marks are usually not picked up during reproduction, so they can be safely used to mark galley corrections.

The typesetter must be able to identify clearly the error in each line. Mark through misspelled words and other grammatical errors and place a caret sign where you wish your correction to be placed. On the border of the galley opposite the error, write the correct spelling of the word. Spell out grammatical corrections in detail.

When a new punctuation symbol is required, place the correct symbol in the margin opposite the line to be corrected and place a caret through the incorrect symbol.

When a word or short phrase is omitted, clearly mark the break in the sentence with a caret. Write the missing words on the right-hand border, using the circled word "omitted" above them.

If you wish to delete a word or phrase, mark through it in the text and place the following symbol in the margin, meaning delete and close up the space between type: ⌀

Finally, mark the correction as either a PE or an AA—a printer's error or an author's alteration—if your typesetter has assured you that he will charge only for AAs.

Have the Typesetter Wax Corrections

When corrections are made, be sure to ask that the back side be waxed. Waxed corrections can be easily placed in position, using a mild pressure. This is more convenient than having to place glue on a narrow strip of paper. Typesetters have waxing machines that can apply wax to corrections easily and quickly.

Proofread Typeset Corrections

Before leaving the typesetter when you pick up corrections, proofread them. If you have extensive corrections, you can expect to find more errors in them. Most of these will be misspellings, although a few omissions may also occur.

When possible, have a second person read the original galley (plus any omissions) to you, as you read the corrections.

Pasting Up Corrections

When you have single lines to correct, use the following procedure:

1. Use a *scissors* to trim single lines to the correct size. Do not use an Exacto knife, as a slip can mar the correction.
2. To align the correction, use an Exacto knife for fine adjustments.
3. Line up the *last letter* of the correction with the last letter of the galley line.
4. Then align the "legs" of similar words. The letters *g, j, p, q,* and *y* have legs that can be made out through the paper of the correction.
5. To align horizontally, use a "headliner ruler." This ruler is transparent and has numerous parallel lines along its length.
6. To align vertically, use a clear, plastic triangle.

When the correction is perfectly aligned, place a sheet of paper over it before burnishing the correction lightly with your finger. Otherwise, you may scrape off part of the typesetting.

This process can be made easier by the use of a light box or light table—a box or table with an opaque glass cover and a light beneath, which allows you to see the original through the correction.

Pasting Up Galleys
and Illustrations
to Boards

23

Many author-publishers think pasting up a book is a complicated procedure. They pay as much as a thousand dollars to have their book pasted up by a graphic designer or printer. Before you waste money hiring someone to do this job, review the simple instructions in this chapter.

Pasting up a book involves three steps:

1. numbering your galleys;
2. cutting galleys into page-lengths; and
3. pasting up these page-lengths to boards.

The result is "page boards," also referred to as mechanicals or repro. This is camera-ready copy from which the printer can shoot negatives.

Equipment Needed

Most of these items you already have. The rest can be purchased at any art supply store.

Layout Boards

Layout boards are white sheets of paper with light blue guidelines indicating the size of the text page and margins. They can be the thickness of ordinary paper, or somewhat thicker. Order as many boards as there will be pages in your book.

Layout boards are available at printing-supply firms. When they are not available at these outlets, use ordinary graph paper with light blue lines.

Other Materials

You will need the following:

1. Exacto knife—for fine-cutting and positioning during paste-up.
2. Light blue pencil—for marking galleys and boards.
3. Large scissors—for cutting galleys.
4. Clear piece of acetate—to measure galleys.
5. Tape—for taping galleys.
6. Metal ruler—for use with Exacto knife.
7. Headliner ruler—for aligning.
8. Plastic triangle—for aligning.
9. Rubber cement—for gluing.
10. Rubber cement eraser—for picking up excess rubber cement from galleys.
11. Rubber cement solvent—for diluting the rubber cement or removing galleys from boards when mistakes are made.
12. Valve-Spout container—for applying the solvent.
13. Liquid Paper correction fluid.
14. Staedtler eraser—for removing marks.
15. Graphic art tape—for outlining illustrations and underlining chapter headings.

Preparing Yourself

As during other critical stages of your book, your mind should be clear before beginning a paste-up. When you're tired, it's easy to paste up a section or galley in the wrong order. Or to place a page number on the wrong side of the page. Or even to place the wrong chapter title at the beginning of a chapter.

While these errors can all be corrected, why not avoid them by doing your paste-up in a refreshed state of mind? Take frequent breaks.

Be sure to wash your hands before starting the paste-up.

Checklist Before Starting

————1. Have all the corrections been made to your galleys?

————2. Is your hand-drawn artwork ready?

————3. Are all photos sized?

————4. Have you made rubyliths for your photos?

————5. Have chapter title headings been typeset?

————6. Have running heads been typeset?

————7. Have page numbers (also called "folios") been typeset?

————8. Is your front matter typeset?

————9. Is your back matter typeset (with the exception of the index)?

Numbering Your Galleys

Cast-off the entire text again. Include the front matter and back matter. Estimate the index page number count as precisely as possible. Your index cannot be typeset until your book pages have been numbered.

Did this final cast-off coincide with the third cast-off described in an earlier chapter? If not, make the necessary adjustments.

Once a final cast-off results in an even-numbered signature, you can number your galleys. Use the light blue pencil for numbering, also drawing lines at the edge of the text dividing pages.

As suggested in Chapter 12, begin numbering your book with Arabic numbers on the half-title page. If you use another system for numbering your book, it's more likely that errors will occur.

Make Dummies for All Blank Pages

A common mistake is failing to make a board for each page of your book that is to remain blank when printed. The back of your Table of Contents page may be blank, as may many of the last pages of chapters.

On the boards of blank pages, write on the face the words BLANK PAGE. Then your printer won't think that the board is missing. Of course, use a light blue pencil.

Starting Your Paste-Up

Paste up one chapter at a time. Before cutting the first page of a chapter, make sure you have made allowances for the chapter title headings.

Number Boards of First Chapter

Lay out enough boards for the first chapter. Number them for each page, placing the numbers in the lower left-hand corner when even, and the lower right-hand corner when they're odd. Use the light blue pencil.

Cut Galley Pages of First Chapter

With a scissors (not an Exacto knife), cut the first page of the first galley. Trim its sides to one-eighth of an inch from the text. This facilitates aligning the page to the blue guidelines. Do not cut off more than one page of the galley at a time.

Arrange Your Lighting

In order to align galley pages to boards, use direct overhead lighting, plus lighting from each side. This eliminates all shadows.

Use Rubber Cement

If you use ordinary glue, you may tear a galley or illustration if you need to remove it from a board. Rubber cement forgives your mistakes. When a mistake is made, you can safely and easily remove the galley from its board by squirting rubber cement solvent between them.

When applying rubber cement to the back of a galley page, turn the galley page upside down before bringing the rubber cement over the page. This eliminates the possibility of spilling rubber cement on the typesetting.

Glue the corners of smaller items, or the upper center and lower center of larger items. Excess rubber cement can be removed with the recommended rubber cement eraser.

Aligning Galleys to Boards

Rubber cement dries quickly, but still allows time to align your material. First, align the lowest line of the text with the horizontal blue line at the bottom of the board. Use the plastic headliner ruler.

Then, use the plastic triangle to align the galley page vertically. An Exacto knife will be helpful in making fine adjustments.

Pasting Up Numbers

Was your page-number sheet waxed? If not, get it waxed before you start.

Cut ten numbers at a time off this sheet. Use a large, sharp scissors. While the Exacto knife is necessary in aligning numbers, don't use it to cut numbers unless you're an expert with it.

Pick up numbers using the Exacto knife. Remember that even numbers belong on the left-hand side, odd numbers on the right.

Pasting Up Running Heads

Running heads can be pasted up at the same time as page numbers. Just remember to paste up chapter title running heads on odd-numbered pages only. Do not center running heads at the top of your pages if you also have section and sub-section headings. They'll conflict with each other and confuse your readers.

Final Check

After completing your paste-up, run the following check of page boards:

1. Are all odd-numbered pages numbered on right-hand corners?
2. Are all even-numbered pages numbered on left-hand corners?
3. Are all pages in order?
4. Are chapter title running heads on upper right-hand corners of odd pages?
5. Did you forget any illustrations?

Pasting Up
Boards to
Signatures

24

After pasting up galleys to boards, most author-publishers turn the page boards over to their printer. The printer must then paste up the boards to large sheets of paper called signatures.

Why not do this job yourself? It is simple to do and will save you 10 to 15 percent of your printing costs.

What Is A Signature?

A signature is a large sheet of paper upon which pages of your book are printed. When properly folded in halves two times (for an 8-page signature) or three times (for a 16-page signature), the page numbers are in the correct numerical sequence.

Pick up a blank sheet of paper and fold it in half, then fold it in half again. Open up the sheet. You will see four equal-sized sections on each side of the sheet. This is what an 8-page signature looks like. They would be numbered as in Fig. 24-1.

Number the sections on your sheet of paper, and then fold it back into two halves. If you fold it properly, the numbers will be in correct sequence. Did you write the numbers along the upper row upside down? When folded, they'll be right side up.

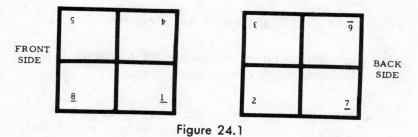

Figure 24.1

A 16-Page Signature

Now pick up another sheet of paper and fold it in half three times (one more time than for an 8-page signature). Open the sheet and you will see eight equal-sized sections on each side of the sheet. This 16-page signature will be numbered as in Fig. 24-2.

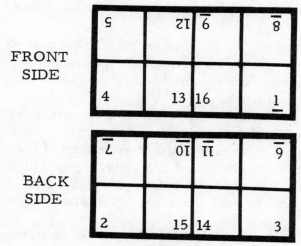

Figure 24.2

Where Do You Get Signature Sheets?

After you select your printer (as explained in Chapter 26), ask him or her to supply you with three items:

1. A *master signature sheet,* which shows the outline of your book page's trim size. You will align your page boards within this outline.
2. A *dummy signature,* on which page numbers are placed to guide you in the pasting up of page boards.
3. Enough blank signature sheets to paste up all your page boards.

Pasting Up To Signatures

If you follow the steps given below, pasting up should be the easiest task you will have to do in the making of your book.

1. Using 8½" × 11" sheets of paper, make a *dummy numbered signature* for each signature of your book. Use the dummy signature given you by the printer as a guide in numbering.
2. If your printer drew your book's trim size on only one section of the master signature, make an outline of the trim size on each of the other sections of the master signature. Make this outline in heavy pencil (or ink), as it will be your guide during the pasting up of your boards to signatures. Tape it permanently to a large tabletop.
3. Check to see that the blank signature sheets provided by the printer can be divided into four equal parts lengthwise. There may be an extra eighth- or quarter-inch at the end of the sheet, for which you must make allowance. If there is, simply draw a vertical line separating this excess amount from the balance of the signature, or trim it off.

4. While your *dummy signatures* should have numbers written on both sides, do *not* paste up page boards on both sides of a single blank signature. You could, but it's easier to use two separate signature sheets for each dummy-numbered signature sheet. Label one sheet "1A" for its front, and a second sheet "1B" for its back. By using two sheets for each dummy signature, there is less chance that pieces of your paste-up will become dislodged.

5. Number two blank sheets for each dummy signature sheet of your book.

6. Align the first numbered sheet (1A) over the master signature sheet, which has been permanently taped to the top of a table. Temporarily tape the blank sheet over the master signature sheet.

7. Are all your page boards the same size? If not, trim them with a scissors so that they are. You should trim them so the outline on the master signature sheet acts as a guide in aligning each page board.

8. Align the page boards for the front (1A) of the first numbered signatures. If you have 16-page signatures, these will be page numbers 5, 12, 9, 8, 4, 13, 16, and 1.

9. Place the page boards for pages 5, 12, 9, and 8 upside down. Remember to place the upper row of page boards upside down for all signatures.

10. Place a liberal amount of rubber cement at the top and bottom of each board and align them in proper sections.

11. When you're finished, double-check your paste-up by:
    a. comparing numbers on pasted-up signatures with those on dummies; and
    b. checking that all page boards along the upper row of signatures are upside down.

12. Make a large container for the pasted-up signatures. Store them flat. Don't fold them.

13. Tell your printer to double-check your work.

Preparing Photographs for the Printer

25

When you tell a printer that your book will have photographs, you will be asked if you're going to deliver "camera-ready copy." The printer is asking if your photographs will:

1. be mounted on boards,
2. be cropped to desired photo areas,
3. have reduction or enlargement percentages calculated, and
4. when necessary, have rubyliths prepared.

Making rubyliths is a simple procedure that can be mastered in a matter of minutes. If you have numerous photographs, making your own rubyliths can save you hundreds of dollars in graphic designer and printing fees. It will permit you to submit "camera-ready copy."

Mounting And Cropping Photographs

Quite often, you will not want to reproduce an entire photograph on your book page. In such cases, outline the area of the photograph you wish reproduced using the following technique.

1. *Never use a scissors* to crop a photo in order to outline the area of the photo to be reproduced. The printer needs the outer margins, even though they will not appear in the book. Leave the entire photo intact.
2. Tape the photo to a board (sheet of heavy paper) using double-edged tape.
3. Using onion-skin paper, cut an overlay for the photo and tape it to the upper margin of the photo.
4. Using a pencil, lightly place cropmarks on the overlay, outlining your *Desired Photo Area* (DPA). Never place cropmarks directly on a photo.
5. Measure the height and width available on your book page for the DPA.
6. If the space available on your book page is sufficient for the DPA, the next step is to make a rubylith of the DPA.

In many cases, however, it will be necessary first either to reduce or enlarge the DPA.

Reducing A Photograph

If a photograph must be reduced to fit the available space on your book page, follow these steps:

1. Trace the dimensions of the DPA on a plain sheet of paper (Fig. 25-1).
2. Draw a diagonal line, a, through the DPA (Fig. 25-2).
3. Decide the exact height or width—whichever is the critical distance—that you wish the photo to be on your book's page. Use centimeters for ease of calculating.
4. If height is the critical distance, using a vertical measurement *from the baseline of the DPA,* mark the desired height on the diagonal line b.
5. If the width of the book page is the critical distance, measure from the left margin of the DPA outline and mark width on the diagonal line b.

6. Draw a vertical line, c, from the baseline of the DPA to the point b on the diagonal line, and draw a horizontal line, d, from the point b to the left side of the DPA. The enclosed rectangle is called the Reduced Photo Size (RPS).

7. Subtract the height of the RPS from the height of the DPA, then divide the result by the height of the DPA to find the percentage reduction (see Fig. 25-3); for example, if the height of the RPS is 6 centimeters, and the height of the DPA is 8 centimeters, then subtract 6 from 8 to get 2 and divide 2 by 8 to get ¼ or 25 percent reduction.

You now have the percentage reduction required to permit this photo to be reproduced on your book page. Write this percentage on the board holding the photo.

As a rule, do not ask your printer to reduce a photograph by more than 50 percent. It is better to have your photo lab furnish a new print, smaller in size, from the original negative.

Enlarging A Photograph

When it's necessary to enlarge a photograph, follow these steps:

1. Trace the DPA on an onion-skin overlay (Fig. 25-4).

2. On another piece of paper (Fig. 25-5), draw a new rectangle having the height that is available on your book page. In this example, it is ten centimeters.

3. Place the onion-skin overlay of the DPA in the lower left-hand corner of this new rectangle (Fig. 25-6).

4. Draw a diagonal line, a, on the DPA, and extend it to the top line of the new rectangle (extending the width of the rectangle as we've done in the example).

5. Where this extended line intersects the top line, b, of the new rectangle determines the width of the enlarged

photo. You now have the exact size of the *Enlarged Photo Size* (EPS) for your book page.

6. Subtract the height of the DPA (6 cm) from the height of the EPS (10 cm). Divide the result by the height of the DPA. This is the percentage (67%) by which your photo must be enlarged. For example, 6 subtracted from 10 is 4, which, divided by 6, is ⅔ or 67 percent. Thus your photo must be enlarged by 67 percent.

As a rule, do not ask a book printer to enlarge a photograph more than 100 percent. Have your photo lab provide a new print from the original negative.

Making A Rubylith (Window) For Your Photograph

The next step is to make an overlay, out of acetate, the size of each photo that will appear in your book. These acetate overlays are called amberliths or rubyliths, depending on the color of acetate used. Either color accomplishes the same result. Which one you use depends on which is available at your local college, art supply, or stationery store.

They are necessary because photographs cannot be pasted up with text, which requires a different negative. You must still plan for them, however, by placing an acetate overlay over the precise area they will occupy on your book page. These overlays create a "window" in the negative that your printer shoots of pasted-up galleys (page boards).

The amber or ruby color of the acetate blocks all light and the resulting space on the negative is clear. This clear space defines the exact area in which the printer should place the halftone of the photograph when making printing plates.

As described in Chapter 14, a halftone is a "printer's negative" of your photograph. It breaks up the image of the photograph into tiny dots for printing purposes.

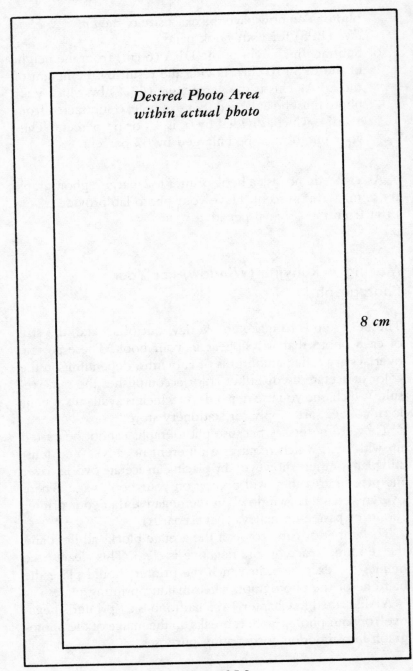

Desired Photo Area
within actual photo

8 cm

Figure 25.1

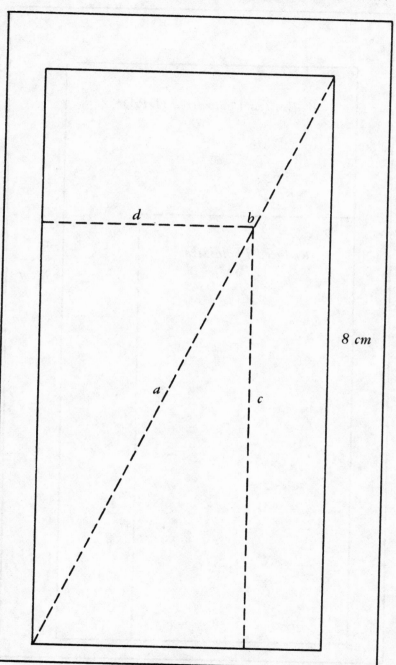

8 cm

Figure 25.2

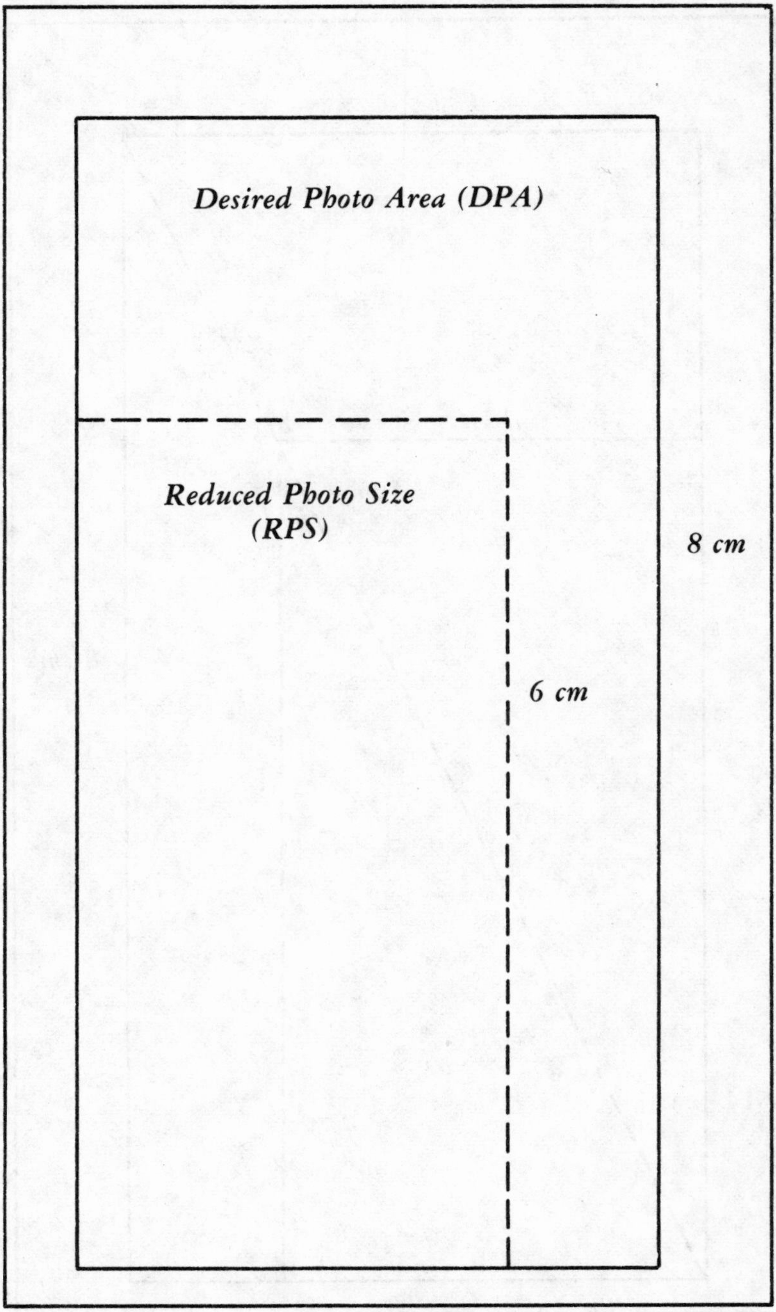

Desired Photo Area (DPA)

Reduced Photo Size
(RPS)

8 cm

6 cm

Figure 25.3

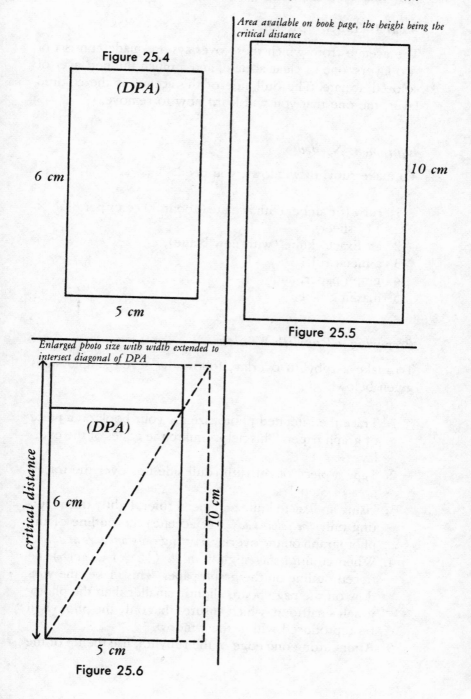

Figure 25.4

(DPA)

6 cm

5 cm

Area available on book page, the height being the critical distance

10 cm

Figure 25.5

Enlarged photo size with width extended to intersect diagonal of DPA

(DPA)

critical distance

6 cm

10 cm

5 cm

Figure 25.6

What Is Rubylith Acetate?

The acetate from which these overlays are made consists of two layers: one of clear acetate, and a much thinner layer of colored acetate. The dull side of the acetate is the colored layer, the one that you will learn how to remove.

Equipment Needed

To make rubylith windows, you need:

1. ruby (or amber) lith acetate (about 80 cents per 8½" × 11" sheet),
2. an Exacto knife (with new blade),
3. a metal ruler,
4. graph paper, and
5. masking tape.

Preparing a Rubylith Window

To make a rubylith overlay, follow the seven simple steps given below:

1. Trace the intended photo size for your book on a piece of graph paper. This helps square the edges of the overlay.
2. Tape a piece of rubylith (dull side up) over the traced area of Step 1.
3. Using an Exacto knife and metal ruler, lightly trace (cutting only *the colored layer* of acetate) the outline of the photograph on the overlay, cutting only *one edge at a time.*
4. When cutting, stay slightly *inside* (⅟32 of an inch) the traced outline on the graph paper. This makes the window on the page board slightly smaller than the photograph's halftone, which ensures that only the photo will be reproduced within the window.
5. After cutting one edge of the rubylith, use the tip of the

Exacto knife to lift off an *outer corner* of colored acetate from the layer of clear acetate. Once you've lifted a corner of the acetate, catch this corner with a piece of tape. Then lift it off the clear acetate.

6. Repeat this process with the three other edges of the outline. The end result is a rectangular piece of colored acetate within a perimeter of clear acetate.

7. Position this overlay over the precise area on your page board where the photograph should be printed. Attach with transparent or white tape, being careful not to cover any of the text.

Experiment with a scrap piece of acetate, cutting only as deep as necessary to remove the colored layer of acetate. With a little practice, this procedure will become easy. Do not seek the assistance of a graphic designer in making these overlays until you have tried doing it. It's not difficult.

Halftones At The Printer

Using instructions you've written on the boards to which the photographs are attached, the printer makes halftones of your black-and-white photographs. They are made by rephotographing the photographs you submit through a screen. The resulting negative is composed of dots. The eye blends these dots together—you may require a magnifying glass to see them. Otherwise, a halftone resembles an ordinary photographic negative.

Different-Quality Halftones

Newspapers do not require high-quality reproduction of photographs; therefore their photographs normally have either 65 or 85 dots per linear inch. Most photocopy machines produce 85 dots.

A book's photographs should have 120 to 133 dots per

linear inch. If your book displays fine art, you might even use a finer screen, such as 150 dots. The term "line screen" is often used to describe the dots per linear inch of an illustration or photo.

Obtain Proof if Photo Is of Poor Quality

When your photograph is of poor quality, ask your printer to make a "proof" from its halftone. This is similar to a print from an ordinary negative, and it reveals how the photograph will look when printed in your book.

Obtaining a proof is also a good idea when you wish to print a color photograph in black and white. Some color photographs print well in black and white, but others will not. There are no hard and fast rules. Having a proof made is called "pulling a proof" in industry jargon.

Working With Color Photographs

The printing of color photographs is known as "process work" because it requires numerous steps, including:

1. preparing a color transparency, or a color print;
2. making color separations, one negative for each of the photograph's four basic colors;
3. making a proof (either a set of color keys or a cromalin) to inspect the quality of the color separations; and
4. printing each of the four colors, which requires four separate runs through the press.

Should You Submit a Transparency or a Color Print?

You can submit either a transparency or a color print to the firm that makes color separations for you. A transparency resembles a color slide, and it is more difficult to judge its quality than that of a color print.

If a flaw exists in a transparency, it may not become evident until it's blown up in the color separations. Even professionals have difficulty spotting flaws in transparencies.

When printers or graphic designers insist on using a transparency to obtain color separations, ask them to guarantee the quality of the separations, which means that you pay only upon your approval. Otherwise, you may have to order a second set of color separations—and pay for them—if a flaw in the transparency turns up.

This book recommends that you have color separations made from color prints. These prints should be submitted in the same size that they will be reproduced in your book, so that the firm making the color separations knows exactly what it has to furnish to you and has no excuse for poor-quality reproductions.

Making Color Separations

Your photograph must be separated into the four basic colors: black, red, yellow, and blue. Each separation resembles an ordinary black-and-white negative, but the image is not reversed.

Few printers make their own color separations. Those firms that do usually specialize in this work. A graphic designer can be helpful both in selecting a color separator and in judging the quality of the resulting color separations.

Color separations come in varying levels of quality. An advertising brochure for a lawn mower does not require the same quality reproduction as a book cover. Ask your graphic designer to recommend which level your book should have. The better the quality, the higher the cost.

Requesting Color Keys or a Cromalin

Since they are only black and white, it is difficult to check the quality of color separations simply by looking at them. You should also order a proof of the color separations: either color keys or a cromalin.

Color keys are four sheets of clear acetate, each of which has one of the four basic colors of your photograph printed on it. The colors blend together when the four sheets (blue, red, yellow, and black) are aligned on top of each other. The result is an excellent indication of how the printed photograph will appear.

A *cromalin* resembles an ordinary color print and provides the same image as a color key, except it's on a single sheet.

Printing Your Color Work

The precision required for color work causes some printers to shy away from this business. For this reason, the most economical printer for your book pages may decline to print a four-color cover.

Four-color printing requires the printers to make four plates, one for each color. First, they print the black ink, then the paper must run through the press three more times as the other colors are added. Each run must be perfectly aligned so that the margins of all the colors will match. The printer must also select the correct shades of these four colors so the overall color combinations will result in a proper color reproduction. If any error occurs, the printer must start over again, and this can be expensive.

Printers who have little experience with color work may furnish excessively high quotes in order to be assured of not losing money on your job. Avoid such printers.

Use the same procedure for choosing the printer of your color work as you did for selecting the printer of your book's signatures. Be sure to obtain samples of previous color work from each printer you interview.

Use The Terminology You've Learned In This Chapter

If you use the terminology in this chapter, professionals will be more likely to quote competitive prices and deliver high-quality work.

> *Halftone*—line screen (or printer's negative) made for a photograph.
>
> *Board*—heavy paper to which artwork and galleys are attached.
>
> *Desired Photo Area*—area of photograph that you wish to appear in book.
>
> *Reduced Photo Size*—size of photograph reduced to fit book page space.
>
> *Enlarged Photo Size*—size of photograph enlarged to fit book page space.
>
> *Rubylith*—acetate overlay placed on page board where photograph will appear.
>
> *Amberlith*—same as rubylith, but in orange acetate.
>
> *Window*—clear space created on negative by rubylith overlay.
>
> *Camera-Ready Copy*—artwork that can be immediately photographed by printer.
>
> *Proof*—a checking copy of artwork, made before printing begins.
>
> *Process Work*—the printing of color.
>
> *Transparency*—artwork for color print, which resembles a color slide.
>
> *Color Separations*—black-and-white negatives isolating each color to be printed.
>
> *Color Key*—a proof of color separations, four separate acetate sheets (one for each color).
>
> *Cromalin*—a proof of color separations, resembling a color print.

For more detailed information on the subjects covered in this chapter, pick up a copy of *Pocket Pal* from your local art supply store. To obtain a copy of this book directly from the publisher, send a check for $3.75 made out to "Pocket Pal," to:

POCKET PAL
P.O. Box 100
Church Street Station
New York, NY 10046.

Choosing and Working With a Printer

26

Your biggest expense will be the printing of your book. This chapter reveals how your book can be printed for as little as half of what most author-publishers are charged for their books.

The Printing Process

There are normally seven steps to printing a book:

1. pasting up page boards to signatures;
2. making negatives from the pasted-up boards;
3. making halftones of photographs (if your book has photographs);
4. making blue-lines from negatives;
5. stripping (taping) negatives and halftones to flats;
6. burning (making) plates from flats; and
7. printing signatures from plates.

In the previous chapter, we have already discussed how you can save 10 to 15 percent by doing Step 1 yourself. You can save an equal amount by skipping Step 4, the inspection of blue-lines.

What Are Blue-Lines?

Blue-lines are photographic prints of the negatives described in Step 2. It is customary for printers to furnish blue-lines so one last inspection can be made of what will be printed. After you approve them, your book is printed. Errors found later are your responsibility, not the printer's.

When collecting quotes by telephone, ask if the quoted price includes blue-lines. This question should be asked after the printer has quoted you a total figure. Most printers will say yes to this question.

Later, when you're bargaining with the few printers who have provided the lowest quotes, ask: "How much money can I save by skipping blue-lines?" You may save quite a bit.

Inspect Negatives, Plates, and Signatures

Instead of inspecting blue-lines, inspect your book's negatives, plates, and signatures. Negatives can be easily inspected on a light table. Plates and signatures can be inspected as they're made.

Most printers will be glad to have your help in inspecting negatives, plates, and signatures. How to make these inspections is described later in this chapter.

What To Tell The Printer When Gathering Quotes

Start by telling printers that you're "collecting quotes" for your book. Don't let a printer think that you're not collecting quotes from other printers also.

Be prepared to provide the following information concerning your book:

1. the size of your book page (trim size);
2. the number of signatures your book will have—in either

8- or 16-page signatures, depending on the capability of each printer;

3. what type of paper you wish to use;
4. how many books you wish printed; and
5. how many halftones must be made.

Do not tell a printer yet that you intend to paste up your own page boards to signatures, or that you don't want blue-lines to inspect. Save this until you start bargaining, which is discussed later in this chapter.

What To Ask Printers

Just as you should get quotes from ten typesetters, also get quotes from ten printers. The more you call, the more likely you'll obtain a bargain price for the printing of your book.

During publication of the author's *Slim* book, one printer bid $4,275 to produce a thousand copies of its 224 pages. The signatures were eventually printed for only $2,200 (which included forty-five halftones).

After providing the necessary information to a printer to work up a quote, you should ask the following questions:

1. When can you start printing my job? This should be within a few weeks of receiving camera-ready copy.
2. How long will you require to complete my job? You can usually double most estimates you receive.
3. Are blue-lines included in this quote? If they are, don't say anything yet about not needing them.

The highest quotes you collect will usually come from larger firms, especially those in high-rent locations. Your low-est quotes will probably come from small, family-owned print-ers. Quite often, a small printer will offer better quality work, too.

Most printers cannot give you an instant answer over the

telephone. They will require time to work up a quote. If they do not call back within a reasonable time (a few days), call them. Good printers are usually busy.

Bargaining With Printers

After you've obtained quotes from all the printers contacted, arrange appointments to see the three or four printers with the lowest prices at their plants.

Interview the Highest Bidder First

Interview the printer in this group who provided the highest quote first. Test your ability to converse in printing terminology with this printer. Remember, the more intelligent you sound when interviewing printers, the more likely you'll receive professional service. By the time you interview the lowest bidders, you'll be more comfortable discussing your job.

Always Obtain Firm Bids in Writing

At the appointment, ask for a bid in writing. If the printer is hesitant to give you a bid in writing, look for one who will—even at a higher price.

A written bid does not have to be a lengthy formal agreement. It should simply answer all your questions and specify what the printer will deliver and for what price.

How to Pay the Bill

If you have established your own company, printed impressive business cards, dressed nicely, and learned how to sound experienced, a printer may not ask you to pay all of your bill ahead of time.

It's not uncommon for a printer to ask that a portion of your bill be paid in advance. The problem with paying the entire amount in advance is that you lose control of quality. If delivered books are below the expected standard, there is little you can do about it. The printer may or may not be concerned with correcting problems.

When asked to pay in advance, say that you normally pay *upon delivery.* Then change the subject. If that doesn't work, then negotiate prepayment of only one-third to one-half of the total bill.

Go to another printer rather than pay in full in advance, even if it means paying a higher price.

How to Bargain for a Competitive Bid

There are a number of questions you can ask a printer in the attempt to reduce the price of your printing. They are:

1. Is there a more economical page size for your book? It's possible that your initial page size will result in a significant amount of wasted paper (which you pay for).
2. How much will you save if you don't request blue-lines?
3. How much will you save if you paste up your page boards to signatures?
4. How much will you save by placing rubyliths on page boards where photographs are to be printed?
5. Can you save by using a paper stock that the printer already has on hand?
6. If you have enough page boards to fill half of the last signature, ask how much an additional signature would cost. If you eventually use one less signature, ask that the bill be reduced by this amount.

Keep track of how much the printer offers to reduce his initial price for each of the above items.

Keep Your Flats

Always specify that you want the "flats" that are made for your book. These are large boards, usually made of goldenrod paper, on which the film for your book is mounted, so they will include all the negatives and halftones for your book. Have this written into the contract.

It's better for you to store them after the printing is completed. You'll probably keep them safer; moreover, if you have had problems with the printer, you may wish to use another printer the next time.

Recover all the pasted-up boards also. If they are on signatures, tell the printer to leave them on signatures.

Working With Your Printer

Once you've turned in camera-ready copy to your printer, you must wait until negatives have been made from signatures.

Inspecting Negatives

Inspect negatives at the printer, using a light table. This is a table that has an opaque glass cover, with a light beneath. Look for the following problems on negatives:

1. Scratches or spots that require retouching.
2. Missing material, especially page numbers and running heads.
3. Poor reproduction of text (fading or blurring).
4. Page order on signatures (take a set of dummy signatures to double-check the page order).

Write notes down on a sheet of paper for corrections. You cannot write on the negatives.

Inspecting Plates

While it is not practical to read plates, you can still check them for the same problems listed for negatives.

Also look for letters (or groups of letters) that are filled in. The letters *e* and *o* are often filled in. When this happens, the plates require additional scrubbing.

When a plate is scrubbed too hard, the printed image often becomes too light. This problem usually goes unnoticed—even by the printer—until the signatures are actually printed.

Inspecting Signatures

Arrange to be at the printer when your signatures start coming off the presses. Inspect them and request reprinting of any that are not adequate.

Before the printer burns a new plate, check the negative on the flat from which the plate was made. If the negative is at fault, just making a new plate will do no good.

In a few cases, it may be necessary to paste up new page boards. After the printing of your book is completed, inspect the signatures one more time before they are bound. Make the printer redo any that are of poor quality.

Dealing With Printing Problems

On the average, half of your printing jobs will have problems even if you take all the precautions suggested in this book.

The typesetter will have excessive errors and equipment breakdowns that delay you. Your printer will deliver wrinkled signatures, make poor halftones and print them, and also have equipment breakdowns. The bindery may break the spine of some of your books, deliver damaged covers, and even lose a few copies.

Expect these problems. Don't be overly disappointed when they occur. While you must live with such problems, you don't have to pay for them. Figure what percentage of delivered books are unsalable and do *not* pay for them.

Once again, make sure that you don't pay the entire bill in advance.

Pricing Your Book

27

Have you been debating how to price your book ever since you began writing it? At first, you may have set an extremely high price, thinking the book-buying public would pay any price to read your message. Later, you may have decided your book deserved the widest possible distribution and set too low a price.

The solution to this dilemma is simple.

Don't Print A Price On Your Initial Book Cover

As recommended in Chapter 15, do not print a price on the cover of your first edition. Once you print a price on the cover, you're stuck with it.

If you price your book too high for the bookstore trade, lowering the price will make the book appear as if it is being dumped. On the other hand, if the price has been set too low and it is printed on the cover, you cannot raise it until you order a second printing (or dust jacket in the case of a hardbound book).

Do Bookstores Need a Printed Cover Price?

Many bookstores place their own price tags on books. If you wish to place a price on your book, use a *pencil* to write it on the upper corner of the half-title page.

Don't mar your book by using a pen. Many of your books placed in bookstores will be returned to you, especially if they've been displayed spine out.

When these copies come back, you'll want to resell them to other customers. You'll be able to erase the penciled price in cases where it's been necessary to raise your price.

How Large Publishers Price Their Books

Large publishers have more latitude in pricing their books because their unit cost is much lower than that of most small publishers. Whereas a small publisher's unit cost may be $5 with a thousand-book print run, the same book might have a unit cost of $2 with a ten-thousand-book print run. This permits them to market their books at a much lower price than we can.

The *Huenefeld Report,* a respected biweekly newsletter for book publishers, offered the following advice on October 31, 1977:

> The pricing formula which has worked best for a major portion of those dozen publishers with whom the Huenefeld consultants have worked intimately in recent years is simple and explicit. It says that a book should be priced for the trade or mail order markets, at *eight times* the anticipated unit production cost of a first printing consisting of the maximum number of copies your marketing team is reasonably sure it can sell within a year.

This advice is often repeated in other references. But it is not feasible if you are a small publisher. With a $5 unit cost, you would have to price your book at $40.

The *Huenefeld Report* qualifies its advice by stating:

That one year quantity need not actually be the eventual print quantity. Your business office may decide to pay a premium for short run production to keep from tying up money in inventory.

Prudence dictates that you follow this basic advice. Even if you have the money to print more than a thousand books, you may be better off gauging the size of your book's market before printing in excess of a thousand books.

Pricing For Mail-Order Sales

To survive, most mail-order books must be priced at no less than $15. The most successful mail-order books are often priced in excess of $20. See Chapter 44 for a discussion of mail-order costs, and you will understand why $15 is a minimum for a mail-order book.

Most of the early buyers of your books are going to be readers of reviews and other publicity that you've generated. Many of these orders will be received by mail. If you've underpriced your book, mailing and package expenses may erode much of your profit. Reviews and publicity may or may not mention additional charges for postage and handling.

Exceptional Reviews

If you have an exceptional book, it may receive favorable reviews from important trade magazines (*Library Journal, Kirkus Reviews, Publishers Weekly,* and *Booklist*). These reviews will generate substantial orders from libraries.

If you have labored to write and publish an exceptional book, you should be well compensated for your time and investment. If you do not offer your book at the highest price at which it can reasonably sell, you may not recover its production costs, plus the value of the time spent writing it.

Minimum Hardbound Price

The minimum price for most hardbound editions should be $12. If you believe that your book has the potential of gathering favorable reviews from trade journals, then price it at least $2 to $5 higher than this minimum. It's also a good idea to check current prices of books similar to yours.

The cost of hardbinding varies according to how many books are being bound, and how they are to be bound. If you plan to hardbind a first printing of one thousand books, then your unit cost will range from $1.50 to $1.75, depending on the size of your book and style of binding you select.

On the other hand, if you need only a few hundred hardbound books, the unit price may be as high as $4.00 to $6.00, so you may find it cheaper to convert softbound books to hardbound form at a cost of $3.00 to $4.00 apiece. See Chapters 28 through 31 for a complete discussion of these options and costs.

Pricing For Retail Outlets

As your book gathers reviews, you'll receive orders from bookstores. You may even wish to generate this business before receiving reviews.

If you've priced your book high enough to provide a fair return on your investment and time, this price may be too high to compete in bookstores. You may wish, therefore, to lower its price. Your book will be competing with thousands of others in retail outlets. Competitive books in these stores may be priced at your break-even point.

Spend some time in a large bookstore to check the prices of similar books. This will inevitably pull your price down. As mentioned earlier, it's difficult to compete with publishers who print minimum runs of ten to twenty thousand books.

A good example of what you may have to do occurred when the author's first book was released. Reviews and publicity were favorable and a large number of library orders were forthcoming. There was no price resistance at the softbound price of $7.95 and hardbound price of $12.95.

Later, when the softbound edition was introduced to the book trade, the immediate response was that it was overpriced. A major wholesaler would not carry it.

After giving the matter serious consideration, it was decided to lower the softbound price to $5.95. Volume orders were immediately received at this price. Three distributors each purchased a thousand books.

When reprint rights were eventually sold to William Morrow and Company, they reduced its price by another dollar.

How Profitable Is Bookstore Business?

After lowering your price to get into bookstores, you must then give up an additional fraction of its value in the form of a discount. Bookstores prefer to buy books at a discount of 40 percent or more, even when purchasing as few as ten books. They need this discount to stay in business.

This may leave little profit, if any, for you in such sales, at least with your first printing. Sales to bookstores wil! not be reasonably profitable until a second printing reduces your cost per book.

While you may not make much money lowering the price of your book to encourage bookstore sales, you may recover nicely if strong bookstore sales encourage a large publisher to purchase reprint rights to your book.

If you're beginning to think pricing decisions are difficult, you're right. First, decide what your goals are. Once you've decided which market to strive for, your decisions will be easier.

Second Printing Profits

Don't expect to make a large profit on your first printing, especially if it's only a thousand books. If you break even, consider yourself fortunate.

The sale of your second printing, however, should yield a healthy profit. You no longer have typesetting costs, graphic designer fees, establishing-your-company expenses, color separation expenses, and the like. Your printer will charge less for a second run, as negatives and halftones are already stripped into flats. Your initial promotion costs are out of the way, too.

Printing a Softbound Cover

28

Designing Of Covers

If your book cover has only one color, it will be easy to print.
You can select almost any printer who provides a low quote.

When the design of the cover involves lettering only, with
one color, then the services of a graphic designer should not
be necessary. Simply select the typeface for the lettering, have
it set within the dimensions of your cover, give the result to
your printer, and your work is done.

Two- or Three-Color Covers

For a two- or three-color cover, you may need a graphic designer. Tell your printers what you wish to do, as they may
have the capability to fulfill your needs. If they can't, ask them
to recommend a graphic designer.

Review Chapters 14, 15, and 25 for explanations of the
various alternatives to color artwork.

Four-Color Covers

A four-color cover is also known as a full-color cover. Successful full-color printing requires skills that many printers, in the
author's experience, do not have.

When a full-color cover involves a color photograph, many printers will shy away from this business or will quote excessive fees to attempt the job.

Color Separations

Color separations are generally necessary when printing multi-colored covers. Larger printers often make their own color separations, while smaller firms may have to contract out this work.

When a smaller printer is asked to arrange for color separations, you will:

1. pay a markup, which may double the cost to you; and
2. rely on your printer's evaluation of the quality of the separator's work.

Neither of these is advised. An independent graphic designer is often the best source for selecting a firm to provide color separations. This graphic designer will also be a specialist in judging the quality of color separations provided.

Obtain Dummy Signatures From The Printer

In order to determine the thickness of your book, ask your signature printer to give you a dummy book, or bulking dummy, consisting of the same number of folded signatures as will appear in the finished book.

The graphic designer needs this dummy to measure the width of the spine for your book's cover. The printer of your cover should be given this dummy too, to double-check that the cover is being printed with the correct spine width. This way, any mistakes made will not be your responsibility.

Have Advance Review Copy Typesetting Done

Have you arranged for the typesetting of advance review copy covers? This is a minor expense.

Having these covers printed should cost less than $50. After printing a hundred copies, the press is stopped and this typesetting is scraped off the printing plate. Then the balance of the covers are printed.

Chapter 15 discusses these covers in more detail.

Protective Coatings

Do not fail to have a protective coating applied to the cover of your book. It should not cost more than $75 to varnish a thousand covers. If you do not go to this expense, the artwork (even lettering) on the cover will tend to smudge or scrape off when your books are stacked during storage or shipment.

Available coatings usually include varnish, liquid lamination, film lamination, or an ultraviolet application. Varnish is the least expensive and is suitable for books with mainly a mail-order market. If you expect your book to receive heavier handling, as in bookstores, consider going to the expense of a slightly heavier coating. These coatings also add a reflective quality to your covers, enhancing the appearance of the book.

What To Tell Printers When Getting Quotes

Many author-publishers use the printer of their signatures to print their covers as well. This is fine if the prices quoted are competitive and the quality of the previous work is acceptable.

Printers require the following information in order to provide you with a cover quote:

1. the number of covers to be printed,
2. the trim size of your book,
3. the type of cover paper desired (the printer will provide samples, and you can look at other book covers for ideas),
4. the number of colors on the cover,
5. the type of artwork to be submitted,
6. the source of color separations when necessary, and
7. the type of protective coating desired.

Printers of color work may require a few days to work up quotes. Again, when they do not call to provide quotes when scheduled, call them.

Avoiding Wrinkled Covers

Have the printer of your book cover call your bindery before printing the cover. It is important that the cover be printed according to the way the bindery will bind the cover, either with the grain or against it.

What To Ask Printers

Ask potential printers of your cover if you can see examples of their work that are similar to your job. Ask to keep these examples when spare copies are available. They can be used to compare the promised quality with the quality of your job.

If a low-bidding printer cannot show you an example of the type of cover you require, go elsewhere. Don't gamble with your money or time.

Did You Check Around For Quotes?

Do not depend on the most economical printer of the first phase of your book to recommend the best source to have your cover printed. The printer of signatures of the author's third book recommended another printer for its dust jacket whose quote ($357) was triple the quote ($119) of the printer who eventually did the job.

Except for color separators, you should not depend on your graphic designer to recommend other professionals, either. The graphic designer of the author's *Slim* book recommended a printer for its full-color cover who quoted $1,475 for a thousand covers. High-quality covers were printed by another printer for $495.

Design For A Hardbound Cover At The Same Time

Always design your softbound cover so that it can also serve as a cover of a hardbound edition. Chapter 29 explains how the same cover can be used for both editions.

To do this, simply extend the color of the spine an eighth of an inch onto both the front cover and back cover of your softbound edition. When you convert softbound books to a hard-cover version, the spine increases in width approximately one-quarter inch due to the thickness of the boards of the hard cover. In extending the spine of your soft cover, you allow for this difference.

By designing this "convertibility" into your softbound cover, you will save as much as $2 to $4 per copy for small printings of a later hardbound edition.

As you should before taking delivery of any contracted work, inspect it before paying for it. Don't look at just the top. Look in the middle of the stacks, too.

How Should Your Book Be Bound?

29

Your choice of binding will depend on the expected market for your book, the number of books being bound, and the size of your book, among other factors. If you expect to market your book by mail order, there's no need for a hardbound edition. Hardbinding simply increases your binding and shipping expenses.

Basic Binding Methods

There are seven basic methods of binding your book:

1. side-stitching,
2. saddle-stitching,
3. riveting,
4. spiral,
5. plastic comb,
6. perfect binding (glue), and
7. hardbinding.

Side-Stitching

This is the least expensive method. The left-hand sides of the pages are simply stapled together; when tape is used to cover the staples, it's called Holland tape.

Side-stitching can be done to a book of several hundred pages. The disadvantage is that the book won't lie flat when opened.

Saddle-Stitching

A saddle-stitched book is stapled directly on its fold—hence the term "saddle." Use at least three staples in order to qualify for the reduced book rate at the post office.

This binding is usually limited to books that are less than a quarter-inch thick, or less than eighty pages, unless unusually thin paper is used.

Riveting

This method is similar to side-stitching, although much more expensive. Rivets are driven through pre-punched holes.

This is a good method of binding bound galleys, which a few trade magazines require for review purposes. This technique is also called "velo binding."

Spiral

This method is often employed for extremely short-run books that are being used to test-market a book via mail-order sales. It is popular for cookbooks, automotive manuals, and other books that must lie flat when in use.

Holes are punched and a metal or plastic wire in spiral form is woven through the holes. This method, too, is expensive, running as much as 70 to 90 cents per copy.

Bookstores and libraries don't particularly like books with spiral bindings, as they cannot be stacked neatly or displayed spine out.

Plastic Comb

This resembles the spiral form, in that the book can be opened flat. Its name describes its form. It is less expensive than the spiral form, though, being often available at 40 to 70 cents per copy, depending on the book size.

The advantages are that it looks better than staples and is far less expensive than perfect binding when only a few hundred copies are being bound. In addition, the comb can be printed with the usual spine information.

Perfect Binding

The term for this form of binding is a misnomer. A "perfect bound" book has its cover glued to its pages. If the covers are improperly glued, they can become detached from the pages of the book. Or the individual pages can loosen and fall away.

Nevertheless, this is the most common form of binding for softbound books. It is also far less expensive than the spiral or plastic comb methods when a thousand or more books are being bound. At 1985 prices, it costs approximately 30 cents each to perfect bind a thousand standard-size books.

Hardbinding

Hardbound books are also called "casebound" books. Their pages can be either sewn or glued together. Then a heavy paper is wrapped around the spine, which is called an endpaper. Thick boards of cardboard or plastic material are sized, covered with either cloth or similar material, and then glued to the spine of the gathered pages.

Binding a hardcover can cost three to five times more than binding a paperback. For just a few hundred books, it can run as high as $4 to $6 per book.

The author suggests that this form of binding not be used for an initial printing, as primary demand for such binding comes from libraries. Wait until such demand occurs. Chapter 31 describes how softbound books can be easily converted to hardbound form as needed, at reasonable cost.

Binding a Softbound Edition

30

Having your signatures bound is the last step in the production of your book. In the past, it has been traditional to bind a new book in hard cover first. Later, if sales warrant, a lower-priced softbound is released for wider distribution. The logic behind this rationale is weak, especially for a small publisher.

In most instances, it makes more sense for a small publisher to issue the less expensive softbound edition initially. A hardbound edition is warranted only if library demand or other special circumstances develop. Then the small publisher can convert softbound books to hardbound as needed.

Bind For Your Market

Disregard tradition in the binding of your books. Consider your market and bind accordingly.

When to Bind in Soft Cover

If you expect the demand for your book will be primarily in bookstores, then bind your book for this market—in soft cover, where your price will be competitive.

A softbound book is also a wise choice for the author-publisher with limited funds. As mentioned earlier, binding in hard cover adds another $1.50 to $1.75 to the cost of each book (in runs of no fewer than a thousand books).

When your expected market is a mail-order one, also bind in soft cover. A mail-order customer does not care whether a book is hardbound or softbound. He simply wishes to purchase the information at a reasonable price.

Recipe books and repair manuals can be softbound, too. You may wish to use a plastic comb or spiral binding, which permits pages to lie flat when the book is opened.

Major reviewers prefer to review books that are available in hard cover. The fact that you have a hardbound edition available can be spelled out on the cover of your advance review copies. On this cover, you simply list the price of both bindings.

Binding In Hard Cover And Soft Cover At The Same Time

If you are extremely optimistic (as most author-publishers are the first time) and have adequate funds, you may choose to bind in both soft cover and hard cover. The author did this with his first book, and the gamble worked. Both library and bookstore orders were forthcoming, but the title was irresistible: *Hemorrhoids: A Cure and Preventative.* There were forty million sufferers, the book was prepared well, and no competition existed. The resulting profits from the combined printings were superior to what they otherwise would have been.

Keep a Reserve of Unbound Signatures

This book does not suggest that you gamble. An alternative to initial hardbinding is to leave a number of your signatures unbound. Then if library demand for your book develops, you can quickly bind a hardbound edition. Otherwise, these unbound signatures can be used to bind more softbound books.

Converting Softbound to Hardbound

The most economical alternative is to bind all your books initially in soft cover, and then convert these to hardbound books as needed.

To find firms that convert softbound books to hardbindings, pick up your telephone and call a few libraries. Most libraries do this type of converting all the time. Simply ask the acquisition librarians at these libraries whom they use to convert their softbound books.

If local libraries cannot help you, you can write to the following address to locate such a bindery:

LIBRARY BINDING INSTITUTE
Suite 51
1421 E. Wayzata Blvd.
Wayzata, MN 55391

When you've located a reasonably priced converter, have a few books converted to check the results. Often, these firms insist on a minimum order of ten books. If the quality of the converted books is acceptable, you have an inexpensive method of meeting demand for your book in hard cover.

Obtaining Quotes From Binderies

There are fewer binderies than there are printers in your locale. You may even find that it's necessary to seek out binderies some distance from where you live. Start by asking your signature printer whom he or she uses for binding jobs. Also consult the classified section of a large telephone directory.

Other author-publishers you've met can probably refer you to reliable binderies.

What the Bindery Must Know

Be prepared to furnish the following information to binderies:

1. The finish (trim) size of your book page.
2. The head trim (side of the book to be bound).
3. The number of books to be bound.
4. The number of signatures in your book.
5. The folding requirements of the signatures.
6. The inserting requirements for signatures.
7. The gathering requirements for signatures.

The "trim size" of a softbound book is the exact size the page will be in the finished book. The "head trim" of most books is the left-hand side of the folded signature.

When a signature is "folded," it is folded into halves until its pages are in the proper sequence. Signatures may require "inserting" when one signature must be inserted inside another. Then the signatures for each book must be arranged in proper order by "gathering" them.

What to Ask the Bindery

Ask if the bindery uses a machine to insert and gather folded signatures, or if this work is done by hand. If it's done by hand, ask how much you can save by doing this work yourself. In the case of the author's *Bond* book, a one-quarter savings in the binding bill for a thousand books resulted when the author and his wife spent an afternoon inserting and gathering signatures.

When a bindery provides a quote, usually in the form of a cost per copy, ask what their quote number is. Should you later decide to use their services, they can quickly refer to their quote when you provide them this number.

Many binderies offer free pickup and delivery. Ask if there are any charges in your area, as these can influence the total cost of binding, especially if you have to go outside your local area to find a bindery.

Also ask that the books be packaged in boxes weighing no more than forty pounds. If you don't specify the weight of delivered and boxed books, you may receive sixty- to seventy-pound boxes, which will be difficult for you to move, store, and ship.

Check For Defective Bindings Immediately

When you receive bound books, always check the quality of the bindings immediately. If a company truck delivers the books, open at least one box and inspect all its books in the presence of the driver. If any irregularities appear, make a note of them on the receipt that you sign for the books. Also contact the bindery to detail the problem as soon as you've checked the rest of the boxes.

In one instance, the author discovered that a third of a shipment had badly wrinkled pages. These books were unsalable. The damage had occurred during folding, which was done at the time the books were bound. Since payment had to be made on delivery, a telephone call was made to the bindery while the delivery truck waited. Payment was made after deducting 33 percent from the invoice figure.

In a second instance, a bindery broke the spine of every other book due to poor adjustment in their binding equipment. As delivery was being taken at the bindery, the author summoned a "quality control" person and proceeded to open the rest of the boxes. Each box had the same problem; every other spine was damaged. The bindery agreed to bind additional books at no cost as compensation. If time had not been taken to inspect these books, this adjustment might not have been forthcoming. The bindery was located a hundred miles away, and a trip would have been necessary to prove the extent of the damage.

Check your books, invoice forms, promotional flyers, mailing labels, and all other printed material when you take delivery. This is the best time to ensure that appropriate adjustments are made to correct printing errors.

Binding a Hardbound Edition

31

There are two methods of hardbinding your book: binding the original signatures, or converting softbound books as described in the previous chapter. Which method you should use depends on how you plan to market the book and where the demand for it occurs.

When To Bind In Hard Cover

If you are binding a book that is expected to have a library market, be a gift, or be purchased by collectors, then bind in hard cover.

Libraries prefer hardbinding and will pay a premium for it. Buyers of gift books prefer the fancier binding. Collectors also favor hardbound books.

Having Signatures Hardbound

If you choose to bind a hard-cover edition, the binder must be given the following information:

1. The number of books to be bound.
2. The weight of paper used to print signatures.

3. The number of pages in the book.
4. The finish (trim) size of the book pages.
5. The head trim (side to be bound).
6. Whether a rounded or squared spine is desired.
7. The type of flyleaf paper preferred.
8. Whether flyleaves are to be printed on.
9. The binding material desired.
10. The color of material for the hard cover.
11. Spine decoration.
12. Front cover decoration.
13. Folding requirements (if any) for the signatures.
14. Insertion requirements (if any) for the signatures.
15. Gathering requirements (if any) for the signatures.
16. If dust jackets are to be placed on the books.

Most binderies do not make dust jackets. Dust jacket printers, who are discussed in the next chapter, must be contracted separately.

Most people prefer a rounded spine on books, although more can be printed on a square spine.

The flyleaf of a book is the heavy paper between the covers and the first and last pages of the book. The printer must be told what type of paper to use and whether it is to be printed on.

It is difficult to select a material and color for the hardbound cover unless you personally visit the bindery to view available alternatives. If you choose material that is already in stock, you might be able to save a small amount.

You will be charged for imprints on the spine or front cover of your book. The spine must be stamped with the book's title and at least your last name. You can also stamp any image you wish on the front.

Wrap Your Own Dust Jackets

When you have dust jackets, don't let the bindery wrap them around your books. When books with dust jackets are stacked

Binding a Hardbound Edition 217

in boxes at a bindery, their dust jackets often become scratched or smudged. By doing this job yourself, you can eliminate the possibility of such damage.

The following chapter describes how to wrap your own dust jackets.

Have the Books Delivered in Small Boxes

Remember, do not have books delivered in boxes that weigh over forty pounds. Smaller containers are easier to move, store, and ship. Small boxes can also be used to pack orders.

Printing Your
Dust Jacket

32

Don't assume that you need a dust jacket. If you already have a softbound edition and intend to convert it into a hardbound book, you don't need a dust jacket. Your softbound cover serves this purpose.

If you don't have a softbound edition to convert, you can still avoid the expense of a dust jacket by having the front cover of your book stamped at the bindery. You will be charged for the metal die to make the stamping, but this may cost less than printing a dust jacket. You can stamp an image on your cover from any good quality black-and-white line illustration. Review the books in your local library to check out books with stamped covers.

While reviewing books in your library, you may observe that many of the hardbound books that were purchased with dust jackets no longer have them. For economic reasons, many libraries discard dust jackets. They must place a cataloging label on the spine of each new book. If this label is placed on an unprotected dust jacket, the label may have to be replaced soon when the dust jacket becomes dilapidated. Rather than replace labels, many libraries simply throw the dust jacket away when they cannot afford to protect it with an acetate covering.

Designing A Dust Jacket

The artwork for your softbound cover can also serve for a dust jacket. An advantage of a dust jacket is that it has more room for promotional copy, because it has flaps.

The front flap should discuss the high points of your book in detail. Your credentials and other promotional material belong on the back flap. If you have written other books, they also should be listed on the back flap.

Flaps should extend at least 3½ inches inside the book covers. This permits the printing of promotional copy and is sufficient to keep the flap inside the book.

When designing your dust jacket, make it 1/16 of an inch shorter than the height of the hardbound cover. If you do not make the dust jacket slightly smaller than the book height, it will quickly take on a ragged appearance when handled in a bookstore or library.

Before printing the dust jacket, obtain the precise measurements of your bound book, particularly the spine width. You can ask your bindery to provide these figures, or wait until you receive bound copies of your book.

After collecting a few reviews, you may wish to print a new dust jacket. The originals can be placed on books for mail-order sales, while the new dust jackets can be wrapped around bookstore copies.

The Importance Of Flap Copy

Jacket copy is the first impression potential readers will have of your book, and reviewers sometimes repeat flap copy as it stands with few alterations. Spend time writing strong copy for your dust jacket. Have your best editors review these words. They may be crucial to your book's success.

This advice applies equally to the copy on the front cover, the half-title page, and the back cover of a softbound edition.

Obtaining Price Quotes

To obtain price quotes, printers will need the following information:

1. the number of dust jackets required,
2. the size of the dust jacket when laid flat,
3. the paper quality for the dust jacket (take a sample with you to the interview),
4. the number of colors on the dust jacket,
5. the type of artwork to be submitted,
6. who will furnish color separations, if needed, and
7. the type of coating desired for the cover.

Be sure to call several printers when obtaining quotes. Remember when the author was quoted $357 by one printer and $119 by another?

Ordering Your Printing

It is suggested that you not have the dust jacket printed until your hardbound book is in hand. That way, you eliminate all possibility of error in measuring the width and height of the hardbound book.

If you have chosen only one color for your dust jacket, there should be no need to wait more than a week for it to be printed.

Do not fail to have your dust jacket varnished: you would save only $25 to $30 by not doing this. Any color will rub off and smudge other dust jackets when you stack books for storage or mailing—they will look terrible by the time they get to your customers. Even varnish can rub off during shipping, so it's often worthwhile to use liquid lamination, which is more durable and costs only about $30 more than varnish.

Wrapping Dust Jackets

If you have chosen to do this chore as you sell books, here is
the easiest way to go about it:

1. Find where the back flap should be creased (when the
   book spine is centered).
2. On a table or desk where the dust jacket can be folded,
   make an outline of it and mark where the back flap
   should be folded.
3. Using this outline, place the dust jacket on the table and
   slightly crease the back flap at the mark.
4. Place the book face up on the table and insert the back
   flap inside the back cover.
5. Raise the front cover to a vertical position and wrap the
   front flap of the dust jacket within the front cover.

Marketing Your Book

V

Releasing Advance Review Copies

33

To write books is easy, it requires only pen and
ink and the ever-patient paper. To print books
is a little more difficult, because genius so often
rejoices in illegible handwriting. To read books
is more difficult still, because of a tendency to
go to sleep. But the most difficult task of all that
a mortal man (or woman) can embark on is to
sell a book.

—FELIX DAHN, *The Writer's Quotation Book*
(Penguin, 1980).

Have you opened the book to this chapter first? Perhaps
you've already written your book and had it printed. If so, you
may have a problem.

Before you attempt to market your book, two questions
should be asked. Is your book well written? And is it well
designed? Not in your naturally biased opinion, but in the
opinion of others. If others cannot sincerely answer yes to
these questions, then you may be wasting your time and
money attempting to sell an unmarketable book.

How Many Advance Review Copies
Should You Send Out?

In any business with a marketable product, your sales will be a direct function of promotional efforts. Perhaps the best answer to the question of how many promotional copies to distribute is: however many it takes to market the balance of your books.

The author printed 212 advance review copies (ARCs) with the initial printing of *Hemorrhoids* (five thousand copies). After distributing all the ARCs, an additional hundred plain copies were sent to more promotional sources.

If your initial printing is a thousand books, a minimum of one hundred should be ARCs. When you promote your book properly, these books should not last long.

Where To Send Your ARCs

It is not practical to list all the places where you should send or distribute ARCs. As each book is different, each book should be distributed differently. The information in this chapter indicates where your promotion should begin. As long as you have books available to sell, you should continue marketing your book with innovative techniques in new areas. The only limits are your imagination and capital.

By the time bound books arrive, you should have prepared mailing packages with addressed labels for most of your ARCs.

Trade Reviewers

Among the most important persons to receive ARCs are the book review editors of the trade review magazines within the book industry. They are the major source of reviews used by acquisition librarians.

These reviewers are listed in *Literary Market Place (LMP)*, an annual that is available in most libraries. An index for *LMP* appears in the front; look up "Book Review Services," and photo-copy the three to four pages that list them. Then go to a large library and check each publication listed to see if it warrants an ARC. Many do not.

A few of the more important services are described below. Addresses are not furnished, as you should use the up-to-date personal names provided in the latest *LMP*.

Booklist: Published by the American Library Association. A good source for acquisition librarians, but it seldom reviews author-published books. If you try this publication, send "uncorrected proof" copy (described later in this chapter).

Bulletin of the Center for Children's Books: Published by the University of Chicago. Fairly important to children's book acquisition librarians.

Choice: Published by the Association of College and Research Libraries. Reviews books of interest to public, high school, and college libraries.

Horn Book Magazine: Reviews books for children and young adults.

Kirkus Reviews: Reviews all books. Important to acquisition librarians, although known for more negative than positive reviews. Seldom reviews author-published books. If you choose to try this publication, send uncorrected proofs.

Library Journal: The premier book reviewer for acquisition librarians. Reviews all worthwhile books, including those that are author-published. Send uncorrected proofs.

The New York Review of Books: Not published by *The New York Times*. Only reviews approximately five hundred books yearly, many of which are published by the university presses.

Publishers Weekly: Occasionally reviews author-published

books. If you wish to take a chance, send uncorrected proofs.

School Library Journal: Reviews young adult and children's books. Send uncorrected proofs.

Small Press Review: Don't send your book here if it's nonfiction. This is a "literary" reviewer.

There are more than fifty book review services listed in *LMP.* Check all of them to see which specialize in your field. If you cannot locate a copy of their publication in a large library, consider this carefully before sending them an ARC. If a large library does not carry their review publication, then they may have little influence with acquisition librarians.

The trade reviewers listed in this book should receive your ARCs four months prior to their publication date. They require this much lead-time in order to review your book and publish their review.

A few of these book review services prefer to have uncorrected proofs of the books they review. This is what they are accustomed to receiving from the major publishers, so it is wise to go to the extra expense if you believe your book has a reasonable chance of being reviewed in these publications.

An uncorrected proof is simply a photo-copied copy of your galleys, cut up into normal page sizes, to which a plain cover has been attached. Artwork that is not attached to the galleys is included at the back of the proof (properly labeled). The major publishers usually write in page numbers by hand. To make a cover, simply photo-copy the typesetting for your actual cover on a heavy colored paper. Then rivet the book cover and its pages together at a photocopy shop.

For Listing Purposes

LMP recommends in the introductory paragraph of its "Book Review" services section that publishers send two copies of finished books to two addresses, for listing purposes:

REGISTRAR OF COPYRIGHTS
Washington, D.C. 20540

for listing in the *National Union Catalog.*

R. R. BOWKER CO.
Weekly Record Dept.
205 East 42nd Street
New York, NY 10452

for listing in the *Weekly Record,* the *Cumulative Book Index,* and the monthly and annual editions of the *American Book Publishing Record.*

Magazine Book Reviewers

There are two sources of magazine book reviewers: *LMP* and the more complete *Ulrich's International Periodicals Directory.* Both publications should be available in large libraries.

They list hundreds of magazines, specializing in every subject, that review books. Make a list of magazines that sound as if they might be interested in your book.

Select magazines that have reasonable circulations, at least five thousand. Then try to locate copies of these magazines in your library. Check each magazine to see if it reviews books such as yours.

Since available capital may prevent your sending ARCs to all the magazines that might be interested in your book, consider sending news releases to most of the magazines with low circulations. How to prepare news releases is explained at the end of this chapter.

Newspaper Book Reviewers

LMP provides an extensive listing of all the major newspapers in the country with book review sections. It would be a waste of books, postage, and your time, however, to send ARCs to the more than 250 newspapers listed. Most of these papers prefer to review bestsellers by the major publishers. When they do review author-published books, they seldom list an address where books can be purchased.

If you do send ARCs to these newspapers and receive reviews, you may never realize it. Readers of the reviews will have to search out your address in *Books in Print,* assuming this reference has listed your address in time for such reviews.

Perhaps the best advice is to send newspapers a news release, offering a book to those editors who are genuinely interested in your subject.

While most newspaper book reviewers are poor prospects for reviews, feature editors in your own region can be excellent sources of publicity. How to generate this publicity is explained in the next chapter.

Book Review Syndicates

Approximately half (ten) of the book review syndicates listed in *LMP* should receive an ARC. These include:

1. AP Newsfeatures
2. John Barkham Reviews
3. Book Beat by Joan Orth
4. Alan Caruba/Interlude Productions
5. King Features Syndicate
6. Jeffrey Lee Syndicate
7. Jerry Mack—Book Review Service
8. Mid-Continent Feature Syndicate
9. Register & Tribune Syndicate
10. United Press International

Send news releases to the balance, if they review books of your type.

Columnists and Commentators

There are more than 160 columnists and commentators listed in *LMP*. Again, make a list of those who specialize in your book's field. Send ARCs to these few, and news releases to others who review general subjects.

This list duplicates many names that appear on *LMP*'s list of book review syndicates.

Radio and Television Stations

More than 290 major radio and television stations are listed in *LMP*. ARCs should be sent to the nearest stations, and news releases to the balance.

Before sending ARCs to these stations, contact their program directors first to ascertain their interest in your subject.

See Chapter 39 for more information concerning radio interviews, and Chapter 40 for details concerning television appearances.

Adult Book Clubs

There are more than 125 adult book clubs listed in *LMP*, a few of which may warrant ARCs. If you send ARCs to some of those listed, be sure to include terms for the sale of one hundred, five hundred, and a thousand books.

Corporations

The author sold hundreds of copies of *Hemorrhoids* to corporations that manufactured cryosurgical instruments for the treatment of the affliction.

If there are companies that could tie your book into the marketing of their own products, send them an ARC. Include the terms under which they can purchase books also. It's customary to give such buyers a discount in the 50 percent range.

Telephone these firms before sending ARCs, to ensure that books are sent to the correct person.

Professionals

Specialists in the field of your book who are influential in their professions are excellent sources of book sales.

The cryosurgeons listed in *Hemorrhoids* all received ARCs, with a letter requesting their "critical comments." The warm response to these ARCs resulted in hundreds of book sales to medical libraries, medical clinics, physicians and their patients, cryosurgical instrument manufacturers, and even a feature article in the New York *Daily News.*

Similar results occurred when the author's *Bond* book was sent to professional acquaintances. Many of the persons who might be sent an ARC should be sent a promotional brochure instead (as explained in Chapter 35).

Bookstore Chains

Few author-published books are purchased by the major chains. Walden's bought a thousand of the *Hemorrhoid* books when they were first released, in addition to a thousand of Gerald Steiner's *Home For Sale By Owner.* These were exceptions, not the rule.

Chapter 41 of this book suggests that you postpone contacting the major chains until you've established a sales record at local stores.

If you wish to offer your book to these outlets immediately, contact their buying agents directly. The two major chains are Walden Book Company and B. Dalton/Pickwick. Walden seldom purchases books from one-book small presses until they have an established sales record.

WALDEN BOOK COMPANY
Attn: Small Press Buyer
201 High Ridge Rd.
Stamford, CT 06904

B. DALTON BOOKSELLER
Attn: Small Press Buyer
7505 Metro Blvd.
Minneapolis, MN 55435

If you are impatient to offer your book to the chains, at least read Chapters 41 and 42 before contacting these outlets.

Requests for Free Copies

If your book receives national reviews, you can expect to receive a number of requests for free books from persons or publications that are not listed in *LMP*.

As a rule, send ARCs to persons making these requests. If you doubt their authenticity, send them a letter explaining that you receive a large number of requests for free copies and ask them to send you a copy of their publication first.

The author received such a request from a quarterly health magazine that had been started by a Yale medical school graduate. When their publication was requested in turn, the author received an early copy of *Medical Self-Care Magazine.* After an ARC was sent, an excellent review appeared in a subsequent edition. Later, editions of the magazine were sold in book form to a major publisher. Orders for *Hemorrhoids* have been arriving ever since.

You may also receive requests for free copies from college instructors, ministers, private libraries, and so on. If you choose to send free copies out to non-reviewers, use your slightly damaged copies for this purpose. Most of the time the author simply sends a brochure in response to such requests.

Your ARC Cover Letter

Your ARCs should be accompanied by a personal letter addressed to the individual reviewer of each publication. Above all, this letter must be easy to read.

First, say why your book is exceptional—briefly. Then outline its highlights, in list form, not lengthy paragraphs.

Conclude the letter with your credentials. If this is your first book, state your qualifications to write it. Do not sign your own name, as that would signal your book has been self-published. Your book deserves a fighting chance. The sample cover letter below accompanied the author's *Bond* book, with excellent results. A subsequent *Library Journal* review pushed the book into a second printing within three months of its release.

California Financial Publications

We are proud to present this advance reading copy of our latest book for your perusal. It is the *first complete reference* on the subject of investment bonds.

The book is written for practical use by both investors and members of the securities profession. It explains:

. . . what investment bonds are,
. . . how and why their values fluctuate,
. . . how bond yields are determined,
. . . when the best buying opportunities occur,
. . . how to conduct bond research,
. . . where the best values can be found,
. . . how to buy new-issue and seasoned bonds,
. . . the advantages of tax-free bonds,
. . . how to establish retirement bond accounts, and
. . . many other subjects which will enable investors to maximize their income and capital with bonds.

We believe the book will become the reference in its field, as have the author's other books in their respective fields. These books are:

STRAIGHT TEETH: Orthodontics & Dental Care (Morrow)
HEMORRHOIDS: A Cure & Preventative (Morrow)

Both of the above titles have been favorably reviewed by *Kirkus Reviews* (5-1-80 and 12-15-79). *Library Journal* "highly recommended" the latter book, while *Publishers Weekly* has just provided a fine review of the former book (4-25-80).

Thank you for your consideration.

Respectfully submitted,

L. C. Bunnell
Marketing Director

Encl:
LCB:em

3900 Shenandoah • Oceanside, California 92054 •
(714) 941-4096

How To Prepare A News Release

If you decide to send news releases to a large number of publications, radio and television stations, and other reviewers, have them printed. Also consider using the "bulk rate" at the post office when the number of addresses exceeds two hundred. If you mail five hundred news releases, each weighing under an ounce, it would cost $115 at the current first-class mailing rate. The bulk rate total would be approximately $62.50.

Writing a News Release

Using your company letterhead, place the words "FOR IMME-DIATE RELEASE" at the top of the sheet. To the right of this title, place a "contact" name at your daytime location and phone number.

Above all, the copy that is used on a news release must be interesting. You can borrow from the promotional copy on your book covers and half-title page, but down-grade all over-enthusiastic phrases. If the editor receiving your news release thinks you're looking for free advertising, you've written a poor news release.

Ask others if they find your news release interesting. If not, rewrite until it is. It may help to read a few newspaper articles in order to understand how to prepare information in a "news" fashion. Double-space the text.

Conclude the release with the lines:

It is available from (your press), (your address), for $(price), plus $1.50 postage and handling.

If the news release is written so that it can be published word for word as is, you may be fortunate to have the publication include this last phrase at the conclusion of their article.

List a street address prior to your post office box on your news release.

Enclose Photograph and Reply Card

Enclose a professionally taken photograph of either the book or a related subject. Its size should be from $3'' \times 4''$ to $5'' \times 7''$. If you print your news release on high-gloss paper, you can make the photo part of the release.

It is customary to include a reply card to invite editors to request a copy of your book. If you have sufficient capital, print reply cards on the back of stamped postcards.

Invite Articles

Many author-publishers have been successful in promoting their books via magazine articles they have written. Why not invite the editors of publications receiving your news releases to publish an article about your book?

If you wish to do this, add an additional phrase to the end of your news release:

> If your publication would be interested in a full-length article on this subject, please contact (name) at (address), or call (telephone #).

Warning:

Someone has written a "get-rich-quick" book, on sale for $24.95. It instructs its buyers in the technique of obtaining free review copies for resale to willing bookstores. Be careful.

Obtaining Your
First Reviews

34

There are numerous means by which you can collect the first reviews of your book. These suggestions should serve as only a beginning for you.

Newspaper Feature Reporters

Once you've written and published a book, you are an author. As a local author of a new book, you are news.

When you contact local newspapers or magazines, don't ask for their book review editors. Medium to large newspapers receive hundreds of books a day for their book review editors, and yours is just another book to these people. They don't like to explain why they may not be able to review your book, or that it would be many months before they could even consider it.

Ask for a Reporter

Why not bring your book to the attention of someone at the newspaper who is eager for a good story?

Do your homework. Check your local newspaper on a daily basis to see which reporters customarily interview authors. Save the articles these reporters write. If you cannot find articles about authors, then look for feature articles about local persons of general interest.

Call newspapers and ask for these reporters by name. Mention that you have read their articles—even discuss them. In some cases, it may be appropriate and effective to invite the reporter to dinner.

Contact After Deadlines

All reporters have "deadlines" to meet. Before these deadlines, reporters are too busy to be contacted easily. If you telephone at the wrong time, ask when the reporter will be available. Sometimes you can leave a message and be called back, but don't count on it. These are busy, harassed people. But they are also looking for a story. Keep telephoning till you get through.

When you reach a reporter, begin the conversation by saying:

"I read your article on _____. And I thought you might be interested in doing a story on a local author."

Then be quiet. Let them ask what the book is about. Highlight the most interesting points. If your book discusses a new method, stress that. If it reveals fascinating facts, explain them. Be brief—and be ready to answer questions. If you have already written an interesting news release, refer to it during the conversation.

The Interview

Prepare written material about yourself and the book to give to the reporter. This will save the reporter the necessity of writing everything down.

1. Your résumé. Age, work experience, family, education, etc.

2. Why did you write the book?
3. How did you write it? Where? When?
4. How was it published? People admire initiative, so don't
   hesitate to admit the book is self-published.
5. What are the highlights of the book? List page numbers
   with interesting quotes or examples.

By furnishing all this information, you are essentially writing
the reporter's article. That's fine. The article should say what
you wish said.

Most reporters will expand on whatever they're furnished.
The more you provide, the longer your article is likely to be.

What to Furnish the Reporter

An ARC should be given to each reporter, with tabs on those
pages with highlights.

Have a photograph available taken by a professional. Many
reporters will take a photo themselves or bring a photographer with them. More readers will notice your article when it's
accompanied by a photo.

Also give reporters a copy of your brochure, as this provides
ordering information for your book. Asking that the reporter
include ordering information in the article is a touchy matter.
Editors may eliminate this data, as it smacks of advertising. As
a minimum, request that the article state which stores are
carrying your book locally. If the reporter will include your
address, use a post office box. You don't want City Hall calling
to sell you a business tax license. Your home may not be zoned
for commercial purposes, either.

Which Newspapers to Contact

If you're inexperienced in publicizing, contact smaller papers
first. Usually, these will be weekly papers. Even when contacting small papers, ask for a reporter or columnist by name. Cold
calls to editors generally end up as brushoffs.

You may be pleasantly surprised to have favorable reactions at most of the weekly papers you contact personally. This will be because they are more anxious for local news than the larger papers.

After gaining some experience with the smaller papers, go see a few of the local dailies. Don't take your press clippings from the smaller papers with you. All newspapers like to think that they were the first to cover a news item.

If you're rejected the first time you contact a paper, don't give up. Don't assume that you selected the correct person on the first try.

Editing Your Reviews

While your first review may be favorable, it may also be poorly written. In order to use this review for promotional purposes, you may find it necessary to omit extraneous material, indicating these deletions with ellipsis points. This may appear irregular, but all publishers do it. Available space will probably require a certain amount of editing anyway.

Local Librarians

Do not overlook the value of your local library in generating publicity and early reviews. Alida Allison, author of *The Toddler's Potty Book,* contacted her local library and received the following review:

> *The Toddler's Potty Book* treats a sensitive subject with the positive, straight-forward approach many parents have been looking for, but are unable to find through contemporary children's books. That difficult transition from diapers to toilet is not always something that "just happens" in the course of growing up.
>
> Parents need as much help in overcoming their attitudes on potty training as children need in coping with this important phase

of growing up. Young families will find it is a must to have on their bookshelves as families grow and the need arises.

This, among other local reviews, was printed on a promotional mailer that was sent to three thousand libraries—with favorable results.

When reprint rights were sold to a major publisher, this review was placed on the back cover of their edition.

Be a Featured Speaker at the Library

Many libraries have an active speakers' program. Contact your library and ask who coordinates these programs. Make an appointment to meet the coordinator.

On one occasion, the author was invited to appear at an annual book fair to autograph books. A pleasant afternoon was spent selling and autographing more than $100 worth of books. A few excellent contacts were made as well.

On another occasion, the author was invited to provide an evening program discussing his *Slim* book. The Friends of the Library sold books after the lecture. This, too, was a profitable evening. None of this would have happened unless the library had been contacted first. Most libraries appreciate local authors and will go out of their way to help publicize your book.

The author normally offers to donate 10 percent of the sale proceeds at these affairs to the library's book fund. On several occasions when appearing at a library function, the library has purchased books from the author.

If you overlook your local libraries when promoting your book, you may be ignoring a gold mine.

Professionals

Regardless of the subject matter of your book, find professionals (doctors, professors, bankers, attorneys, ministers, and others) who are willing to give you favorable comments on it.

In giving these professionals an ARC, don't ask for "favorable comments." It is far better to ask for critical comments. When you ask for criticism, these critics become psychologically inclined to give you compliments instead.

If your book is worthy, most of the comments you receive from these sources will be favorable.

Industry Contacts

Go to every meeting involving people in the book industry that it is practical for you to attend. You'll meet other authors who have published their books. They will assist you in locating professional assistance in publishing your own book.

At a book publicist's gathering, another writer introduced the author to a woman who subsequently provided reviews for two books in a national health magazine.

As jealous as authors can be of another's successes, we are still glad to see such success. It means that we too can aspire to such heights. You will find that most of the authors you meet will be quite willing to help you, often without being asked.

Be considerate of another author's time. Do not contact an author by telephone unless invited to do so. It is better to write a note, enclosing a self-addressed, stamped envelope. In addition, do not ask another author to recommend an agent; that information must be volunteered.

Don't Get Discouraged

When you're turned down after contacting a newspaper, library, or professional, do not worry about it. In the normal course of contacting scores of people, you're going to run into a certain number who are having a bad day or are otherwise unreceptive. Running into these people is part of the process of publicizing a book. It's necessary to give them a try in order to find the ones who will cooperate.

In contacting local newspaper reporters, the author has had a success ratio of 50 percent. That means rejection half the time. The other half made the experience worthwhile.

Your Promotional Brochure

35

Your promotional brochure should be designed to serve several purposes:

1. as a handout at lectures, autograph sessions, etc.;
2. as an order form; and
3. as a mailing piece, not requiring an envelope.

If you were to print separate items for each of the above, your printing bill would be three times higher than necessary.

How Much Should You Spend?

If you print on one side of a thousand sheets of $8\frac{1}{2}'' \times 11''$ colored paper, the cost of printing your brochure should not exceed $125, including typesetting.

For another $50, you could print on both sides of this sheet. You should do this, as the more information your brochure provides, the better it will sell your book.

Do not print more than a thousand copies of your first brochure, unless you have already gathered all your reviews. If you expect to obtain reviews shortly after your book is released, you may wish to limit this printing to only five hundred copies.

One of the reasons why an initial printing should be limited is that the main purpose of a brochure is to generate mail-order business. The minimum printing for such a mailing is three thousand copies. To print that many brochures, you should wait until you have reviews that will motivate their recipients to buy.

Your brochures must emphasize and exploit these reviews to the fullest. So be patient. Don't rush to print expensive brochures until you have all your ammunition.

What Size Should You Print?

Don't print a promotional brochure smaller than 8½" × 11". If you need more room, use a 17" × 11" sheet to print four 8½" × 11" pages.

What's The Best Color?

Studies have revealed that the goldenrod color draws the best in mail-order brochures. Other strong colors are red and mint green. You may pay a premium of $10 to $20 for colored paper, but it's worth it.

If your brochure is printed on colored paper, you can obtain a two-color effect by printing with a colored ink. Your printer should charge no more than $20 extra for colored ink.

Select a paper thick enough to print on both sides. If you plan extensive mailings, the weight of your paper will not be important as bulk-rate mailing pieces can weigh as much as three ounces.

When you have photographs, use a clay-coated stock. This gives photographs fine clarity, almost equal to that of a photographic print.

Expressing Your Message

Go to your local library and check out Julian L. Simon's *How to Start and Operate a Mail Order Business.*

Every day, we are bombarded with advertising messages: billboards, television commercials, newspaper ads, radio ads, mailing pieces, bumper stickers. We rarely give these appeals more than a moment's notice. Most of the mailings we receive that are obviously advertising, we may not even open. Considering the competition, your brochure must be well prepared.

Grab With Your Headline!

Having only a few seconds to grab your reader's attention, your headline must be powerful. For example, the sample brochure on the following page begins: BURN THIS BOOK!

Outline the Benefits

List the rewards of the book. Don't compose long paragraphs. Your brochure must be capable of being scanned quickly.

Breathe life into the phrases written for your brochure. Stimulate. Your words must cause action, motivating the reader to part with money.

Include Photo of Book and Author

Show your recipients what they are going to get for their money. You can use either a photograph of your book or the artwork for the cover.

It is also effective to include a photograph of yourself. Again, have this photograph taken by a professional.

Sample Promotional Brochure

ADP

ANA-DOUG PUBLISHING COMPANY
424 West Commonwealth, FULLERTON, CA 92632

BURN THIS BOOK!*

On June 6th David Kinchen gave **HOME FOR SALE BY OWNER** a rousing review in the Los Angeles Times — the paper was virtually bombarded by irate Realtors wanting to burn the book. One Realtor group actually threatened reprisals by removing their advertising from the Los Angeles Times.

Why do the Realtors react so violently? Why don't they want you to have this book?

Because this five star* book on home selling is written by Gerald M. Steiner, a nationally renowned X-Realtor, turned consumer advocate. This is without exception, the best and most comprehensive book ever published on the home selling process. This is the first complete step by step program for selling a house without a broker — everything is included from advertising to escrow.

> The following newspapers and magazines, in the interest of the general public, gave **HOME FOR SALE BY OWNER** enthusiastic reviews: Los Angeles Times, Washington Post, National Observer, Whole Earth Catalog, American Library Association, Chicago Sun Times, Los Angeles Herald Examiner, CoEvolution Quarterly, Newark Star Ledger, Seattle Times, Chicago Tribune, Buffalo Evening News, Miami Herald, and the West Coast Review of Books "★★★★★".

So really . . . why waste $3,000 or $4,000 on a Real Estate Broker? When you can easily do it yourself and save thousands of dollars by using this exciting new book.

In **Chapter One** we explain all the tricks of the trade. Also how to defend yourself against the Realtors.

In **Chapter Two** we show you why a home sold 'by owner' will sell faster and for more money.

In **Chapter Three** we will tell you why your present family lawyer isn't any good and how to go about getting a top notch real estate lawyer who will charge only about $250 for the complete transaction.

In **Chapter Four** you will learn how to price your home right so that it will sell fast for the highest possible price. Caution: Realtors are not competent in appraising home values.

In **Chapter Five** you will learn what actually should be done in order to properly prepare your home to sell fast.

In **Chapter Six** you will learn how to complete the Home Information Forms which are supplied with the book.

In **Chapter Seven** you will learn how to write effective, emotional, exciting ads for the real estate classified section — literally hundreds of sample ads are included.

In **Chapter Eight** you will learn how to become a real estate salesman overnight; how to handle objections; how to recognize buying signals; how to use low pressure finesse; and how to help the prospective buyer say 'yes.'

In **Chapter Nine** you will learn how to explain the advantages of owning your home to a prospective buyer.

In **Chapter Ten** you will learn how to emphasize what the buyer wants to hear.

In **Chapter Eleven** you will learn how to hold an Open House. And how to screen out the Lookie Lous — something brokers never do, no matter what they say to the contrary.

In **Chapter Twelve** you will learn exactly what your rights are in regards to the Open Housing Law.

In **Chapter Thirteen** you will learn how to determine if the buyer can afford your home — again something Realtors never bother doing.

In **Chapter Fourteen** you will learn that the real estate contract is actually very simple — all the component parts are explained in layman's language.

In **Chapter Fifteen** you will learn the meaning of Points and how they can affect the net amount you receive.

In **Chapter Sixteen** you will learn how you can assist the buyer in getting financing.

In **Chapter Seventeen** you will learn what Title Insurance actually is and why it is necessary.

In **Chapter Eighteen** you will learn what Escrow is and what the main advantages of it are.

In **Chapter Nineteen** you will learn about the Closing, plus also a check off of documents that should be in the hands of your attorney.

In **Chapter Twenty** you will learn how monthly mortgage payments are computed and what they include.

In **Chapter Twenty-One** you will learn how to translate real estate legalese into everyday English.

In **Chapter Twenty-Two** you will learn all the ins and outs of moving after your home is sold.

In **Chapter Twenty-Three** you will have at your disposal an assortment of all the contracts and contingencies necessary to complete practically every type of residential real estate sale. Even low cost **HOME FOR SALE BY OWNER** signs are available through this book.

There you have Twenty-Three Chapters — 210 big 8½"x11" pages of effective home selling techniques and information that will save you up to $4,000 or more in exorbitant Realtor fees.

Every homeowner needs this book. Even if you're not planning on selling today — when the time comes you'll be ready.

Thousands of homes have been sold 'by owner' using this book. Why not yours?

Order it now!* Use the enclosed postage-paid envelope. Or for immediate delivery call **TOLL FREE 800-528-6050** Ext. 820. Read it for one year and if you are not 100% satisfied return it for a complete refund.

Our guarantee! You have never, ever read anything like it. And it has got to be worth 1,000% more than the small price to any homeowner. So, don't miss it. Just return the postage-paid order form today.

Respectfully,

Doyle Chism
Executive Director

* It's even tax deductible! **Only $15.65**
(Includes postage and handling. Air mail add $2.00)

Speaking Engagements

36

During the time that your book is at the printer and bindery, you should be making appointments to speak to every civic group in your area that utilizes guest speakers at its meetings.

Finding Civic Groups

To locate such civic groups, first subscribe to a local newspaper. Save the announcements of meetings that appear on the social pages, plus any publicity notices.

Contact your local library and ask which civic groups use their facilities. Ask for the telephone numbers of these groups. The bulletin board at the library may list a number of organizations.

Educational institutions such as junior colleges also sponsor meetings of various groups. Contact their libraries or review campus bulletin boards.

Finally, check with your local Chamber of Commerce for listings of local groups. Also contact the Junior Chamber of Commerce.

Obtaining Speaking Dates

Phone numbers listed in newspaper and other announcements will usually be those of officers or membership chairpersons. Ask these persons for the names of their "program chairpersons."

The Program Chairperson

This individual may be in dire need of a speaker within the next few weeks, or it may be six months before another speaker is needed. Normally, there is a two- to three-month wait before most organizations can use you as a speaker. This is why it is necessary to start making speaking appointments several months before you receive bound books.

After explaining the purpose of your call, offer to mail information concerning the book and yourself. Do not offer to send a book, unless specifically requested to do so.

Questions You Should Ask

When a group seems interested in having you appear, make a file sheet of the following questions:

1. name of organization,
2. name of program chairperson (and phone number),
3. time, date, and location of meetings,
4. amount of time assigned to speakers,
5. total membership and normal attendance at meetings,
6. activities at meetings, and
7. desired orientation of your presentation.

If a definite date is not set at the time of your initial call, ask if you can call the program chairperson back at a later date. Program chairpersons are volunteers, and you cannot expect them to be as efficient as persons in a business. It may be necessary to pin them down, pleasantly.

Attach the newspaper article (or other notice by which the organization came to your attention) to the file sheet that you make of each group. It may come in handy later if it has photos of the group's officers.

Preparing Your Presentation

The time allotted for your presentation will usually vary from fifteen to thirty minutes. Whatever time is assigned to you, do not exceed it. You will aggravate instead of entertain if you delay their meeting or detain members in any way. It is vital that you know in advance how long your delivery will be.

Take an adequate number of books to the engagement, plus a few sample copies to pass around during your presentation. Tag the sample copies with labels.

Bring enough promotional brochures to provide everyone with a copy. Many people who are too shy to approach you in front of their friends will order via the mail. The brochure also serves as a reminder that your books are available at a local store.

Audiences love handouts, even if they must return them. Take some or all of the following:

1. a notebook of your rejection notices;
2. photographs used in your book;
3. sample signatures (they'll enjoy trying to fold them back properly);
4. unusual reviews; and
5. other items of general interest.

Pass these out during the course of your presentation.

Do a "Soft Sell"

Civic groups are accustomed to speakers who have something to sell. They sit back and wait for the pitch. Don't make your audiences wait.

Ask that the person introducing you tell the audience that you will be available to autograph copies at the end of the meeting.

You'll be introduced as an author, so it won't be necessary to tell your audience why you're standing in front of them. But make sure to tell them where your book can be obtained. First, tell them which libraries carry your book; then which bookstores. Finally, tell them that books will be available at the conclusion of the meeting, if your host did not state this during your introduction.

Provide Personal Background

You will learn by experience that most audiences initially are more interested in you as an author than they are in your book. Don't let that bother you. If they learn to like you, then they'll become interested in your book, too.

The author usually asks at the beginning of classes and lectures if anyone would like to see his rejection notices. A number of hands normally shoot up.

Audiences are generally interested in every aspect of life as an author. Rejection notices can help satisfy that curiosity and also make your successes seem more impressive.

Provide the same personal background to an audience that you provide to reporters. Then ask the audience if they have any personal questions they'd like to ask you. Be prepared for anything.

Highlight Your Book

Don't bore your audience by reading long excerpts from your book. Select one or two of the most interesting highlights if you wish to read something.

Each highlight should be no longer than two to three minutes. Most audiences are interested in why you wrote the
book. If you can read a portion of your book that answers this
question, it may stimulate more questions. It helps to get on
a one-on-one basis with your audience as soon as you can.

The following highlight from the author's *Slim* book describes a motivating experience:

> A few years ago while lying in the sand among a group of sun-
> worshippers, I asked a lovely woman nearby what kind of diet
> she had to stay in such excellent shape. Before telling me about
> her diet, she said, "I haven't always been this way. After having
> my daughter, I put on 60 pounds." Her friends insisted this
> was true, however hard it was to believe looking at her. She had
> no stretch marks and her skin was quite firm, as was the rest of
> her body. So I asked what caused her to lose the extra 60 pounds.
> She said, "My husband said I had fat feet! That really made me
> mad."

The audience is then told that this woman used a vegetarian
diet to lose weight, in addition to getting rid of her husband.

Solicit More Questions

After explaining how your book came to be written, ask your
audience if they have any questions concerning its subject. If
they don't, keep bringing up provocative points until they do.

Later, you'll find that the persons asking most of the questions will be the ones who become book buyers. Repeat all
questions for the audience before answering them, and don't
brush off any question asked, however simple it may be.

Allow Time to Autograph Books

Leave adequate time for autographing books at the conclusion
of your presentation. It's helpful if someone else is available
to handle book sales for you.

You'll find that you're not nervous at these engagements. The reason is that you're the "expert." You're the specialist on your book's subject. When you are knowledgeable about your subject and have prepared your presentation, these engagements should be rewarding.

Autograph
Sessions

37

Being featured at an autograph session can be one of the finest rewards of becoming an author. Or it can make you feel like a caged animal in a zoo, if the advance planning has been poor. Entertainer Steve Allen, who has been autographing books for more than twenty-five years, warned in an article in *Publishers Weekly* on June 5, 1981, "I do not suggest that in the 1980s every such experience is a disaster; merely that failure is the norm and success and competence the increasingly rare exception."

The most common location for autograph sessions is a bookstore. You will learn that they're not necessarily the best locations, at least not for author-publishers.

Autographing At Bookstores

Most bookstore owners will be receptive to holding an autograph session for you. They have good reason to be receptive, as your presence will help pull customers into their stores. You are free publicity for these stores.

Contact the store manager by telephone first, to set up an interview to discuss the autograph session. Then personally meet the manager to set a date for the autographing.

The Consignment Arrangement

After setting a date for the session, the next step is to place books with the store. Both independent and chain bookstores will prefer a consignment arrangement. They will ask for a 40 to 50 percent discount. Begin by offering 30 percent, and compromise at the 35 to 40 percent level.

The consignment agreement you sign is not a purchase order. After the autograph session, you must personally count the number of books sold and then write up a sales invoice.

Who Generates Publicity?

You do. Few bookstore managers will offer to generate publicity, even when you become a well-known author with a major publisher.

Ask if the manager will permit you to display a poster announcing the autograph session in a prominent window, along with a stack of your books. If the answer is positive, you are fortunate, as windows are normally reserved for best-selling books.

Have a poster announcing your autograph session made for this purpose, which can double as a poster for the autograph table. Do not letter it yourself, unless you are a graphic artist.

Don't expect a bookstore to share the cost of advertising to promote the session. It is normal for the publisher to contact local papers, radio stations, and TV stations.

The best publicity you can generate will be a feature article in your local newspaper, announcing both your book and the autograph session. Ask the reporter to mention the autograph session at the end of the article.

Also contact local radio and television stations to announce the session. Offer to be interviewed, stressing why your book is of local interest. Arranging such interviews is covered in Chapters 39 and 40.

Bring Your Own Equipment

You cannot assume that the store will make any preparations whatsoever prior to your arrival. This means you should plan to set up your own equipment, including:

1. a folding table, with a cloth cover;
2. a sign stating "Local Author" and your name, to be attached to front of the table (bring a few pins);
3. a standing poster featuring your book, its dust jacket, and/or a newspaper article publicizing the session;
4. brochures to hand out to all passersby;
5. a tall stool to sit on (you should be elevated to be seen more easily, as well as to be on a level with browsers who stop to chat); and
6. a small dish of snacks (optional), which will not transfer from fingers to books.

Bring an extra box of books to leave in the trunk of your car. The books for your table should be price-marked by the store a few days ahead of time.

The Day Arrives

You arrive at the store. Space has not been arranged for your table, as previously agreed. Your books are located only after a ten-minute search. The manager is out to lunch and you begin to lose the feeling that you're an honored guest.

If necessary, select your own location. It should be near the entrance of the store, where there is maximum traffic. Catch customers both entering and leaving the store.

Set up your own table. After placing the books, posters, brochures, and snacks in place, make sure you've remembered the stool.

People will naturally stop to look over your books. Be sure to hand them one of your brochures—it's a good way to get the interest of shy browsers. In addition to autographing books, you may be asked for free advice. Don't be surprised if a few people ask you to autograph books they have purchased weeks or months earlier.

Regardless of the results of the session, you should have an enjoyable afternoon. Talking with strangers about your book is always interesting. If you're lucky, you may even be invited to a party or two. Expect anything. Other writers and authors will come by to introduce themselves. They may wish to discuss how to publish their own books.

Autographing At Libraries

Invite the "evening program" chairperson at local libraries to combine a lecture and autograph session for your book. If you locate libraries that offer such programs on a regular basis, the cooperation you receive will be the opposite of what can be expected from bookstores.

They will probably make a poster to announce your lecture-autograph session in their lobby, plus handouts. They may even arrange for newspaper publicity.

Even when libraries do not handle most of the preparations for you, they will at least assist you. The financial arrangements with libraries are superior, also. It's appropriate to offer the library 10 percent of the sale proceeds of your books as a donation. Or you can ask if they'd prefer to have a few free books.

At most library autograph sessions, you will sell two to three times as many books as you would have at a store. Book fairs sponsored by libraries are also good locations to autograph books. Whenever you see one publicized, contact the library sponsoring it.

Attending Book Fairs

38

Do you have delusions of grandeur about the demand for your book? If you don't, you're not a typical new author. Dreams keep us writing.

However, if you think that all your book needs to "take off" is to be displayed at a major book fair, you're going to be disappointed. Of the hundreds of success stories the author has seen, read of, or heard of, *none* has been due to an exhibit at a book fair. Don't be misled by the advertising you receive from exhibitors. Save your promotional money for more productive activities.

Fairs Are Social Events

While you won't sell many books at these gatherings, you can meet important people. If the location of the fair is attractive, you can even enjoy a vacation. The 1982 American Booksellers Association (ABA) convention was held on Memorial Day weekend in Anaheim, California. The convention center was sandwiched between Disneyland, Knott's Berry Farm, and the Pacific Ocean beaches.

The author has attended numerous regional fairs, two national ABAs, and one World Book Fair (held in Frankfurt,

West Germany). At each of these fairs, important contacts were made within the book industry.

At regional fairs you have the opportunity to meet the management of printing companies, binderies, paper suppliers, and other publishers, both large and small.

Exhibiting At Fairs

If you insist on exhibiting your book at a fair, at least do it in an economical manner. How best to exhibit a single book depends on the size of the fair.

Regional Fairs

At regional fairs, the cost of a booth will be at least $200. By the time you add the cost of gas, food, and accommodations, it will probably cost you $450 to $500 to exhibit your book.

Why not share the cost of a booth? That way you will have time to visit the booths of other small presses. By the time your book is in print, you should have met several other author-publishers. You may even be able to share living expenses with co-exhibitors.

As stressed earlier, do not go to a fair expecting to make money selling books. After expenses, you won't. Such profits will come indirectly in the future, from savings in your next publishing venture, contacts with other author-publishers, and so on.

National and International Fairs

LMP lists more than eighty regional and national book fairs (under "Book Trade Events"), many of them in such specialty areas as music or religion.

The annual ABA fair is by far the largest of the national fairs and an experience that every author should enjoy. The location changes every year. Dates and sites are announced in the spring editions of *Publishers Weekly.*

At a national fair, you may wish to hire the services of a professional exhibitor. Numerous exhibitors are listed in *LMP* under "Exhibits." Exhibitors usually reserve space at all major fairs, including many international fairs. Then they try to offer their services to enough publishers to cover their expenses. When they cannot cover their expenses, they cancel out. Be prepared to hire another exhibitor if this happens to you.

Do not hire a professional exhibitor if you do not plan to attend the fair. The exhibitor may have hundreds of books on display, many of which will be spine out. If the exhibitor knows that you are not attending, your book will probably have low visibility. Even when they know you're attending, your book may be displayed spine out.

The fees these exhibitors charge to display a book range from $75 on up. Many exhibitors will also offer to act as short-term agents for small publishers for a commission of 10 to 15 percent. For the duration of the fair, this may be a good idea. If your book is represented on an agency basis by your exhibitor, it's more likely that it will be prominently displayed.

If you do hire an exhibitor to act as your agent (at a fair you attend), the extent of the exhibitor's effort may simply be to refer you to major publishers who have expressed an interest in your book.

International Fairs

Annual book fairs are held in Brussels, Bologna, Jerusalem, Montreal, Quebec, Warsaw, Toronto, Frankfurt, and London. Pick your vacation.

The major fairs are in Frankfurt and Bologna. Frankfurt, the largest in the world, is called the World Book Fair. Bologna holds the largest annual convention for children's books.

Frankfurt's fair is in mid-fall. Accommodations should be arranged at least a year in advance. The fair is so large that it's impossible to view all the booths. Simply viewing the English-language books is a major undertaking.

At the Frankfurt Fair, the author concluded negotiations for the British Commonwealth rights to his first book. While negotiations had been initiated earlier, the interest generated by several other publishers improved the terms of the final agreement. The book was displayed and represented by an exhibitor.

Plugging Your Book
on the Radio

39

If you enjoy talking about your book, then you will enjoy radio interviews. Radios, just like newspapers, are looking for local news—which is you.

Contacting Radio Stations

There is no shortage of radio stations. Start by calling the nearest stations and asking for the program director. Then ask this person if the station has a program that does author interviews. Get the name of the person who handles these programs and propose doing an interview. Be prepared to explain why the radio's listeners would be interested in your book.

Do not send your book to a radio station unless you have talked to the program director first. Otherwise, you could be wasting a book and postage.

Preparing The Interviewer

Quite often, an interviewer will not have time to read your book. For this reason, always mark the most interesting passages with a felt-tipped marker. Then place tape on the margins of these pages, so they can be turned to quickly. Generally speaking, the larger the radio station, the less time your interviewer will take to review your book.

Prepare a List of Provocative Questions

Having prepared for lectures and newspaper interviews, you should know the highlights of your book. Use these highlights to draw up a list of questions, and send this to the interviewer ahead of time.

In answering these questions, use examples from the book to illustrate your points. The examples must be brief. You cannot ramble on the radio, or you'll lose your listeners. There should be active conversation between the interviewer and you.

Practice With a Tape Recorder

After writing down the questions and answers, with examples, use a tape recorder to test their length and how they sound.

Try to shorten your answers as much as possible. The briefer the answers, the more ground you'll be able to cover.

Provide Other Reviews Also

When you give your book, plus questions and answers, to the interviewer, include your newspaper reviews with the package. Mark the strong points made in these reviews, as they may act as a guide to the interviewer, who has little time to prepare.

Handling The Interview

As you enter the radio station booth, you become an entertainer. So enjoy yourself. Having prepared well, you can relax and act as if you're sitting in your own living room, chatting with a friend.

The actual interview that is aired may be one-third to one-half of the time that was devoted to interviewing you. When you are unsure how to respond to a question, ask that the question be rephrased. Don't try to answer questions if you don't have good answers.

Don't Say "My Book"

Instead of saying "my book," repeat the title of your book. This is how the listener will remember how to order the book at a bookstore. Repeat the title whenever possible.

Another reason for repeating the title is that some listeners may have tuned in late. They won't know what you're talking about unless the title is repeated.

Say Where the Book Is Available

This can be a problem, without the assistance of the interviewer. Discuss this subject openly before the interview. Ask how listeners will know how to buy copies unless they're told.

It's best to have the interviewer state where your book is available. Prepare a large label on the back of your book from which the interviewer can read out ordering information to listeners.

Handling Spontaneous Interviews

Some interviewers prefer not to tell you what their questions will be ahead of time. They believe it makes the interview more spontaneous and interesting. That's fine. Handle questions the same way you would if you were in your living room. Most interviewers using this technique plan to edit the results heavily.

Arrive Early for the Interview

Plan to arrive early in case directions turn out to be confusing. This also provides time to familiarize yourself with the station. You will probably sit in a relatively small room with the interviewer. The only other person nearby will be the technician handling the taping equipment.

Bring an Extra List of Questions

There will be occasions when the interviewer has not prepared at all. Even the list of questions you supplied earlier will have been misplaced. Make sure you have brought a copy of the material you furnished earlier.

The interviewer should be able to assimilate every major point on this preparatory sheet within one minute, which may be all the time he or she has. You're expected to do the entertaining, so be prepared. When necessary, take the interview into your own hands. If the interview is live, use station breaks to suggest the next questions to be asked.

Make a Copy of the Interview

Always make or obtain copies of radio interviews. They will help improve your next performance and may be useful in selling your book to a major publisher. You can also quote from them in promotional material.

Appearing on Television

40

Television talk shows are anxious to interview well-known authors of best-selling books. Most authors will appear for no fee, as they're glad to get the publicity. Talk shows such as "The Tonight Show" and Merv Griffin select their guests with great care. When a large publisher's resources are behind you, it's possible you might appear on one of these shows . . . if you have written a bestseller.

As an author-publisher, concentrate your energies on local stations. Cable and public service stations may be your best bet initially. Experience gained at radio station interviews will serve you well.

Contacting Television Stations

By consulting a TV guide, or a friend who watches TV constantly, you can quickly compile a list of local talk shows on which authors are interviewed. Contact these stations to obtain the names of their program directors.

When program directors appear interested in your book, send a copy to them. It should be prepared in the same manner that you prepared books for radio interviews.

Preparing The Interviewer

Remember to take an extra copy of the book when you go to the interview. It may be the one that appears on the show. Also take the original artwork or photographs of any subjects in the book that might make good closeups.

Television hosts are notorious for not previewing authors' books. The list of questions, answers, and anecdotes that you prepared for radio interviews will be even more important to the success of television interviews. Further streamline this material for television, as you may have to share air-time with other personalities.

If time permits, suggest relevant portions of your book the host may wish to read, particularly those that are amusing.

Many talk show hosts are quite willing to inform their viewers where your book can be obtained. Tape this information to the back of your book, and point it out to your host just before the show.

Are You Worried About The Audience?

If you're worried about confronting an audience at your first TV interview, don't be. The small local stations at which you have your first interviews will probably not even have audiences. The room you'll be in may be smaller than your living room, and the camera so small that you won't notice it.

If you are fortunate enough to have an audience, it will enhance your interview. The audience can ask questions, which will keep the conversation moving.

The TV interview will be edited, just as most radio interviews are. Just be sincere, interesting, and add humor whenever possible. They'll keep your best and edit the rest.

Handling The Interview

Speak with fervor. Sound genuinely concerned about your subject. Remember how you wrote your book? In a fury!

Whenever you make a point, be prepared to offer specific examples illustrating this point.

And be concise. There are three good reasons to be brief:

1. Never bore the audience (even if you cannot see them).
2. By being brief, you can cover more territory in your book.
3. Give the host plenty of air-time. They have egos; they like to hear their own voices. If they wish to extoll the virtues of your book, don't interrupt them. Those listening will be far more impressed by another's compliments than your own favorable opinions of your book. Encourage these compliments by careful planning.

Some hosts enjoy badgering their guests a bit. If so, stand your ground. When the host says something you believe to be incorrect, cordially present the more accurate view. Do not let anyone (host or member of the audience) sway you from your beliefs. Don't compromise yourself. A little controversy will make the interview far more interesting to the audience and other viewers. The audience may even express support for your stand, especially if the host makes a custom of badgering guests.

Maintain your sense of humor in all situations.

Marketing to Bookstores

41

Do you believe that all you have to do is place your books in bookstores—even on consignment—and they will automatically sell out?

There are too many books written and published each year to be sold, or even displayed, in bookstores. This is a considerable problem even for major publishers, who have promotional resources vastly superior to those of small publishers.

The chronic over-supply of books, combined with the limited capital of most small publishers, poses a serious dilemma. This is not the worst of it, though. There are seven additional stumbling blocks for a small publisher who wishes to sell to bookstores.

1. Shelf space at many stores is now controlled by computer-measured sales. To get a book on the computer is nearly impossible for an author-publisher unless a chain store or large wholesaler chooses to pick up your book.
2. To place books in stores, most author-publishers must consign them. In most cases, the expenses involved in doing this preclude real profits. The time involved in placing books, returning to count sales, and returning again to invoice the books is not profitable if you have only one book that sells fewer than ten copies monthly.
3. Bookstores, even large ones, pay slowly. It is not uncom-

mon to receive payment for books six months after they've been sold. You may be thankful simply to get paid at all. Author-publishers (and other small presses) are the last to get paid by independent stores, chains, and the wholesalers who stock stores. This can cause havoc with your cash flow.

4. If stores accept your books, on any basis, they will not be prominently displayed in most stores. Normally, your books will be displayed spine out.

5. Displayed spine out and receiving little publicity, a significant number of the books you place on consignment will be returned. This percentage often reaches as high as 40 percent for even the major publishers.

6. Returned books will seldom be in resalable condition; many will be in too poor a condition to give away. But if you do not refund the store's money (if it has paid for them), the store will not accept your books in the future.

7. There being more than nine thousand bookstores in this country, the headache of invoicing that many different accounts will probably be beyond your physical resources, even if your book sells well.

The information in the balance of this chapter will tell you how to minimize the above problems—*if* your book is one of the few that has a market in bookstores.

Sales Require Publicity!

Have you followed the advice provided in the previous eight chapters? If you haven't, how will book buyers know that your book is available in the stores?

Have you hit the local newspapers, contacted civic groups, called your local library, arranged autograph sessions, and arranged both radio and television interviews? When you know that publicity will appear within a week, then you can place books in local bookstores.

Approaching Your Local Bookstore

During the period when you're organizing a publicity campaign, map out the stores within a reasonable distance. Call their managers, explain that you have a book you'd like to place on consignment, and describe the upcoming publicity for the book. Make a list of those stores that will accept your book.

Make Display Cases

Before placing books in a store, make a display case that will hold ten books. You may be able to obtain ready-made display cases at one of your local stores, if they are disposing of them.

Take your books to stores in these cases; they're the only chance your books will probably have to be displayed face out. They make a nice compact package, which can be placed in a small space. Attach your business card to the side of the case, so clerks will know how to contact you when their supply of your book is getting low.

Ask the manager to locate the display case on the counter next to the cash register, so that everyone who comes into the store will notice the availability of your book. Ask for this privilege for one week. This is highly desirable display space, so the technique has a better chance of success in independent stores than in the large chain stores.

Make Display Posters

Space is usually at a premium in most bookstores. For this reason, it's a good idea to prepare display posters that can be placed in windows of the store.

Place a dust jacket of your book on these posters. If you don't have a dust jacket, use a good facsimile of your book's cover.

Keep hand-lettering on these posters to a minimum. They

must be neat, if the manager is to agree to place them in a window, and even then, competition for window displays is keen.

Place at Least Ten Books in Each Store

By placing ten books with a store, there is a better chance that they will be displayed face out. When ten books are displayed face out, they usually take up no more space than if they were displayed spine out.

Be bold. Ask if the manager has enough room to display your books face out. If the manager hesitates, suggest that the store display them face out for one month only.

If the manager declines to display your books face out, then place only three or four books with the store. If you give more than that, the balance will probably be placed in a storage area.

Prepare an Invoice

Even though your first "sales" to a store will probably be on a consignment basis, prepare an invoice with your terms at the time the books are placed. If it's on a consignment basis, state that on the invoice in order to avoid confusion in the future.

Most stores accept books on consignment for ninety days only. At the end of that time, you are required to come to the store, do an inventory of books sold, and make out an actual sales invoice. Do not expect the store to do this for you. If you do not return, you'll never get paid for books sold or recover unsold books.

What Should the Sales Discount Be?

The sales discount granted on the books is a matter of negotiation. Offer a 30 percent discount initially; most stores will ask for 50 percent. Suggest a compromise at a middle figure, using the word "compromise."

Restocking Your Books

You'll probably return in a week to see how your books are selling. Don't be surprised if they are all still there. If you have not generated enough publicity for your book, it's time to wake up.

Expecting people to buy your book without even telling them it exists is like expecting them to find a needle in a haystack. It's not too late. If you want to sell your thousand books, start a genuine publicity campaign.

Your books may be displayed spine out by now, with your display case nowhere in sight. Stores dispose of other publishers' display cases, so don't be too disappointed if they didn't save yours. Your poster may have met the same fate.

After two or three weeks, if you've generated a fair amount of publicity—and your book fills a genuine need—you may have to restock the store. Ask the manager if you can write up an invoice for the sold books and replace them with new books. If your books have done well, the manager may simply tell you to write up an invoice for all the books, thereby canceling the consignment arrangement.

Many stores, particularly the chain bookstores, will write up a purchase order on their forms. You'll receive a copy to place in your files. Even so, make out an invoice of your own, in order to keep track of when the bill is paid.

Local independent bookstores often pay their bills at the time they're presented, while chains may take three months to a year to pay you.

Keep Good Records of Local Sales

Considering all the work you've done to generate publicity, making display cases and posters, placing books in stores, and then restocking these stores, you'll be fortunate to earn $1 per hour for your time.

Nevertheless, keep excellent records of your sales to local

stores. These sales will have considerable influence on the buying decisions of the large chain stores. While the profits on local sales may be nil, the fact that you've generated demand for your book is invaluable publicity.

Don't Overlook Specialty Stores

If your book makes a good gift, it may do well in stationery stores. Be imaginative in selecting retail outlets for your book.

The author found that an excellent market for the *Hemorrhoid* book existed in health food stores. A small health food store in his hometown sold more than a hundred copies of this book during its first eighteen months. A display case was prominently placed by the cash register for one month, and the books were later moved to the general bookcase. The sales at this store were instrumental in selling the book in volume to the largest book wholesaler to national health food stores (see the next chapter).

If your book relates to health, place it in health food stores; if it relates to music or exercise, try record or sporting-goods stores. It may sell far better there than in bookstores.

Selling To The Chains

After you've established a strong sales record locally, offer your book to the chains. As mentioned earlier, Waldenbooks seldom purchases from one-book publishers; the same is true of Crown Books. A complete list of bookstore chains can be found in *The American Book Trade Directory*. Call your local libraries until you find one with this reference.

Before sending a sample book to these chains, telephone them first so that you are sure to send your books to the proper department and person.

278 How to Publish, Promote, and Sell Your Own Book

Composing Your Letter

In communicating with chain bookstores, it's important to stress the ability of your book to garner publicity. The author's letter to Waldenbooks, which resulted in a purchase order for one thousand copies of *Hemorrhoids,* is included here. Note the enthusiasm of the letter and its short paragraphs. Be sure to enclose an ABI form with your books. It suggests that you know what you're doing.

The letter mentioned at the bottom of the example was from Barry Kramer, reporter for *The Wall Street Journal.* Concerning his article on the subject of hemorrhoids, he revealed: "Of all the stories I ever wrote for *The Wall Street Journal,* it got the most reader response. . . ." Kramer's letter was certainly helpful in establishing this book's popularity.

The letter to Waldenbooks was sent before the book had been placed in local outlets. Waldenbooks had earlier picked up Jerry Steiner's book.

Both Waldenbooks and B. Dalton utilize a system called "category buying" to select books from publishers. B. Dalton introduced this system in 1981, and Waldenbooks began category buying effective January 1, 1983.

Under this system, the central merchandising department of the chain makes all purchasing decisions. Each category of books has a group of buyers responsible for selecting the books in that category. They use best-seller lists and information compiled from computerized cash register systems to purchase both new titles and backlist titles.

Category buying does not encourage wide distribution of small press books. Under this system, small presses will have far more difficulty establishing their books in these chains.

Policies change periodically, which is one of the reasons you should contact the buyers of the chains before sending them an ARC.

347 Mermaid   Box 963   Laguna Beach, CA 92652
(714) 498-0542

December 14, 1977

Waldenbooks Company
Attn: Thomas Simon
179 Ludlow Street
Stamford, Conn 06902

Mr. Simon:

Jerry Steiner *(Home For Sale By Owner)* has strongly suggested that a copy of this book be provided to your offices. It was received from the printer last week and is self-published.

The following newspapers intend to feature the book as a *news article:*

San Diego Union	Lew Scarr (Medical Editor)	714–299–3131
Santa Ana Register	Kari Granville (Medical Editor)	714–835–1234
Los Angeles Times	Harry Nelson (Medical Editor)	213–625–2345

and James Bacon (syndicated columnist—including LA *Herald Examiner*) intends to feature the book in his column. 213–748–1212

These newspapers are the first, third, fourth, and fifth largest in the state. Each of the named individuals has received an advance review copy and has been personally contacted by myself. In each case, the response has been enthusiastic (high incidence in the industry helps).

More than one hundred advance review copies have been forwarded to the normal trade reviewers.

In discussing the placement of the book with local Waldenbook stores, each manager contacted has requested the book on consignment.

The purpose of this communication is to allow for a more formal arrangement. Should you prefer to handle the book on such a basis, our volume discount on orders is:

10–49	40%	(net 30
50–199	45	days, and
200–up	50	100% cash
		refunds
		with
		resalable
		returns.)

Please call us collect with your preferences.

Best regards,

Robert L. Holt

(Enclosed are copies of the ABI form, the only other widely read info on hemorrhoids, and a letter which indicates the response to be expected from newspaper articles on the subject)

RLH:1c

Obtain Payment Before Filling Re-Orders

A smaller chain of bookstores also purchased the author's first book soon after it was released. A month and a half later they re-ordered, but they hadn't paid for the first books yet. The author told them the second shipment would be sent when payment had been received for the first one. Payment was received immediately.

You should request payment from both chains and independent bookstores before filling additional orders; otherwise, serious cash-flow problems might develop. Examples of what can happen are explained in the following chapter, on wholesalers.

What Discount Should Be Offered?

When sending an ARC to the chains, be sure to list your discount policy. This is important in any future discount negotiations.

If you are asked for a higher discount than 50 percent, state that you normally do not grant a higher discount unless it is on the basis of "no returns." This means that a buyer cannot return books for a refund.

Another reason for going to a higher discount is if you request prepayment of the order. Try to hold the line at 55 percent when requesting prepayment on a thousand books or selling them on a "no return" basis.

The retail discount policies of both a major and a small publisher are shown below. These were in effect on January 10, 1985.

Large Publisher		Small Publisher	
1–4	20%	1	25% prepaid only
5–24	40	2–9	30
25–49	41	10–499	40
50–99	42	500–over	50
100–249	43		
250–499	44		
500–1,999	46		
2,000–over	47		

Avoiding Delinquent Accounts

Your past experiences with managers of bookstores have probably been pleasant. You have found most of them to be quite intelligent, gracious, and sensitive.

As a new author-publisher, you may be inclined to give them the benefit of the doubt. You may even assume that the average manager will be anxious to further your literary career by actively assisting in the sale of your books.

When you receive out-of-town orders for your books from bookstores, you don't hesitate to fill their orders immediately, granting them up to a full 50 percent discount to assure their profitability. You may even absorb the postage charges.

Your faith and confidence in these managers begins to fade, though, when you discover that approximately half of them do not pay for ordered books within six months of shipment. Those who pay after six months must usually be reminded by repeated dunning letters.

What will gall you the most will be the 25 percent who do not pay for your books at all. They may have "lost" your invoice, gone out of business, be too short of cash, or simply feel little obligation to pay debts to out-of-state small publishers. These non-payers will include well-known names in the book-selling business.

You're left with the gnawing feeling that you've been mistreated. You've lost the value of the book, its mailing package, postage, invoice, and time spent packaging and mailing the book. Most of all, these bookstore managers have stolen the hundreds or thousands of hours that you spent in writing and publishing the book.

How do you avoid this experience? It's simple. Whenever you receive an order from a bookstore, return it with a request for prepayment, as described in Chapter 41.

Virtually all the stores will prepay for their orders within four to six weeks, without even a protest. They must fill orders for their customers.

It may surprise you to learn that it is not necessary to grant a discount on your single-copy orders. Most bookstores will still prepay these orders at no discount, in order to satisfy their customers.

Selling to Wholesalers

42

On April 16, 1981, an article entitled "The Little Guy Gets Paid Last and Can Least Afford It" appeared in the *Los Angeles Times*. In it, Archie Kaplan, head of Environmental Planning of New York, stated:

Holding up money for small businesses is usual practice for some companies. These companies profit from the float between what they owe and what they have to pay. As a matter of course, they just don't pay on time to suppliers wherever they can get away with it, and it's small business that's most vulnerable.

The article later explained why small businesses are often taken advantage of:

Most are too small to have their own credit collection department. Almost none have in-house lawyers or even lawyers on retainer. Few even have separate accounting departments. In fact, says Sue Bohle, head of a public relations and advertising firm in Los Angeles, "the principal has so many other responsibilities pulling at his time that he doesn't get around to checking back receivables as often as he should, and he finds out his clients are 60 to 90 days overdue when he suddenly doesn't have the cash to pay his own bills."

284 How to Publish, Promote, and Sell Your Own Book

This can happen to you.

An additional warning was issued by the *Huenefeld Report* on July 24, 1978:

> An important segment of the U.S. book trade is made up of wholesale distributors who buy and warehouse the most popular titles of several hundred publishers, and provide one-stop shopping plus fast delivery to bookstores, libraries, and schools in the regions where those warehouses are located. Because they often resell books at substantial discounts (especially to bookstores), these wholesalers operate on thin margins, and a number of major ones have gone bankrupt in recent years.

Among the saddest predicaments related in the pages of *Publishers Weekly* are the occasional reports from small presses left "holding the bag" when one of their wholesalers has gone out of business.

This almost happened to the author when his first book was published. The Waldenbooks purchase of one thousand books described in the previous chapter was placed through a wholesaler.

During the printing of the author's first book, credit information was exchanged with more than fifty other small presses. Several hundred wholesalers and bookstores were placed on a list as frequent slow payers and outright nonpayers. Of all the names repeated on this list, the most frequent was that of this wholesaler.

Properly cautioned, the author insisted on prepayment for the thousand-book order. By numerous letters and telephone calls, the wholesaler tried unsuccessfully to persuade the author to send the thousand books prior to payment. After wasting two months, the wholesaler finally sent a check (which was immediately put through for collection).

A few months later, the wholesaler folded. Another large wholesaler assumed their accounts. Whether payment would have been received for the thousand books if prepayment had not been requested will never be known.

Credit was extended to other wholesalers during the next few years by the author. During this time, four of these wholesalers went out of business. No notification was ever received; their bills were simply not paid. Fortunately, their orders seldom exceeded ten books at a time.

While credit was granted to wholesalers, the average length of time required to receive payment for books was two and a half months. Delinquent accounts were frequent, with a significant number extending for as long as a year.

Many wholesalers would not pay until the time came to re-order, and then only after specific payment was requested.

Conversations with other small presses have revealed that the author's experience is not unique.

As a consequence, the author now requires prepayment from all wholesalers who are obviously filling orders for their customers. These prepayments are normally received within three weeks of the request.

No wholesaler has ever questioned a request for prepayment from the author.

Discounts to "Order-Taking" Wholesalers

The experience described above also prompted the author to revise his discount schedule downward. The following schedule is recommended to other author-publishers when filling orders to wholesalers who have done nothing to generate the orders they are placing.

Books Ordered	Discount
1	0%
2–10	10
11–25	15
26–up	20

At the 1982 American Booksellers Convention, the president of a large Western publisher revealed that their maximum discount is also 20 percent. However, you should be aware that most mainstream publishers grant discounts to wholesalers that are considerably higher.

If your book receives favorable national reviews, many libraries will place their orders through a favored wholesaler. Such wholesalers are simply "order-takers."

A number of other small publishers have questioned why "order-taking" wholesalers are granted any discount at all. They cite the June 2, 1975, *Huenefeld Report,* which surveyed those factors that influence acquisition librarians. This report revealed that "list price, discount, and availability through wholesaler supplier" were not determining factors in the buying decisions of acquisition librarians. The conclusion of the report was that "once the librarians decide they want your book, non-literary factors seldom discourage them from getting it." In other words, you, as a small self-publisher, are in an enviable position: the librarians want your book, and the wholesaler wants to supply it to them. The wholesaler may agree to buy your book, even if you offer no discount.

Working With "Marketing" Wholesalers

There are a number of wholesalers who do "market" books. If you book is suitable, they will purchase it in quantity and attempt to sell it for you.

To work with these wholesalers, it is necessary to grant discounts comparable to those granted the chain bookstores that purchase in quantity. Prepayment is out of the question.

Each year, *Publishers Weekly* discusses the wholesalers who deal with small presses, usually in a feature article. Their October 2, 1981, article, "The Ups and Downs of Getting Small Press Output to the Retail Book Market," should be read by all author-publishers considering sales through a wholesaler.

Be forewarned that these distributors can rarely make a profit dealing with a one-book publisher. Your book must be quite exceptional in order to be accepted.

Ingram Book Company, the largest wholesaler to retail

bookstores, voiced a similar problem when discussing dealings with a small company that had only one trade title:

> It's kind of a delicate situation. *The Mathematical Experience* is a book that does have potential in the market, but it also poses a lot of potential problems for us internally. We might get returns on the book after we've already paid for it, and with a specialized publisher, there won't be any other titles we'd want to use our credit on.

Demand for *The Mathematical Experience* pushed it into four printings totaling 35,000 books during its first six months. Nevertheless, Ingram was still hesitant to distribute this book.

If you wish to encourage these wholesalers to carry your book, approach them in the same fashion you approached the large chain bookstores. Mail an ARC with a cover letter, then follow up with a telephone call to their buyer.

Advertising with Wholesalers

A number of wholesalers invite publishers to purchase advertising space in catalogs that are mailed to customers of the wholesalers. While these wholesalers may deny it, most of them turn a tidy profit marketing space in such catalogs.

A few wholesalers, however, offer catalog space at cost, allowing publishers to pay with books instead of cash.

For example, a full-page ad in Nutri-Books' catalog for the author's first book was paid for with a hundred books. This ad was instrumental in notifying health food stores throughout the United States that the book existed.

Co-Op Wholesalers

It's not uncommon for a group of small presses to band together, forming a co-op to market their collective output to libraries and retail stores. If you get involved in such a venture:

1. do not commit more than a bare minimum of books to the co-op inventory warehouse; and
2. do not fill replacement orders by the co-op until they've paid for the books they've already sold for you.

If you disregard the above advice, you may become a victim instead of a beneficiary of such a consortium. Network Inc., a co-op of thirty-eight West Coast small presses founded on July 1, 1982, collapsed financially in 1984. The result of this collapse was described in a *Los Angeles Times* article of November 11, 1984:

> Some Network publishers are out of business for good, others are regrouping, and all lost money—from several thousand dollars to more than $100,000.

The intent of this chapter is not to discourage small presses from doing business with wholesalers. The intent is to help make such business profitable.

Distributors

The differences between a distributor and a wholesaler are small but distinct. At times, a firm may act as both.

The distributor demands a larger discount that averages up to 60 percent. In return for this large discount (which often leaves little profit margin for a small press with low press runs), the distributor agrees to market your book *actively* in the region he serves. In theory, the salespeople of such a distributor will physically carry your book into retail outlets and solicit orders for it, your book will appear in the sales literature of the distributor, and it will be exhibited at book fairs attended by the distributor.

Where Do You Find Distributors?

Your initial efforts to find distributors for your book should be concentrated among the:

1. distributors listed in *Literary Market Place,*
2. recommended distributors from other small presses, and
3. distributors utilized by retail outlets that carry books similar to yours.

The 1985 edition of *Literary Market Place* (see your local library) lists 129 distributors. Some of these are simply individual sales representatives, while others are among the largest "wholesalers" listed elsewhere in *Literary Market Place.*

Obviously, you shouldn't send a copy of your book to each of these 129 firms. Rather than choosing randomly, select the largest firms listed and contact them first—by telephone. They'll often have "800" telephone numbers.

If you have followed the advice in this book and become active in small press organizations in your region, then you should have met the owners of many other small presses. Ask them which wholesalers and distributors they use. The more such contacts you make, the larger your list of reputable distributors. By using your local small presses for references, you may be able to avoid those distributors (and wholesalers) who pose poor business risks—those firms that may be in financial difficulties or pay their bills poorly on a "normal" basis.

Finally, you can find distributors by walking into retail outlets in your region of the country that already carry similar books to yours. These don't necessarily have to be bookstores, although bookstore owners will recommend distributors to you if you make the rounds of local stores.

After obtaining a list of recommended distributors from bookstore managers, be imaginative and check other retail outlets. Do your local drugstores carry books like yours? If so, ask the drugstore owner how his books are acquired. If you have a book on gardening, then go by your local nurseries and see how they obtain their books. If your book relates to health, check the health-food magazines available at health-food stores. Distributors are listed in these publications (see their book ads). The health-food-store owner probably buys books through a jobber (another word for distributor) who offers mostly non-book products. Maybe local grocery stores, stationery stores, department stores, or gift shops carry books. Check with them, too.

How to Contact a Distributor

The most effective method of initially contacting a distributor is by telephone. You've got to find out who his "buyer" is.

Once you have the name of the buyer, this person will normally ask that you send a copy of your book along with its local sales record and publicity. Don't expect the book to be returned.

After the buyer has considered your book and decides to carry it, you *should* be contacted with an order. When you haven't heard from the buyer within 30 days, re-contact the distributor. He may wish to carry your book, but simply hasn't taken the time to contact you. This can happen half the time, so take the initiative yourself after an appropriate wait.

Bargaining With a Distributor

The terms of business with a distributor will vary with each firm. The most important are:

1. the discount of the book,
2. how quickly he'll pay for his orders,
3. the distributor's return policy (or yours), and
4. how freight charges are paid.

The distributor may attempt to dictate these terms to you. If so, don't despair. Still try to bargain with him. Use humor and advice from other small presses. Always state the terms you would prefer to any distributor. Once both the distributor and you have stated specific figures, then you should offer to "compromise by splitting the difference." This has seldom failed to work for the author.

Offer a 50-percent discount when the distributor demands a 60-percent discount. After some positioning conversation, then offer to split the difference at 55 percent. If that doesn't work, state that you normally grant a 60-percent discount when you sell your books on a non-returnable basis. If you happen to know the terms this distributor is giving other small presses in your region, you've got leverage there, too. Do your homework.

While a distributor (and other wholesalers) will agree to pay for books in sixty to ninety days, in practice this time period may stretch out to six months or longer. Even a written agreement on paper means little. You may not be paid at all unless you repeatedly demand payment. Your best guarantee of being paid is when your book is selling and the distributor wishes to re-order. At that time, encourage the buyer to contact the "accounts payable department" of the distributor for payment *before* you ship a second load of books out. Be businesslike when making such a demand. In many cases, he's simply waiting until you make such a request before paying for your books. The distributor's attitude may be to let you "finance his inventories" as long as possible. This is common among most businesses, so don't let your emotions get out-of-hand.

In cases where the distributor has been unable to sell a significant portion of your books, eventually he'll return the unsold copies and pay for the balance of your books. This may happen after six months or a year, depending on how well you're staying on top of the situation. Again, be businesslike and be willing to take the initiative to make things happen . . . even if you must make repeated requests for your books and the check.

In negotiating a returns policy, do not ask that your books be returned before they've had an adequate time period on bookstore shelves. The author recommends *six months.* If you request your books be returned within six months to a year in order for a refund to be made, you're giving your books plenty of opportunity to sell. As mentioned earlier, many distributors will stretch out their payment policy in order to see whether your books are selling first. If they suspect they're going to have to return most of your books to you, then they'll prefer to not pay for your books until they know precisely how many were sold in retail outlets. Essentially, when this happens, you've been working on a consignment basis with the distributor. When you stop to think about it, you can't blame the distributor for attempting to reduce his financial risk.

Freight charges will also vary among distributors. It is common for the publisher to pay the charges to ship books *to* the distributor. Often, small presses will require minimum orders before paying freight charges. It is also common for the distributor to pay the cost of shipping returns *back* to the publisher, although many distributors will attempt to pass this cost along to the small press. If this happens, it's up to you whether to assume such charges.

In bargaining for the terms under which you sell your books to distributors, be careful. If you're not flexible, a good distributor will simply decline to carry your book. And if you're too flexible, you may leave yourself such a pitiful profit margin that you're almost "giving your book away."

Using A Major Publisher As A Distributor

It isn't uncommon to notice a few books in stores that have been published by a small press but are being distributed by a major publisher. The inside of the dust jacket or backcover of a trade paperback often reveals this type of arrangement. The smaller publisher is hoping the national sales force of the major publisher will effectively push his books.

In such instances, the discount given the major publisher is quoted in a "dollar-price" per book, rather than a percent of its retail price. This dollar-price is normally 25 percent of the book's price.

Due to the "discount" granted the larger publisher, these arrangements are seldom profitable to a small press unless the number of books printed in their press run exceeds ten thousand copies.

If you have the capital for such press runs and contacts at major publishers, this may work well for you. Usually these arrangements are made only with small presses with considerable track records in the business.

Should You Become A Distributor?

If you have the resources and necessary time, there's no reason why you can't distribute other small press books that are related to yours (and even a few that aren't).

An author of my acquaintance, Diana Lindsay of San Diego, California, recently became a distributor for the publishers of the first two books she authored. Dissatisfied with the overall sales of her first two books, Diana decided to self-publish her third book.

After getting her third book in print, Diana's next step was to contact her earlier publishers, prestigious California houses. She inquired if she could distribute *her titles* with these firms. They readily agreed to this request and offered her discounts of 50 percent and more when she explained the scope of her marketing plans.

Diana's third step was to offer to market the *other* books printed by these publishers—at the same high discounts to herself. They quickly agreed to do so.

Her fourth step was to contact a few other small presses with books she found attractive and similar to her own. Several of these small presses offered their books to her at a 60-percent discount. Diana now offers more than twenty book titles when she enters a bookstore as a distributor, and when she gives lectures to civic groups (which she does at least once a week).

On a recent afternoon, she obtained more than a thousand dollars' worth of book orders after canvassing bookstores. Diana finds greater success among independent bookstores and other retail outlets that are not served by the major wholesalers and distributors.

In the past, she earned a royalty of 75 cents each time the publisher sold a copy of her book. For selling the same book at her lectures, she now earns $8.00 per copy. Of course, her profit margin on books sold through bookstores is considerably less, but it is still an impressive *multiple* of her previous income level per book.

For the first time in her career as an author, she's realizing a fair return for her time. Plus, her relationship with her previous publishers has changed. They're now working *together,* and selling many more books.

Having more than one title to sell to a bookstore manager, Diana is far more likely to make a sale when she walks into a store or contacts them by telephone.

If you're willing to work hard and be imaginative, maybe you should contact a number of small presses that carry books similar to your own. If you can become enthusiastic about these books, there's no reason you can't distribute other books in addition to your own.

Selling to Libraries—
the Cream of the Business

43

A well-written manuscript on a subject that has not been adequately covered in the past and that is properly packaged in book form can become a gold mine if it is favorably reviewed for libraries.

This is a goal for which all nonfiction writers should strive.

Not only will a large number of libraries purchase your book at full price, but the books sold to libraries become permanent advertisements to the library patrons. On the last page of your book, you tell these readers how to purchase additional copies. These subsequent purchases will become a source of continuing income to you.

How Do Libraries Choose Books?

Acquisition librarians are busy people. They usually base their acquisition decisions on the recommendations published by several trade publications, including:

1. *Library Journal*
2. *Publishers Weekly*
3. *Kirkus Reviews*

4. *Booklist*
5. *The New York Times Book Review*
6. *Choice*

If you are favorably reviewed by *Library Journal,* or any combination of the above publications, you are virtually assured of a successful first printing (assuming your first printing was a thousand books).

The question of how to obtain these reviews is answered in the first part of this book. If you're going to publish a book, write it well enough so that it will sell.

Selling Books To Libraries Without Favorable Reviews

Other references in the publishing field suggest that you can easily sell your unreviewed book to libraries by sending out mass mailings. This is rarely true. The same references indicate that you should rent a booth at a library association convention. This, too, is poor advice.

Librarians' purchases are based on reviews. If you cannot gather favorable national reviews, then gather as many favorable local reviews as possible. Using the guidelines discussed in Chapter 35, print a promotional brochure suitable for mailing to libraries.

As the next chapter explains, it will be important that you share the costs of any mass mailing with others. Otherwise, it will be unprofitable.

There are numerous sources where you can purchase mailing lists for libraries. Among the more reliable lists are those compiled by R. R. Bowker Company (the publisher of *Library Journal, Publishers Weekly,* and *LMP*) and the American Library Association. Write to these addresses and request their latest information concerning mailing lists for libraries.

MAILING LISTS
PUBLISHING SERVICES
AMERICAN LIBRARY ASSOC.
50 E. Huron St.
Chicago, ILL 60611

R. R. BOWKER COMPANY
205 E. 42nd St.
New York, NY 10017

Should You Give Discounts To Libraries?

If you receive reviews that encourage libraries to purchase your book, a small fraction of their purchase orders will request a discount. If you grant these discounts, you are giving money away.

Asking for a discount is a fair request, certainly, but few author-publishers can afford the luxury of granting it. While libraries can purchase more books for patrons if they receive discounts, these discounts are your profit margin.

The author has never lost an order from a library by refusing to grant a discount.

Successful Mail-Order Techniques

44

The last three chapters may have seemed slightly discouraging. This chapter on the subject of mail-order sales is also meant to be sobering.

New author-publishers must function in a state of euphoria, of unbounded enthusiasm. When it comes to spending your promotional dollar, however, it's necessary to sober up. Don't throw your money away.

Resist—or ignore—the books that describe how easy it is to make a fortune in mail-order sales. Most of the information from these sources is misinformation.

Have you read Julian L. Simon's *How to Start and Operate a Mail Order Business* yet, as suggested in Chapter 35? While this book is written in textbook form, it is still vital reading for anyone considering an investment in mail-order promotions.

Mail-Order Booksellers

More books are sold by mail than are sold in bookstores. This does not guarantee, however, that mail-order sales of your book will be a bonanza.

The vast majority of books sold by direct mail are marketed by large book clubs, consumer catalogs, and other mail-order outlets. These businesses have several advantages over you.

You Have Only One Book to Sell

A book club often has hundreds of books from which their customers can choose. You have just one from which to recover the costs of your mailing.

One way to survive with only one book is to set a high price for it. The profit for each sold book will be much higher; but if the price is too high, you may sell too few books to break even.

Another method, suggested earlier, is to share the cost of a mailing with other author-publishers. This reduces your break-even point substantially, but it also reduces the number of books you will sell compared to the results of a mailing that was not shared.

Limited Capital

Large mail-order firms have the capital to test mailing lists, in order to identify their most lucrative markets. To test a sufficient number of lists to find those with the most potential may require mailings of one to three thousand brochures to as many as ten different lists.

The cost of ten different test mailings would be almost prohibitive to an author-publisher. (How to figure the costs of a mailing is explained later in this chapter.)

A large mail-order firm also has an extensive list of people who have responded to their past mailings. If this is your first book, you have nothing of this sort.

Have You Tested?

A common failing of author-publishers is not testing their advertising copy. Are you so enthusiastic about the value of your book that you cannot resist the temptation to purchase expensive advertising space for it right away?

Space Advertising

Before purchasing such expensive advertising space in a magazine, newspaper, or other media form, you must determine the following:

1. What publication is likely to result in the best returns?
2. What size ad will pull best?
3. How should the ad be worded?
4. When should the ad be run?
5. How much will the ad cost?
6. What the return percentage is required to make money?

A mistake in any of these six areas can result in a poor return.

Direct-Mail Advertising

When planning a mass mailing, you must determine:

1. what lists to purchase,
2. what size mailings to send,
3. what type of paper to print on,
4. how many pieces to include in the mailing,
5. how to word your message,
6. when to send the mailing,
7. what the total cost will be, and
8. what return percentage is necessary to make money.

Before committing your time and limited capital to a mail-order effort, make sure you're not wasting this time and money.

Space Advertising

After reviewing Simon's book and the latest *LMP* (more than thirteen hundred magazines are listed), you should be able to select a few mediums in which to place ads.

Always review a copy of any publication you are considering. You can do this by going to the largest library in your locale, or by requesting a sample copy from its publisher.

Selecting the Publication

Does the publication have numerous mail-order ads in it? If it doesn't, find one that does. If readers of the publication are not accustomed to buying items directly from ads in the publication, they probably won't respond well to your ad either.

If the publication does contain numerous mail-order ads, look through them to see how many books are advertised. If other books are not advertised there, then look elsewhere for publications that do advertise books.

Now that you've narrowed the field to the publications that contain mail-order ads for books, select those that are in the same field as your book. If there are no publications that qualify in this area, then at least place your ad in publications that advertise books in the same broad category as yours (self-help, poetry, fiction, etc.).

These should be mail-order ads, not ads that are intended to pull customers into bookstores. The book review sections of newspapers contain ads for books; their intended purpose, however, is to generate bookstore, not mail-order, sales. When in doubt, write to a few of the book advertisers in these sections and ask them what their results were. Be sure to phrase the question properly:

I'm considering the placement of space advertising in the _____ and I noticed your ad last month. Would you recommend that I place an ad for my book there, too?

Do not ask directly about the results of their ad. They may exaggerate. Also, include a self-addressed, stamped postcard with your inquiry.

How to Test

The most common method of testing is to do a smaller-scale ad or mailing first. If the results indicate potential profitability, then place a large ad or do a larger mailing. How large a test ad or mailing to use is determined by your computations of the required return percentage for a profitable full-scale ad or mailing. How to determine the required return percentage of an ad or mailing is explained later in this chapter.

When available, a classified ad is an inexpensive method of testing a publication. If the classified ad returns well, then the larger display ad might do well also.

Be sure to key your test ads and mailings in order to check the return on each effort. How to key ads is explained later in this chapter.

Size of Your Ad

The larger the ad, the more returns it will pull. If you determine by testing that a publication is ripe for your book, then design an ad that is large enough to display a photograph of yourself or your book, plus room for a coupon. This will usually be in the range of sixteen square inches.

This size ad will be expensive in large circulation publications and may be beyond your budget. If so, you can risk a smaller ad. The problem with a small ad is that it may not contain sufficient information to induce the interested reader to part with money. How much information would you require from an ad to part with your money? Probably quite a bit.

The sample ad for Jerry Steiner's *Home For Sale By Owner* has pulled quite well in several publications. Its printed size, 3¾" × 4⅞", is sufficient to catch the eye of anyone who reviews the page it's displayed on.

Vital Components of Your Ad

There are four vital components to any ad. First, it must draw the reader's eye. It must stand out on the page. In Steiner's ad, "BURN THIS BOOK" reversed on a black background does this job.

Review book ads in other publications to see how they accomplish this goal. Be bold in devising your own.

Next, after getting the reader's attention, remember that you have five to eight seconds to deliver the gist of your message. This must motivate your reader to consider your offer seriously. In this short period of time, you must offer your reader an irresistible benefit.

The third step is to describe your offer. Limit the use of adjectives and adverbs. If your nouns and verbs are strong, you don't need modifiers. You also don't have unlimited space in which to describe your book. If you can list what others have said about the book, it will be more effective than your own superlatives.

With the fourth and final step, you must close the sale. A coupon generally improves the return of an ad. Always offer a money-back guarantee, which also improves your response. Some ads suggest the reader send a postdated check that won't be cashed for thirty days, in case the buyer wishes to return the book.

Many ads by large advertisers ask the reader simply to send for their book and be billed later. This also improves the response, although many persons may not pay for the book. If your publication and mailing costs are low, it may not hurt to lose a few books. This amounts to a free trial offer, so do not be disappointed when you never hear from some of the respondents.

Keeping a Record of Sales

The advertising record sheet shown here can be used to track each of your ads or mailings. Use these sheets to determine the profitability of your promotional efforts. Let results guide your promotional expenditures.

When to Run Your Ad

When to run your ad depends somewhat on the nature of your book. If the book is a gift item, it may do well in the late fall.

ADVERTISING RECORD SHEET

● Publication _____   Date of Issue _____

Amount of Space _____   Key _____   Cost of Space _____

DATE	1	2	3	4	5	6	7	8	9	10	11	12	13	14	15	16	17	18	19	20	21	22	23	24	25	26	27	28	29	30	31	Total No. of Inquiries for Month	Total No. of Orders
JAN. I / O																																	
FEB. I / O																																	
MAR. I / O																																	
APR. I / O																																	
MAY I / O																																	
JUNE I / O																																	
JULY I / O																																	
AUG. I / O																																	
SEPT. I / O																																	
OCT. I / O																																	
NOV. I / O																																	
DEC. I / O																																	

Interval Since Publication Date	INQUIRIES		ORDERS		SALES Total in $	Cost of Ad Per $1 of Sales	Cost of Follow-Up Per $1 of Sales
	Total No.	Cost Each	Total No.	Cost Each			
3 Months							
6 Months							
9 Months							
12 Months							
● TOTAL							

Diet books, as well as outdoor recreation books requiring good weather, may do well in the spring and summer.

Review the information in Simon's book to determine when your book can best be displayed in ads. Also take the time at your local library to see when most book ads appear in the publications you've selected.

No hard and fast rules apply, although the summer and holiday periods are usually not recommended for general books.

The Cost of Your Ad

To obtain the cost of placing space ads, write to all the publications you're considering and ask for their

1. rate card,
2. mechanical requirements, and
3. a sample copy of their publication.

The rate card will tell you how much the different sizes will cost, and the mechanical requirements tell you what must be submitted to the publication to run your ad.

The higher the circulation, the more expensive will be the space. Always check the paid circulation to make sure you're getting adequate coverage.

Mechanical requirements vary with each publication. Some will typeset your copy, while others may request a velox (black-and-white transparency) of your ad.

Computing Required Return Percentage

As a rule, a fair return on space ads is one-tenth of 1 percent of the circulation of the publication. It is rare that you will do better than this percentage.

Before placing an ad in a publication, you must compute its potential return based on its circulation and your combined publication and advertising costs. Since your publication costs are already fixed, these computations may determine the size of ad you can afford.

For example, let's assume you're considering an ad in a magazine having a circulation of a hundred thousand. One-tenth of 1 percent of a hundred thousand means that the maximum return on that circulation would be one hundred sold books. Will one hundred sold books be profitable?

Add up the following costs:

1. the cost of the space ad;
2. the cost of preparing the artwork for the ad;
3. the cost of a hundred books;
4. postage and packaging for a hundred books; and
5. the value of your time.

Do your costs exceed the sales proceeds of one hundred books? If they do, then you'll have to buy a smaller ad space, find a magazine with a larger circulation, or abandon the idea of space advertising.

How Long Must You Wait for Results?

Within thirty days, 50 percent of the orders should have been received. By ninety days, 99 percent of the orders should have been received. It is not necessary to wait the entire ninety days when testing, but certainly wait thirty days.

Key Your Advertising

Failure to key their advertising is a common error of over-enthusiastic author-publishers. If you do not key your advertising, there is no way to test the number of returns received from each ad.

There are various ways of keying your ads. The simplest method is to alter the price of your book slightly for each ad placed. A more common method is to alter your return address for each ad. If your mail is normally delivered to a street address, add a "Dept. A" or "Suite 200" to the address. Then use "Dept. B" or "Suite 300" for the next ad.

If you use a post office box, add a letter to the number. Place a dash between the number and letter used, such as:

P.O. BOX 222-A.

Then make your next ad, P.O. Box 222-B.

Setting Up An Advertising Agency

By forming your own ad agency, you will save 15 percent of your advertising costs. This is because most of the magazines and other publications in which you would place advertising grant a 15 percent discount to advertising agencies.

To form an ad agency, simply print up or photo-copy "insertion orders" and open a bank account for the agency.

Insertion Orders

An insertion order is the form used to place an advertising order with a publication. The sample insertion order on the following page can be used to design your own form.

Permission is granted to photo-copy this insertion order to make your own orders. Simply design a new letterhead and place your address over that shown.

The following steps describe how to fill in an insertion order. See numbers on sample.

1. Place the name of your publishing company on this line.
2. Your "product" is a book (include its title).
3. "Space" is the size of your ad (quite often this must be taken from mechanical requirements of the publica-

PUBLISHER'S ADVERTISING AGENCY

2830 Chicago St.
San Diego, CA 92117
(714) 276-8646

INSERTION ORDER

ORDER NO.   DATE

TO PUBLISHER OF

CITY AND STATE

(1) PLEASE PUBLISH ADVERTISING OF (advertiser)

(2) FOR (product)

(3) SPACE   TIMES

(4) DATE OF INSERTION

(5) POSITION

(6) COPY   KEY

(7) ADDITIONAL INSTRUCTIONS =

(8) RATE   •

(9) LESS AGENCY COMMISSION   PER CENT ON GROSS   •

(10) LESS CASH DISCOUNT   PER CENT ON NET   •
                                                        ───────────
(11)   ▶

PER _____

IMPORTANT — We Must Have Checking Copies — **IMPORTANT**

tion). After "times," place the number of times you wish your ad to run. Until you've had the opportunity to test an ad once, do not schedule multiple times.

4. It may not be possible to specify a particular "date," but you can usually specify a date after which your ad should appear.

5. The "position" is where in the publication you wish your ad to appear. For some positions you will pay extra.

6. Your "copy" is what you are submitting. It may be simply typesetting (for a classified ad), a velox (transparency for a display ad), or other requirements. The "key" is to tell the publication how you wish multiple insertions to be keyed. Each insertion must have a different key if you are to tell how each fares.

7. Use the "additional instructions" to clarify your insertion order. If you're submitting just typesetting for a classified order, type the ad in this space.

8. On the "rate" line, place the cost of your ad, according to the rate card of the publication.

9. Place "15%" after the word "commission" and compute this amount. Place the dollar amount at the end of the line.

10. If you pay cash in advance, place "2%" within this line and deduct 2 percent from the net rate (after deduction of the 15 percent agency commission).

11. At the bottom of the column of figures, place the net cost of your ad.

Sign on the PER line. Use your name, as the publication may find it necessary to contact you should any questions arise in placement of your insertion order.

The CHECKING COPIES that are requested at the bottom of the insertion order are copies of the actual ad printed by the publication. This permits you to check the accuracy of the ads. In the author's experience, one out of every four classified ads has been incorrectly printed. On such occasions, the publication is asked to rerun the ad. Errors in display ads are rare, as you normally submit camera-ready copy.

Direct-Mail Advertising

If you have designed a promotional brochure that can double as a flyer in your direct-mail promotions, you will save the expense of printing another flyer.

A properly designed flyer will eliminate the need for printing order forms and mailing envelopes as well.

Computing Your Required Return Percentage

Before committing both time and money to direct-mail promotions, first determine how many books must be sold to recover your planned costs. Direct-mail promotions are considered successful if they result in a return of 1 to 3 percent. It is rare that you will receive a response that is greater than 3 percent.

For example, let us assume that you receive a response of 2 percent on a mailing of 3,000 brochures. This means you've sold 60 books. In order to do this, you will have to pay for the following:

1. publishing 60 books,
2. printing 3,000 brochures,
3. obtaining a bulk-rate mailing permit,
4. mailing 3,000 brochures,
5. packaging and mailing 60 books,
6. renting mailing lists, and
7. printing 3,000 envelopes (optional).

Sample costs for mailing 3,000 brochures with a return of 60 sold books are listed at the top of the following page:

60 books @ $4 ea.	$ 240
3,000 brochures	250
bulk-rate permit	80
mail 3,000 brochures	375
mailing books (60)	60
mailing lists	150
Total	$ 1,155

If your book is priced at only $10, you will lose money. Even if it's priced at $20, you will barely make money.

In this example, if you shared the costs with another author-publisher, you could save half of $605 (the total of the bulk-rate permit, brochure postage, and the mailing lists).

You will still lose money on a $10 book; a $20 book, however, will yield a profit of $347.50 ($1,200 less $852.50).

Of course, these computations have not taken into account the value of your time. You will probably spend weeks preparing a mailing of three thousand brochures.

Before you plan any mailing, check out the economics. Cut your direct-mail costs as much as you can. And raise the price of your book as high as is practical. Keep adjusting your mailing until it has a chance to be successful.

Obtaining Mailing Lists

If your library has it, the best source of mailing lists is the *Standard Rate & Data Service's Mailing List Directory.* It contains more than fifty thousand lists, half of which are to consumers.

The latest issue of *LMP* lists numerous firms dealing in mailing lists. Compare prices from a number of these firms before making any purchases.

The Size of Your Mailing

After testing a mailing list, it's best to send out at least three thousand brochures. Less than that does not give you a good opportunity to recover your expenses.

If the three thousand mailing does well, do a larger mailing, according to your available resources.

Never do a large mailing without testing.

Preparing Your Message

The only difference between preparing copy for space advertising and for a direct-mail flyer is that the flyer has more room.

Current postal regulations permit you to mail three ounces of material with each piece of a bulk-rate mailing. This includes the weight of the envelope. Use this maximum weight for your material or to share with others to minimize your costs.

An Order Form

If you insert a separate order form, keep it simple. The form below is suggested.

CALIFORNIA HEALTH PUBLICATIONS

347 Mermaid   Box 963   Laguna Beach, CA 92652
(714) 498-0642

Please ship _____ hardbound copies of *Hemorrhoids* by R. L. Holt.

Retail price $12.95 (plus postage).
*Special Library Price on direct orders: $10.95 (plus postage).

TERMS: Net 30 days

Buyer's
Signature _____

Ship to

Bill to _____

Street _____

City _____ State _____ Zip ____

Cust. Order No. _____ Date _____

Code Each Mailing

Just as your space ads should be keyed, your mailings should be coded. Use the same methods as you used for space ads. An additional method when order forms are included is to mark their edges with a felt-tipped marker.

Obtaining a Bulk-Rate Mailing Permit

A bulk-rate permit costs $80 initially; $40 for the "permit imprint," and $40 for the "mailing fee," which is renewable annually. The "mailing fee" permit expires each year on December 31.

This permit allows you to mail envelopes weighing no more than three ounces at the current rate of 11 cents each. The minimum number of envelopes per mailing is now two hundred. All of these figures are subject to change and should be checked at your local post office before planning a mailing.

Fulfilling Your Orders

45

This is the pleasurable part of being an author-publisher. The excitement of pulling orders out of envelopes does not diminish even after many years.

How you fulfill these orders has a great deal to do with your level of profitability. Discounts, packaging, and prepayment requests have been extensively discussed in previous chapters. By this time, your invoices and mailing labels should be printed and ready for use.

Handling Your Mail

As your promotion gets under way and reviews begin appearing, your incoming mail should increase substantially. The following steps will be helpful in handling this mail efficiently.

Open Mail on Left-Hand Side

Open the left-hand side of envelopes (as you face their addresses). This makes the envelopes easier to stack and file. If the top of the envelope is opened, other letters will tend to become hidden under its flap when it is filed.

Do not tear the return address portion of the envelope as

it's opened. Your letters will be filed alphabetically, according to the customer's name on this address.

Marking Order Envelopes

All envelopes containing orders should be marked as such when they are opened.

Write the number of books ordered, followed by a notation of which edition (hardbound or softbound) is being ordered. If you have more than one book, also write down an initial designating which book is being ordered.

When checks are enclosed, remove them and write the amount on the face of the envelope. Then circle the amount. This designates the order as prepaid.

If an order arrives from an individual but no check is enclosed, you have to make a choice. Should you send a book with an invoice, or should you send an invoice requesting prepayment? It's suggested that you mark these envelopes "RP," meaning that you will request prepayment.

Pull Invoices When Paid

If a check is received in payment of an invoice, pull your invoice copy from the "Accounts Receivable" file. Mark it as being paid by placing the current date on the invoice just above the original date.

By pulling and marking paid invoices at the same time their checks are removed from envelopes, you make sure that you will not forget to do so later. Otherwise, you will be sending out dunning letters unnecessarily, alienating potential customers for your next book.

Individual Orders

Many of your orders will be from individuals who have noticed reviews of your books or have used the information on the last page to order additional copies. Most of these orders will be prepaid and will require no more than typing an address on a mailing label.

Some reviews will fail to list the price of your book. In addition, some people do not know where to look in a book for order information. In such cases, you'll receive requests for books before payment.

Initially, you may be inclined to fill such orders before payment. Two out of three people will pay for your book immediately. The third will be one of those people who find it difficult to pay bills on a timely basis, if at all. After a year of chasing these people (they include doctors and professors) with repeated reminders to pay their bills, you'll decide to return all individual orders with prepayment requests. To prepare such requests, follow the same procedure as described for bookstores later in this chapter.

Library Orders

Since libraries always pay their bills, it isn't necessary to request prepayment for their orders. A few libraries will ask for a discount. Such requests should be politely declined, as suggested in Chapter 43.

It is a general practice to pass on your postage and package costs to libraries and other single-copy purchasers. Use your own judgment in levying these charges on multiple-purchase buyers.

When preparing library orders, always check to see that the invoice should be sent to the same address as the books. Sometimes the book should be sent to the library and its bill to City Hall.

Use the following procedure to fill in an invoice for a library order. (A sample invoice is provided in Chapter 17.)

1. Assign and type invoice number.
2. Type date the invoice is prepared.

3. Type shipping address for invoice, if different from that of book.
4. Type shipping address for book.
5. Type purchaser's order number, or date of purchase order if no order number is provided.
6. Type date books are to be shipped.
7. Type book quantity of purchaser.
8. List brief book title and your last name, plus softbound or hardbound when you have both editions.
9. Use UNIT PRICE column only when order is for more than one book.
10. Place price of book(s) in TOTAL AMOUNT COLUMN.
11. Place postage and packaging charge below book price.
12. Type total of all charges.
13. Write assigned invoice number above return address on order envelope.

Step 13 is necessary in order to trace purchase orders when questions arise later.

Occasionally, you'll receive prepaid orders from libraries. These libraries are trying to avoid postage and packaging fees on their book orders. They figure that a seller will simply accept their check and not bother billing them for additional minor charges. They are probably right most of the time.

Bookstore And Wholesaler Orders

Chapters 41 and 42 discussed when to request prepayment, and recommended discounts for bookstores and wholesalers.

When you do not request prepayment from these purchasers, fill in their invoices the same way you fill in library invoices.

Requesting Prepayment

The following procedure is suggested for prepayment request invoices:

1. Remove order from envelope and dispose of envelope (otherwise it may be confused with other envelopes).
2. Type PREPAID above the word INVOICE on your invoice form.
3. Assign an invoice number having the same numbers as your last regular invoice, but add two letters as a suffix. For example, if your last regular number was 316, add "aa" to make 316aa. Use 316ab for the next prepayment request. It is fruitless to use your regular invoice numbering system for prepayment requests, as stores and wholesalers will often fail to mention your invoice number when returning a check to you. You have no way of matching checks to invoices then. This also makes it unnecessary to retain a copy of prepayment request invoices for your own files. Quite often, they cannot be matched up, either.
4. Fill in the rest of the invoice the same way as a regular invoice, except place the word "Pending" in the DATE SHIPPED space, and type the words PREPAYMENT REQUESTED boldly across the open space beneath the description of your book.

When payment is received, you should treat it the same way as any other prepaid order, except that you may wish to fill in an invoice for your own record-keeping purposes. It's not necessary to send a copy of the invoice with the books. Instead, simply enclose the buyer's purchase order with the books.

Following the above procedure will eliminate 99 percent of your slow payers and 100 percent of your non-payers. The only slow payers will be an occasional library.

Dunning Slow Payers

As many as half of the slow-paying libraries you have on your books will be your own fault. They will be cases where you've forgotten to pull invoices when checks were received. For this reason, be cordial when inquiring why these bills "have not been paid."

The following form is suggested when inquiring why an invoice has not been paid:

Acquisition Librarian:

Our records indicate that we have not received payment ($_____) for _____ copies of _____ ordered by your library on _____.

Your order number is _____. We shipped the books on _____. Have you received the book(s)? If so, do you have a canceled check for their payment? We thank you for your courtesy in this matter.
      _____ (name)
      _____ (company)
      _____ (address)

The above request will fit neatly on a postcard. If you've written invoice numbers on your order envelopes as suggested, you will have no difficulty locating their original purchase order (so you can fill in the dunning postcard).

Packaging Your Books

Your books should be packaged so that they will arrive in the same shape as they were mailed. This costs only a few cents extra and ensures that you will not have to replace damaged books.

Shipping Packages

There are four basic types of inexpensive shipping bags. *Utility* bags consist of a heavy kraft paper without cushioning. If your book is small and compact, these may suffice. In lots of a hundred, they currently cost approximately 9 cents each.

Padded bags contain cushions in the form of shredded paper or cloth material. They are useful when minimal cushioning is desired. A 7¼" × 12" padded bag weighs almost three ounces, so this bag should not be used if your book weighs more than 13 ounces. A lot of a hundred padded bags costs in the range of 14 cents each.

Foamlite bags have a layer of foam laminated to the kraft paper. They are heat-sealable, but a stapler can also be used to close them. This bag weighs less than an ounce. When purchased in lots of five hundred, the 7¼" × 12" bags costs about 20 cents each.

Mail-lite bags are light, too, weighing slightly more than an ounce. They have a plastic air bubble lining laminated to the kraft paper. They currently cost about 23 cents each, in lots of five hundred.

To obtain the lowest prices on shipping bags, check with major paper wholesalers in your area. Also check the Yellow Pages, and other author-publishers.

Packing Your Books

When packing multiple book orders, always place a cardboard liner between the spines. Also place cardboard liners around the outer edges of the books, so they are not loose. If they can move around, they will scratch each other. Dust jackets and softbound covers may be damaged, causing the books to be returned.

The best boxes to use for packing large orders are the boxes your books came in. This is one of the reasons you asked the bindery to pack the books in convenient-sized boxes.

Tapes used to seal boxes should be self-adhesive. Use plastic tape to close open edges, then reinforced tape around the entire box. Slightly overlap the mailing label with tape during wrapping.

On single-copy packages, overlap the mailing label with stamps. This helps to ensure that the label stays on.

Selling Reprint Rights to a Major Publisher

VI

Finding an Agent

46

Finding an agent who will sell your work enthusiastically is not easy. If you are an aspiring or new author, it may take years.

A unique chemistry must exist between an author and agent. Each of the following conditions must exist:

1. Both must basically like each other.
2. The agent must respect the author's writing ability.
3. The author must respect the agent's editing advice.
4. The agent must be enthusiastic about the author's subject matter.
5. The author must be patient in awaiting results.
6. The agent must be sensitive in handling authors' egos.
7. The author must be mature enough to handle rejections.

There are also professional requirements:

1. The author's work must be well written.
2. The agent must be a good salesperson.
3. The author's work must have commercial appeal.
4. The agent must be an efficient business person.

With all these conditions and requirements, it is little wonder that few aspiring or new authors find agents who successfully market their work.

If you pursue a writing career, at some point you may cross the line that separates successful authors from those who are not. At that time, finding an agent will not be so difficult. Agents have bills of their own to pay, which causes them to seek successful authors as clients.

After attending a writer's conference in Los Angeles, Art Seidenbaum, book review editor for the *Los Angeles Times,* commented on March 14, 1980:

> Writers are always in want if not in need. And none of us has any right to blame the next of us for asking guidance, help, hints, human response. The trouble with conferences is the way they collect so many wanters in one space for one weekend. Collector Carolyn See (organizer of the conference) even felt so conscience-stricken she announced that no member of the audience was to ask an appearing author about an author's agent.
>
> A good rule, I think. Selecting the proper agent involves complex questions of chemistry, economics, data retrieval and Ouija as well as literature.

Where To Find Agents

The classified section of your telephone directory probably lists agents. *LMP* has hundreds of agents listed throughout the country. Writers' magazines abound with the names of agents, including ads that offer their services.

Your Author-Friends

There are few situations in which author-friends can prove more valuable than when they refer their agents to you.

If your book is worthy, several of these friends may have suggested that you forward a copy to their agents. Introductions from such friends may be necessary for your book even to be considered.

Responding to Agent Advertisements

Within many publications catering to the interests of writers, you'll find ads inviting you to submit your manuscript for a "reading" by an agent. Usually, you must pay a fee for this reading. In return, you will receive what may be constructive criticism.

While these are professionals who know the business, this is often the same response and assistance that you should have received free from editor-friends during the writing of your book.

Many of these same publications abound with ads by subsidy publishers as well. Be forewarned.

Selling An Agent On Your Book

An agent, just like an individual buyer, acquisition librarian, bookstore manager, wholesaler, or reviewer, must be sold on your book. Prepare an attractive book package before approaching an agent.

Your Book's Credentials

Include a folder or three-ring binder of all the reviews and other publicity the book has generated. This should be well organized.

Describe the sales record of your book, including the names of everyone who has purchased copies in volume.

If several printings have been necessary, describe the number of books in each printing. If your initial contact with the agent is in person, take copies of each printing with you.

Your Credentials

In detail, tell the agent what qualifies you to write your book. Why are you *and* your book salable commodities?

An agent must sell both you and your book to an editor. A major publisher will want to know how impressive you can be during interviews with reviewers and interviewers in the media. List all of your personal accomplishments, including those within the writing field (other books), within the subject area of your latest book, and in other areas of work. Do not be modest.

Include a Photograph

Include a professionally taken photograph of yourself with this package. You must appear interesting and provocative. This photograph will help convince a publisher that you are marketable.

Meet Your Agent Personally

The relationship between an author and an agent must be carefully developed. If a personal meeting can be arranged, take the time to interview any agent who might be useful to you.

Do not approach agents by "asking" them to represent you. Be positive. Tell them that you're considering the services of an agent in the marketing of your book to a major publisher. Ask if they would be interested in discussing the matter.

Be enthusiastic in interviewing an agent, and look for a similar reaction from the agent after your book has been evaluated. If an agent is not excited over your book, how will he or she generate sufficient enthusiasm to market it successfully?

Your personal style must be compatible with the agent's personality. Only a personal meeting can verify this.

The Author's Experiences With Agents

Perhaps you will have more reasonable expectations from agents after reading this next section.

The author's first agent was referred by another writer, the author of a health book found on the shelf of a bookstore. This agent was hurriedly obtained when a New York editor expressed interest in the author's first manuscript. The editor suggested that obtaining an agent would be a wise move.

This agent was cordial, but his interest in selling the manuscript evaporated as soon as the New York editor revealed that no offer would be forthcoming after all. The agent didn't even bother to inform the author that the editor would not be making an offer.

A few years later, a second agent was engaged after the author received an offer for reprint rights to his first book and an offer for his second manuscript from the same publisher. An editor at a successful small press in northern California recommended this agent, a person who is frequently mentioned on the "rights" page of *Publishers Weekly* and who represented prominent authors at that time.

This agent:

1. negotiated terms contrary to written instructions,
2. failed to review contracts for accuracy,
3. misplaced contracts and sent them out by fourth-class mail (before they had been signed),
4. failed to forward royalty statements received from the publisher, and
5. was not able to sell rights to either of the author's next two manuscripts, the first of which became the best-selling book in the field of investment bonds.

After the *Bond* book was self-published, this agent was still unable to sell it even though it had been selected one of the top five books published in its field the year it was released.

After canceling the arrangement with this agent, the author immediately sold reprint rights to Harcourt Brace Jovanovich by contacting the publisher directly. The Harcourt edition was then selected by the Book-of-the-Month Club.

Finding the Right Publisher

47

Before attempting to sell reprint rights to a major publisher, that is, to give another publisher the exclusive right to publish your book, you must have a salable product. Has your book gathered favorable reviews and established a reasonable sales record? If so, it should not be difficult to sell the reprint rights.

Choosing The Right Publisher

There are three important considerations in selecting a major publisher for your book:

1. Does it publish the general subject matter of your book?
2. Does it publish in softbound as well as hardbound?
3. Does it have a national distribution network?

Visit Your Local Bookstore

Check the most recently published books in your general subject area (health, business, and so on) at your local bookstore. Who publishes these books? Make a list of at least fifteen publishers that are currently releasing books like yours.

These publishers should be the largest that you can find. You want a large publisher in order to encourage the widest national distribution, as well as to obtain the highest possible advance.

Visit Your Local Library

If you do not come up with fifteen publishers after visiting the bookstore, collect more names at your library.

At the library, check the latest edition of *LMP* for the names of editors at the publishers you've compiled. A large publisher may list several dozen editors, without designating their speciality areas. In such cases, address your correspondence to the editor-in-chief.

LMP also lists the number of books each publisher issued in the previous year. By checking these figures, you can determine the relative size of the publishers on your list.

Contacting The Publisher

The most commonly accepted method of contacting a publisher to sell your reprint rights is to send a query letter with a copy of your book. If you live near the publisher, use your telephone to make the initial contact. In addition to gauging their interest in your book, you can also determine to whom it should be sent. The author's *Bond* book was sold to Harcourt Brace Jovanovich after an initial telephone contact.

Your Query Letter

Your query letter should be one page, single- or double-spaced. Use short paragraphs, double-spacing between them.

Do not compliment your own book when reviews and comments of others are available. When you've had an opportunity to talk personally to an editor beforehand, appeal to his or her stated interests. Sell what they're looking for.

The sample letter on the California Health Publications

letterhead was sent to fourteen publishers, three of whom responded with offers. This letter lists the accomplishments of the book on hemorrhoids in a concise fashion. It can be easily scanned in a minute.

The next-to-last paragraph emphasizes the high incidence (52 percent) of the affliction among all adults over the age of forty. This suggests a wide audience for the book.

Item #6 mentions the enclosure of a review by *Library Journal.* The editor at William Morrow (who acquired the reprint rights) later told the author that this review was one of the main reasons they acquired the book. Enclose the most favorable reviews your book has received.

Your letter to a major publisher must be perfect. Rewrite it until it is. And have another person proofread your spelling and punctuation.

If a publisher is interested, they'll call you. Don't bother calling them, though you may want to send a follow-up letter if you've had no response after a month.

CALIFORNIA HEALTH PUBLICATIONS

347 Mermaid   Box 963   Laguna Beach, CA 92652
(714) 498-0642

December 3, 1978

Hillel M. Black,
Editor in Chief—Adult Books,
WILLIAM MORROW & CO., INC.,
105 Madison Avenue,
New York, NY 10016.

Dear Mr. Black:

The enclosed book—*Hemorrhoids: A Cure and Preventative*—has established itself as one of the best-selling popular medical books of 1978.

Since its publication date of February 28, 1978:

1. libraries have purchased more than 6,000 copies,
2. Waldenbooks has purchased 1,000 copies,
3. the largest bookstore in America (Barnes & Noble, NY) has sold more than 75 copies,
4. Ingram named the book among the "Best of the Independent Press" titles of 1978 and purchased 1,000 copies,
5. Nutri-Books, largest wholesaler to health food stores, has ordered the book four times (100 books each time),
6. the book sold out its first and second printings with no national publicity other than the attached *Library Journal* review,
7. Milestone Publications has acquired Canadian rights, and
8. British Commonwealth rights were sold to Abacus Press.

Success of the book may be attributed to the fact that 52 percent of American adults over forty years of age suffer from hemorrhoids and the book is well written.

As we believe that the book would benefit now by the marketing ability of a national distributor, we are inviting your interest in its softbound rights. Please indicate your interest at your earliest convenience.

Thank you.

Best regards,

Robert L. Holt

Enclosures
RLH:kw

Negotiating Your
Reprint Contract

48

As discussed earlier, it's difficult for a new author to obtain the
services of a professional agent. For this reason, this chapter
discusses how you can represent yourself in the negotiating
process.

What To Offer

In your query letter, offer only North American rights to your
book. This means the publisher will have the right to sell your
book in the United States and Canada. You retain the rights
to all other countries. If this is not specified, you'll end up
splitting advances and royalties on foreign editions of your
work.

It is customary to let a publisher know if you are submitting
the book simultaneously to other publishers.

Retain Mail-Order Rights

Try to retain mail-order rights to at least one of your editions,
too. The hardbound edition, being higher-priced, will be
more profitable to retain.

This right will be non-exclusive, as your publisher must

have the right to market its version of your book by mail-order also.

Retain Movie and TV Rights

If your book has this potential, also try to retain movie and television rights. You may wish to show such a book to a few agents before trying to sell reprint rights yourself.

Your query letter can specify that only North American and softbound rights are being offered. Do not state in this letter that you intend to retain other rights, as these can be bargaining points for later.

Negotiating Terms

Make an itemized list of the terms to be negotiated. These should include:

1. the advance,
2. royalties,
3. mail-order rights,
4. free copies to author,
5. movie and TV rights,
6. other rights,
7. duration of contract,
8. form of payment, and
9. copyright.

Your first contact with an editor interested in purchasing reprint rights may be a complete surprise to you. Since it will probably be a telephone call, keep a clipboard with this list next to your telephone.

If you're organized, you won't be confused when the call comes. You'll sound more intelligent during negotiations. And it won't be necessary to bring up points later that have been overlooked.

Verbal Negotiations

Most publishers will conduct negotiations over the telephone. Only in rare instances will you receive an offer in writing. To avoid misunderstandings, however, it is suggested that you respond in writing to all offers.

Counter-offering in writing accomplishes several goals.

1. You have more time to consider your response.
2. By reducing your counter-offer to written form, it will be better organized.
3. It provides an opportunity to restate the publisher's offer in written form.

If you choose to counter-offer in writing, send your responses to the publisher by one-day mail service. It will cost more, but it's worth it.

The Advance

The size of your advance is the most important negotiating point—more important than royalty levels for 90 percent of all books published. Since only 10 percent of the books that are released each year continue to sell beyond the first year, the royalty levels negotiated for the other 90 percent are irrelevant.

So, concentrate on maximizing your advance. It may be the only compensation you receive for your book.

How do you do this? By offering your book to as many publishers as possible, simultaneously. Let them bid against each other, the highest bidder winning. Make sure, however, that your query letter clearly specifies that you are making a multiple submission.

Royalties

Fortunately, hardbound royalty rates are more or less standard in the industry and usually needn't be negotiated. These rates are:

First 5,000 books	10% of the publisher's retail price
Second 5,000	12½%
Over 10,000	15%

On the other hand, royalty rates for softbound books vary widely. Most publishers will offer you the lowest rates they think you'll accept. They expect you to negotiate. One publisher may offer only 5 percent, and another 10 percent.

There are two different types of softbound books: trade paperbacks (also called quality paperbacks) and mass-market paperbacks. Trade paperbacks are distributed only to bookstores, while mass-market paperbacks are also sold in newsstands, airports, drugstores, and so on. Mass-market paperbacks are predominantly pocketbook size, $4^3/_{16}'' \times 6^3/_4''$, while trade paperbacks are often simply the signatures of the hardbound size wrapped in a softbound cover.

Royalty rates on mass paperbacks are considerably lower. They may start at the 6 to 8 percent level, escalating no further than the 8 to 10 percent level.

A few publishers will attempt to pay you mass paperback royalty rates for editions of your book that are printed in a trade paperback size. Do not allow this to happen to you. Be certain that royalty rates for each size paperback are specified in your contract.

If you decide to sell reprint rights to a publisher that does not print a mass paperback-size book, your publisher may attempt to sell such rights to another publisher. In such cases, the advance and royalties are split, usually equally between the author and the publisher.

Even when your publisher has a mass-paperback line, the firm may still decide to sell mass-paperback rights to another publisher. Unless you are a major author, you will have little control of such sales.

Mail-Order Rights

It's important that you retain non-exclusive mail-order rights to your book (or one of its editions) in order to continue fulfilling the mail orders you receive. These are orders that you've generated, and you're entitled to them.

Since most of these orders will be single-copy orders, few major publishers should object to your retaining this right. Filling single-copy orders is not profitable for a large publisher.

In retaining mail-order rights, also negotiate the right to purchase additional copies of your book from the publisher.

When you run out of your own books, it will be necessary for you to purchase additional copies from your publisher. It is customary for publishers to sell such copies to their authors at a 40 percent discount. The author was able to negotiate such purchases at 10 percent over their cost in one case. Try to get at least a 55 percent discount on purchases exceeding five hundred copies at one time.

Free Copies

It is standard for publishers to furnish authors with six to ten free copies of their books. This barely takes care of your personal needs, leaving no books to provide for promotional purposes.

For this reason, ask for fifty to one hundred copies of your book. The author obtained one hundred copies of the *Orthodontic* book for promotional purposes and fifty copies of the *Bond* book from its publisher.

The *Los Angeles Times* review of the *Orthodontic* book came about as a result of their receiving one of these copies. This was a major review, which would not otherwise have been forthcoming.

When you've successfully published your own book, most publishers will realize the value of local and regional publicity that you can generate for their edition. This publicity may be the only publicity your book receives, other than the standard review copies sent to major reviewers. In negotiating these free copies, ask the editor what publicity and promotional plans he or she has in mind for your book. If they're honest, they may admit they have few or none. This is when you stress what you can do in the way of publicity and promotion.

Tell the publisher to send you copies with "Not for Sale" marked on them, if necessary. In any case, this is a bargaining point. If the company will not yield in this area, ask it to yield in another.

Movie and Television Rights

If it develops that your book has potential in the area of movie and TV rights, obtain the services of a professional agent. If an agent knows that you have such interest in your book, that agent will be anxious to represent you.

Since many books are purchased for production as movies but never produced, it is important that these rights revert to you after a reasonable length of time if it appears that the original buyers will not be using your book.

If your publisher retains these rights, bargain for 80 percent of them.

First and Second Serial Rights

First serial rights are for excerpts of your book that appear in magazines *before* the book's publication. The split of the money received for this right is normally 90/10 or 75/25 in the author's favor. While the sums of money paid for these rights to new authors may be relatively minor, the pre-publication publicity generated by the magazine coverage can be major.

Second serial rights are for excerpts that appear *after* your book is published, and the split of money generated from this source is generally 50/50.

Book Club Rights

It is customary to split book club rights 50/50. The Harcourt reprint of the *Bond* book was sold to the Fortune Book Club, a division of the Book-of-the-Month Club. It had been offered earlier in the author's edition without success.

Attempting to sell your self-published book to a major book club may be similarly fruitless. Book clubs depend on publishers of their books to generate nationwide publicity. Few author-publishers have the capital to do so.

Other Rights

There are numerous other rights cited in the small print of a large publisher's contract. These include rights to condensations, recordings, microfilming, digests, and so on. The author's share in such rights varies from 50 to 80 percent, depending again on the publisher and how the bargaining is conducted.

Duration of a Contract

If your publisher does not keep your book in print, you must be able to regain the rights to your book. The terms may vary from publisher to publisher, but you can usually reacquire these rights by making a written request. If the publisher declines to print additional copies within six months, the rights revert to you.

In such cases, you normally also have the right to purchase their overstock of your book at 10 to 15 percent of its retail price. The plates and negatives may also be offered to you, at their cost plus shipping.

Make sure an acceptable procedure for the reversion of rights is specified in the contract.

Timing of Payment

How the advance is paid is important. Do not let a publisher wait until your book is finally published before making full payment of your advance. It's no longer an advance if they can wait that long.

Try to insist on receiving half the advance upon signing the contract, and the balance upon their acceptance of all revisions to your book. This is becoming the standard in the industry. What if the publisher decides not to publish your book after all? Not only would you fail to receive the full advance, but you will have lost the opportunity to have your book published on a timely basis elsewhere.

It is standard that royalties are computed twice a year, for example, on June 30 and December 31, but seldom paid until three to four months later. Of course, you will not receive royalties until your advance has been covered (earned out).

Copyright

Your book should always be copyrighted in your name. Never budge on this.

The author was told by one author-publisher of an instance where her printer attempted to copyright her book in the name of the printer. If this had happened, she would have lost all rights to her book.

Bargaining

As mentioned already, publishers expect you to bargain; they don't expect you to accept their initial offer. When you are first contacted, carefully write down the terms offered. Repeat them to the editor to assure perfect understanding.

Then ask questions concerning any of the first eight items listed in the previous section that have not been covered already. Make notes of everything mentioned.

When all points have been discussed, ask the editor, "May I get back to you in a few days? I'd like to think this all over."

Do not get into a disagreement on any of the points discussed. Simply note what is offered and make sure the editor knows what you'd like to receive.

Can an Attorney Help You?

If the attorney has no experience selling books, of course not. If you can find an attorney with such experience, he or she will probably wish to act as your agent—in return for a 10 to 15 percent agency commission. If you really think you need an attorney to advise you, hire one on an hourly basis—one who has extensive experience with book contracts.

Never reveal to an editor that you're using an attorney. During negotiations, you have an opportunity to establish rapport with the editor. If you bring an attorney into the picture, you may lose this important one-on-one contact. You might even scare the editor off.

Considering the Offer

Remembering that you're a new author, list the goals of your bargaining. Is the advance reasonable, in your opinion? Have you checked the advances received by other authors for similar books?

Have you waited long enough for any offers that might be received from other publishers? If you wish to delay bargaining with the publisher making the first offer for your book, be certain that this publisher will leave his offer open during your delay. Remember, you should have informed the editor at the beginning that this was to be a multiple submission. Most editors are used to fairly prompt conclusions to negotiations and may refuse to leave an offer open for you. It is customary to ask the first publisher if he'll leave his offer open for a week while you contact other publishers.

Before responding to the editor, carefully list the terms that are satisfactory and those you'd like to improve. Have in mind those terms in which you are willing to give ground in return for better terms in other areas.

Other Subjects Worth Discussion

After discussing terms, there are several questions that should be asked concerning the reprint edition, including:

1. its intended price,
2. its release date,
3. desired revisions (the publisher's),
4. the planned cover,
5. the publisher's promotional plans, and
6. the size of the first printing.

As a new author, you do not have control of these areas. But you might be able to influence the editor's thinking by positive persuasion.

As a matter of fact, your editor may not have that much control over many of these areas, either. The company's marketing department exercises control over most of these points.

When you become a well-known author, you can then be more forceful in determining how your book is published. In the meanwhile, be properly humble. Make your point with as much common sense as possible, then get on to the other matters of your contract.

Responding with Counter-Offers

Your written response should reiterate the current offer. Then it should suggest alternate terms that you'd prefer. Don't be rigid in stating what you would like; leave room for adjustments. At the same time, be confident. Be encouraging to the editor. Mention any recent publicity your book has received since your initial query letter was sent.

Compose the letter in list form. Number each of the terms discussed. Be brief.

The editor will probably respond by telephone again. By this time, you should be even better prepared to communicate.

If you're comfortable doing so, conduct further bargaining over the telephone. At the conclusion of each call, though, write a letter confirming the progress made and send it to the editor.

If you cannot get a 10 percent royalty rate on softbound (trade paperback) printings at the twenty thousand level, then suggest this break-point at thirty thousand or even fifty thousand copies. If an editor asks for foreign rights, don't agree unless you gain ground in another area. Standard foreign rights splits are 75/25 in the author's favor.

If an editor balks at your retention of non-exclusive mail-order rights, ask how profitable single-copy orders are to large publishers. Most large publishers do not even fill such orders —they refer them to wholesalers.

If the publisher won't agree to one hundred free copies, ask for fifty. Be prepared to tell the editor what will be done with the copies. Explain that this will guarantee that the book receives some promotion. If you ask the editor to guarantee promotion of your book, you're likely to get a negative response. Once the book is printed, it's usually out of the editor's hands.

Give and take in these discussions. Be cordial at all times and keep your sense of humor. Try to develop a good working relationship with your editor.

How to continue working well with your editor is the subject of the last chapter.

Working With an Editor

49

Once you've sold your book to a major publisher, you can expect changes in the book's title, cover, format, style, illustrations, photographs, and so on. Having successfully self-published the book, you may find these changes difficult to accept.

As a new author, though, you have little bargaining power to convince an editor to retain the original version of your book. Consider yourself fortunate to have the book picked up by a major publisher; few are. After you've gained more experience (written a few more books), you may be in a better position to control the publishing of your books at a major publisher. Editors will have more respect for you.

Why You Must Get Along With Your Editor

Your goal is to maintain the editor's enthusiasm. This is vital to the survival of your book. Modern editors are no longer simply editors.

They must sell their books to salespersons in their marketing departments. You want the pitch for your book to be strong! If you've made yourself a pain in the neck, your editor may relegate your book to the bottom of the heap when the time comes to persuade the marketing department to promote the book.

When you sold the rights to your book, you relinquished all control over it. If you don't like what happens and you've stated your case with adequate clarity, there's nothing more you can do. Control your ego instead. Hope the mistakes won't hurt your book after all.

Reviewing The Editing

Your editor will probably return a copy of your book with extensive changes marked throughout the text. These changes can be placed into three categories:

1. those that improve your text,
2. those having a neutral effect, and
3. improper changes.

How you handle *each* of these categories may determine whether your editor will consider your suggestions fairly.

Editing That Improves

Recognize editing that benefits your book. Be sure to compliment your editor or copy editor for these changes. Be sincere. Solicit suggestions from them for making further improvements. Be prompt in submitting any requested rewriting.

Editing with a Neutral Effect

If you've waited at least one week before deciding what you think of your editor's changes, you'll realize that many of them do not have a particularly beneficial or harmful effect on your text.

In such cases, do not challenge them. It is better to semi-compliment them, if you make any comments at all. These changes are not worth protesting. Save your time and energy for those that are.

Improper Changes

Countering improper changes will challenge all your skills as a writer. These changes will cause you anguish. Your emotions will not help you now. Common sense and reason are your only allies in convincing an editor to change his or her mind.

If you do a good job of presenting your case, an intelligent, experienced editor may accept half of your challenges. Do not count on doing better than that. If you do, you'll be disappointed. You may be fortunate to persuade an editor to alter anything.

Itemize your objections in a clear form. Ask a friend to review these objections to check their validity. Are they convincing? Do you come on too strong?

What if the Editor Is Firm?

When an editor insists on editing text in what you consider an improper fashion, your next step is to live with it.

Of course, your first reaction will be anger. Direct this anger in a direction other than its cause. You have nothing to gain and much to lose by alienating your editor.

This advice may be hard for a new author to take. Few authors are naturally humble. Develop humility as fast as you can.

Judy Blume is one of the most successful American authors of books for adolescent girls in the last few decades. The following extract from *Judy Blume's Story,* by Betsy Lee (Dillon Press, 1981), describes her first meeting with an editor at Bradbury Press (Prentice-Hall):

Judy had read in *Writer's Digest* magazine that Bradbury Press was interested in realistic fiction for young people, so she had sent them a draft of *Iffie's House.* They didn't accept the manuscript or reject it. Instead, they asked if she would meet with them to talk about it. . . .

Dick Jackson liked the manuscript and with some revision, he said it might work out as a book. "Maybe," he added cautiously. "Now," he said, leaning back in his chair, "what do we know about Winnie? What kind of person is she?" For an hour and a half, Dick asked Judy questions about her characters, about the plot, about where the book was going.

Judy took notes furiously. New ideas began to spin out of her imagination. They talked about tightening scenes, cutting chapters, and adding new dialogue in places. By the end of the meeting, they were both exhausted.

Her book had only begun. Dick said he could not offer her a contract yet. If she was willing to revise the manuscript, making changes they had agreed on, Bradbury would consider publishing it. Maybe.

If Judy Blume had not been humble on this occasion, she might not be the most popular author in her field today.

Put yourself in the editor's place. If you had purchased a manuscript of a book for $10,000 and were going to spend an equal amount on publishing it, wouldn't you want to be in the driver's seat?

As a successful author-publisher, you will find that numerous people approach you to publish their books. Would you publish any of their books without total control of everything? Of course you wouldn't.

When you lose, lose graciously. Above all, maintain your rapport with your editor.

Good luck!

Glossary

Acquisition Editor: Editor who specializes in the acquisition, rather than the editing, of manuscripts.

Addendum: Supplementary information added to the end of a book, often written by another author.

Advance: Money paid to an author for selling a manuscript or reprint rights to a publisher, an "advance" against future royalties.

Advance Book Information (ABI): A brief summary of a book, on special ABI forms, that should accompany Advance Reading Copies when they are sent out for review.

Amberlith: Orange-colored acetate used to make a window on the page board for the printing of halftones.

Appendix: Supplementary information added to the end of a book, often lists of data not considered reference material.

Author's Alteration: A change made by the author in a galley or proof, marked AA.

Back Matter: Material appearing at the end of normal text, such as glossary, index, addendum, appendix, index, and bibliography.

Bibliography: List of sources for information appearing in a book.

Blue-Lines: Proofs of a printer's negatives that are the author's final check before printing

Boards: Paper sheets to which galleys and artwork are attached, also the stiff material to which the cover is attached in bookbinding.

Bound Galleys: See "uncorrected proofs."

Burning Plates: The making of printing plates from negatives.

Camera-Ready Copy: Final material, ready for photography, submitted for printing.

Case Bound: See "hardbound."

Cases: Capitalized (upper case) or uncapitalized (lower case) form of letter.

Cast-Off: The estimate of a book's length before it's printed.

Character: A single letter or space.

Checking Copies: Page from a publication containing an advertisement, sent to the advertiser as proof that the ad was run properly.

CIP Information: Cataloging in Publication, data furnished by the Library of Congress designating labeling information for book spines in libraries.

Clay-Coated Paper: Paper coated with a thin layer of clay for better definition of printed material, used for high-quality art books.

Clip-Art: Non-copyrighted artwork that can be clipped from catalogs available in stationery and artwork supply stores.

Color Keys: Four sheets of clear acetate, each of which has one of the four basic colors of a photograph printed on it, that allows you to check the quality of 4-color artwork.

Color Separation: Breaking down 4-color artwork into four negatives—one for each of three colors, plus black—for printing.

Consignment: The placing of books in a store in which the publisher is paid only upon the sale of books.

Contact Sheets: Sheets furnished by a photo lab on which all prints from one roll of film are printed, usually in reduced size.

Copyediting: Final checking for grammatical errors, consistency, transition, and structural problems in written material.

Cromalin: A proof, resembling a color print, that enables you to check the quality of 4-color artwork before printing.

Cropping: Outlining the area of a photo to be reproduced.

DBA: "Doing Business As."

Desired Photo Area: The area of a photo to be reproduced in a book.

Direct Mail: Selling books in brochures sent through the mail.

Display Type: Large type used for title pages, chapter openings, subheadings, etc.

Dummy Signature Sheets: Blank signature sheets with numbers indicating where page boards should be placed.

Duotones: A halftone from a black-and-white photograph that is printed in two colors, one dark, the other lighter.

Editing: The general review of a manuscript for overall meaning, accuracy, and transition.

Elite: Type size having twelve characters per inch.

End Paper: See "fly leaf."

Enlarged Photo Size: The size to which a photo must be enlarged to appear in a book.

Fictitious Name Statement: A notice published in a local newspaper announcing that you are doing business under a name other than your own, also called a "DBA."

Finish Size: The size of a book after it is trimmed and bound at the bindery.

Flats: Large boards, usually made of goldenrod paper, on which the film for a book is mounted before the plates are burned.

Fly Leaf: The first sheet in hardbound books that is attached to the inside covers.

Folio: A page number.

Galleys: The first proof of a typeset manuscript, usually printed on oversized sheets that can later be cut down to page size.

Gathering: Putting signatures in proper order for binding.

Half-Title Page: The first inside page of a softbound book, the second inside page of most hardbound books, on which only the title of the book appears.

Halftone: A line screen (or printer's negative) made for a photograph.

Head Trim: The side of gathered signatures that is trimmed before being bound.

Headliner Ruler: A transparent ruler with horizontal and vertical lines.

High-Bulk Paper: Paper thickened during manufacture by having air blown into it.

Inserting Requirements: Indicates where signatures must be placed within other signatures during gathering.

Insertion Orders: Forms used in the ordering of advertisements to be placed in a periodical.

International Standard Book Number (ISBN):   The identification number issued by R. R. Bowker and Company for a book.

Justify: To align the vertical margins of a page, usually refers to an even right-hand margin.

Layout Boards: See "boards."

Leading: The vertical distance between typeset lines.

Letter-Spacing: See "pitch."

Line Editor: Editor who specializes in the editing, rather than acquisition, of manuscripts.

Line Illustrations: Black-and-white illustrations that can be pasted up and photographed with ordinary text, having solid black tones only.

Line Screens: Screens that permit varying percentages of color to be printed, also refers to number of dots per linear inch of a halftone.

Mass Market Paperbacks: Paperback books, usually $4^3/_{16}"$ × $6^3/_4"$, that are sold in newsstands, airports, drugstores, etc., rather than just bookstores.

NCR Paper: Chemically treated paper that does not require carbons to make duplicates.

Page Boards: Boards to which galleys and artwork have been attached.

Paste Up: Attaching galleys and artwork to boards.

Perfect Bound: A book in which the pages and the cover are attached by glue.

Pica: Type size having ten characters per inch.

Pitch: The distance between letters in the words of typesetting.

Plastic Comb: A method of binding a book in which plastic teeth fit through notches in the pages.

Plates: Metal or plastic plates used in printing presses to print signatures.

Printer's Error: A correction of an error made by a printer, marked PE; author should *not* be charged for the correction of PEs.

Proof: A photographic print of artwork or type used to check the quality and accuracy of work before the actual printing.

Process Work: Color printing.

Proportional Spacing: The typesetting of letters of differing widths.

Pulling a Proof: Having a proof made.

Quality Paperback: See "trade paperback."

Query Letter: A letter to a publisher describing a book or manuscript offered for submission.

Rate Card: Card or brochure listing the cost of advertising in a publication.

Recto: The right-hand page.

Reduced Photo Size: The reduced size of a photo to be reproduced in a book.

Reprint Rights: The rights to re-publish a book.

Resale Number: A number obtained from the state permitting the purchase of materials used to produce a book without paying sales tax, as tax will be collected when you sell the materials as a finished book.

Returns: Books returned to the publishers by bookstores and wholesalers.

Rivet Binding: The use of rivets to bind a book.

Rubylith: Red-colored acetate used to create a window for the printing of a halftone.

Running Heads: Headings in the top margin of each page telling the reader where he is, e.g., chapter title, part title, author's name.

Saddle-Stitching: Binding a book by stapling along the spine.

Serifs: Fine lines extending from the main strokes of letters.

Side-Stitching: See "saddle-stitching."

Signature: Large sheet of paper on which several pages of a book are printed; when folded, the pages appear in the correct order.

Smyth Sewn: Hardbinding in which signature pages are sewn together with thread.

Space Advertising: Advertising requiring artwork.

Spiral Binding: Binding a book by inserting coiled wire through punched holes in pages.

Straight Copy: Typesetting with no indented material, italics, or other deviations from plain sentences and paragraphs.

Stripping Into Flats: The taping of negatives to plastic sheets before burning plates.

Style Sheet: An alphabetized list, prepared by the copy editor, of words and phrases used in a book to ensure consistency.

Tag Ends: Partial line at extreme top or bottom of page.

Trade Paperback: Paperbacks sold in bookstores only, often the signatures of the hardbound edition in a softcover binding.

Trade Journals: Magazines for the book trade, such as *Library Journal* and *Publishers Weekly*.

Trade Reviews: Reviews in trade journals.

Transparency: Artwork for a color print, resembling a color slide.

Trim Size: The size of a book page after it is bound.

Uncorrected Proof: Photocopy of a book used as "advance reading copy" for review in trade journals.

Varnishing: Protecting a book cover with varnish.

Velo-Binding: See "rivet binding."

Velox: Artwork for black-and-white reproduction, resembling a negative but *not having* a reversed image.

Verso: The left-hand page.

Window: Clear space created on a negative by a ruby- or amberlith overlay.

Index